RAD
HITLER

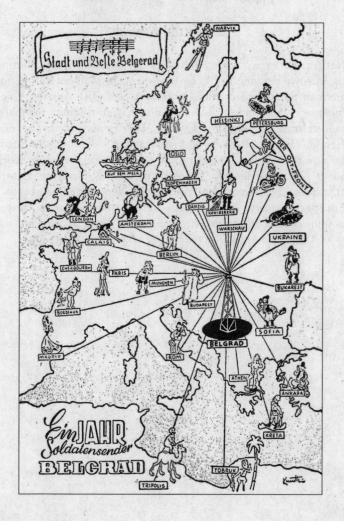

About the Author

Nathan Morley is a journalist and author based in Cyprus. During the last two decades, he has covered events in southern Europe for German public broadcaster Deutsche Welle, ORF Austria, Voice of America and Vatican Radio. Morley has also written for many publications including the *Cyprus Mail*, *Sunday Mail*, *Catholic Herald*, *History Hit*, *Best of British* and *New Europe*. In 2001, he was the recipient International Radio Festival of New York Silver Award for his production of the weekly historical feature 'The Retro Flashback'. He is passionate about twentieth-century European history, and has broadcast extensively on a variety of subjects ranging from Erich Honecker, Berlin at war and the Chernobyl disaster to the history of Radio Luxembourg.

RADIO HITLER

Nazi Airwaves in the Second World War

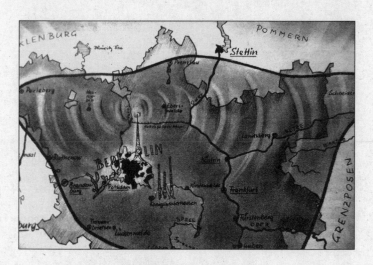

Nathan Morley

AMBERLEY

For my parents,
Mandy and Bernard.

Half-title page: Once the sun set over Europe, increasing the transmission range, the signal from Soldatensender Belgrade stretched from Narvik in Norway down to North Africa covering an audience of six-million soldiers.

Title page: A map (from *Volksfunk*) showing the coverage of *Reichssender Berlin* which promised to capture the 'essence of this city in which all the threads of the empire converge'.

This edition published 2023

Amberley Publishing
The Hill, Stroud
Gloucestershire, GL5 4EP

www.amberley-books.com

Copyright © Nathan Morley, 2021, 2023

The right of Nathan Morley to be identified as the Author of this work has been asserted in accordance with the Copyright, Designs and Patents Act 1988.

ISBN 978 1 3981 1546 0 (paperback)
ISBN 978 1 3981 0447 1 (ebook)

British Library Cataloguing in Publication Data. A catalogue record for this book is available from the British Library.

1 2 3 4 5 6 7 8 9 10

Typesetting by Aura Technology and Software Services, India. Printed in India.

CONTENTS

FOREWORD

The thread that linked the public, the German radio network, and the government was the Haus Des Rundfunks, the stylish red-brick broadcasting centre in Charlottenburg in Western Berlin. From behind its guarded doors, propagandists, reporters, and commentators were shielded from public view, but their voices were heard everywhere. The story of broadcasting in the years of National Socialism is, in fact, a fascinating social and political chronicle of one of the most turbulent periods in German life.

Within these pages, we breeze through fourteen eventful years when the Nazis – which started as a group of discontented fanatics in Munich – were able to construct a vast political machine and become the sole instrument of the state. During that time, they stubbed out parliamentary democracy and established the most brutal dictatorship ever known. For Hitler, radio was an absolutely essential tool. He explicitly emphasised the importance of propaganda in *Mein Kampf*, ascribing it a decisive factor not only in peacetime but for any future war. For him, propaganda was as a means to an end – an instrument for influencing the public, which was not subject to any moral judgment.

By the mid-1930s, with the help of radio, the National Socialists had managed to penetrate every phase of social and individual life in Germany. The main radio network, Deutschlandsender, which broadcast from the aforementioned

Haus Des Rundfunks – a building I was privileged to work in myself for many years – championed coverage of everything from social reform projects, mass tourism, news coverage and music to education, culture and, of course, the demonisation of enemies.

In this work, Nathan Morley – himself a broadcaster who has worked with Deutsche Welle and Austrian Broadcasting, as well as Vatican Radio – deftly walks through the good times and the bad, from the pioneering shortwave broadcasts at the 1936 Olympics and the evolution of television in Berlin, to the darker days of conflict and national strife.

In its persistent efforts to shape world opinion, German radio was able to call upon an extensive network of high-powered transmitters aimed in all directions. The communications empire was, at its peak, employing over 20,000 people on local, national, international and clandestine stations, which produced subversive radio propaganda. Programmes were aimed at Europe, Asia, Africa, India, Australia, the Middle East, United States and South America. There were broadcasts in just about every tongue imaginable, including Faroese.

It is interesting to read about life early in the war, when husbands were drafted and homes broken up. While women were fearful about casualties at the front, soldiers fretted about the physical insecurity of their families – to bridge the gap, radio acted as constant link between separated families. Few Germans of that generation would ever forget the *Wunschkonzert für die Wehrmacht*, a popular variety show playing requests and dedications for the military. Other shows, including *Kameradschaftsdienst*, and *Ankerspill*, became part of the national fabric, as did the mutterings of foreign renegades such as Lord Haw-Haw on Reichssender Hamburg making his outrageous claims, night after night.

For most listeners, it was the reports from the Front detailing military successes which were eagerly lapped up. As you will read, the transcripts of some of the campaigns are included in this book, and take us on thrilling adventures in Holland, France, Norway and Russia. By contrast, from 1942, Germany suffered one blow after another. Stalingrad marked the turning point of the conflict as the struggle for national survival began – that fateful announcement concerning the fall of the German Army was made from the studios of the Haus Des Rundfunks.

On the home front, listeners were mobilised and ate rationed food, as well as suffering a dreadful decline in their standard of living and health. By that time, the public were suffering the horror of intensive bombing of cities and the destruction of homes and personal property, which rounded out the pattern of totalitarian war. As Allied air raids worsened so did the 'achtung' warnings, which became increasingly common on the domestic airwaves, sending the public scrambling for their cellars.

Another area of interest which receives attention in this book is the 'Ordinance on Extraordinary Radio Measures' which threatened lengthy prison terms – and in the worst cases even the death penalty – for those Germans caught listening to enemy stations such as the BBC and Radio Moscow. The story of Hitler's radio is an engrossing read – after years of careful research, the book is a very welcome addition to this fascinating subject.

Wolfgang Bauernfeind

ACKNOWLEDGEMENTS

Over and above the usual acknowledgements, it is important to describe the role in this book of several key survivors from the Second World War who provided thrilling first-hand insight. I would particularly like to thank Peter Meyer for sharing his own extraordinary experiences of the Reichs-Rundfunk-Gesellschaft (RRG). Likewise, I am also deeply indebted to Richard Baier, who, at 93 years old, gave a fascinating account on his important work as a newsreader on Reichssender Berlin, as bombs rained down and the Russians advanced toward the German capital.

My deep appreciation goes to the staff at the Staatsbibliothek zu Berlin and the newspaper archive at Westhafen; both assisted with invaluable archive materials. At the same time, I am very grateful to the Deutsches Rundfunkarchiv (DRA) in Potsdam, especially to Dr Jorg-Uwe Fischer for providing countless transcripts and other materials. Likewise, Niclas Sennerteg, author of *Tyskland talar*, a study of the RRG's Swedish wartime service, shared his valuable research. Other important material was garnered from the National Archives in London, while Simone Humphries helped decipher the William Joyce diaries, which turned out to be important to this book. Margot Blank at the Deutsch-Russisches Museum in Karlshorst gave me valuable help and background to the notorious Propaganda Companies, which, as you will read, weave their way through the pages of this book. Heartfelt thanks are also given to broadcaster and historian Wolfgang Bauernfeind in Berlin for his kindness and sharing his knowledge, given his long association with Sender Freies Berlin (SFB), and latterly Rundfunk Berlin-Brandenburg (RBB).

The wartime history of German radio itself is impoverished in terms of archives. I wasn't far into my secondary research when it became clear the vast bulk of transcripts and records from 1943 onwards, when the war swung against Germany, had been lost during the Allied bombing or destroyed after the conflict. Thankfully, British and American government monitors, the BBC, the British police and newswire press services had kept a keen ear on German radio, much of which is stored in the pages of journals in the British Newspaper Archives. These reports provided a fascinating record of every new horror or outrage broadcast on home and foreign services from the period of Stalingrad until the collapse of Germany. Over the past few years, I have had nothing but kindness from the staff at the library of the Topographie des Terrors, which is home to a unique collection of material related to the state security apparatus and Berlin at war.

I was extremely lucky in the encouragement, tips and advice given by friends, associates and colleagues at NDR in Hamburg, Deutsche Welle in Berlin and ORF in Vienna. Finally, I would like to send a special thank you to my former Vatican Radio colleagues Charles Collins, now managing editor at *Crux*, and Christopher Altieri, Rome bureau chief at the *Catholic Herald* for their kind support. Also, it goes without saying my gratitude is also sent to commissioning editor Connor Stait at Amberley Publishing for his faith in, and dedication to, this project.

I

THE DARKENING

On 1 February 1933, two days after being appointed Chancellor, Adolf Hitler opened one of the darkest periods in the modern history of mankind. Dressed in a grey flannel suit, he stood before a microphone emblazoned with the Funke-Stunde logo at the Reich Chancellery in Berlin. 'His whole body quivered and shook,' noted financier Hjalmar Schacht. Despite being an old political hand and accomplished speaker, this moment marked the first time the 43-year-old Austrian had ever spoken over the radio. Then, just after 22.00, speaking in a dry and sombre tone, Hitler reeled off a declaration of policy. He announced two four-year plans to 'repair the damage of the past fourteen years', with a promise to save farming and launch an attack on unemployment. As the speech went on, he gave details of a new compulsory labour service along with a pledge to eliminate economic distress and overthrow 'Communistic disintegration'.

As for the public at large, hearing his voice for the first time, the speech turned out to be uninspiring to the point of boredom. Even Hitler seemed unimpressed with his pale performance, which lacked the energy and enthusiasm he gained when whipping up an audience or rally.[1] Hitler's radio inexperience could be forgiven. For years his Nazi Party had unsuccessfully lobbied the national radio company Reichs-Rundfunk-

Gesellschaft (RRG) for airtime through a series of petitions, demonstrations and even veiled threats.

Before being allowed on air, Hitler had fought in the political arena in various ways. During the 1932 election, he threw his energy into reaching mass audiences by using Lufthansa, the state-owned airline. Over the course of two months, he flew over 30,000 miles wading into crowds, shaking hands and addressing meetings. His travelling roadshow featured a cast of Nazi star turns, including 'deputy Führer' Rudolf Hess, future aviation minister Herman Goring, and Robert Ley, the Nazi specialist on labour relations. Hitler was able to address as many as five separate rallies a day, 23 in all over a period of just a week. His message was clear: Germany's fleeting dabble in democracy, the Weimar Republic, which had been dogged by misfortune – war guilt, the seizure of prized territories, crippling inflation and severe unemployment – was over.

Although the novelty of Hitler's vigorous 'flight over Germany' won over some voters, the effort could never match the impact of radio, which had blossomed from a fraught enterprise when it began in 1922 into a thriving concern. During the early twenties, the Reichspost, which owned and controlled broadcasting infrastructure, handed responsibility for output to nine new independent regional stations.[2] Local culture, political structure, and transmitter coverage limitations determined broadcasting boundaries. For example, citizens of Bavaria located in the south-eastern corner of Germany had different tastes and interests from listeners in the northern district of East Prussia, and so on.

Once developed, the network beamed programmes from stations in Berlin, Leipzig, Breslau, Konigsberg, Hamburg, Köln, Frankfurt, Stuttgart, and Munich.[3] The president of the Radio Corporation of America, James G. Harbord, declared Germany had made more progress in radio by 1925 than any other country, second only to the United States. *Leeds Mercury* correspondent Elizabeth Craig went a step further. She wrote a laudatory piece from Berlin insisting German radio was superior not only to British but also to American output. 'In a word,' Craig reported, 'the German wireless programmes are now filling public want.'

When 'Attention! Attention! Berlin', comes imperiously across the wireless in German, the listener knows that whatever attention is called for, it will be for something very worthwhile to a great mass of the German public.

They cater equally for the new poor, whose wealth and chances vanished during inflation, and the new rich, who yearn secretly for culture they do not have, as well as for the huge army of poverty-stricken people, of aged, of sickly, of workless, who day in and day out can be charmed into forgetting their cares by listening in.[4]

For the most part, news and political propaganda was not broadcast due to the fear of diminishing newspaper circulation, but even with the absence of current affairs, the programming on the regional channels was praised. Dr Karl Rottgardt, a well-known academic, purred that the best artists in Germany, including the Berlin Philharmonic Orchestra, along with educational content from the leading university professors, achieved instant popularity and accelerated the rate of social change. Furthermore, frequent national link-ups made it possible for noted singers and personalities to reach every corner of Germany.

The Reichs-Rundfunk-Gesellschaft (RRG) was established in Berlin in 1925 and acted as an umbrella organisation of the nine regional broadcasters, with Hans Bredow – a visionary once known as 'Germany's Marconi' – as chairman. Bredow, a tall, portly man with a disarming smile, had served as an executive at Telefunken, as well as director of the Department for Wireless Telegraphy and Secretary of State for Telecommunications.

During the turbulent years of the twenties, when inflation was rife and unemployment high, Bredow oversaw the installation of a longwave transmitter at Königs Wusterhausen, south of Berlin. With a 900-foot mast – the highest in the world, with the exception of the Eiffel Tower – he launched Deutschlandsender in 1926 as a national educational network offering speech programmes relayed from the nine regional stations. Operated by Deutsche Welle, its main goal, according to director Professor Dr H. Schubotz, was to unite the country to form a large cultural community and allow citizens from all districts to 'participate in the spiritual life of the nation'. Schubotz compared Deutschlandsender to an 'adult education centre' with a schedule divided into general and vocational output. His office was also responsible for answering and analysing mail from listeners. 'Our lectures have become popular across Germany, but also for Germans living abroad on the borders of the Reich, especially in Poland, Romania and Czechoslovakia,' Schubotz reflected.[5]

Deutschlandsender expanded activities to pedagogical broadcasting, with closed lectures for dentists, doctors, veterinarians and lawyers, supplemented by vocational training programmes, alongside features on home economics, farming and business.[6] Other initiatives, such as language courses in English, French and Esperanto, gained widespread support. There were talks on religious studies, natural sciences, global politics, the work of the League of Nations, poetry, books and music history programmes.

On top of regional relays, Deutsche Welle produced the only daily national weather report, as well as remote broadcasts from the International Science Congress in Berlin, German Hygiene Congress in Dresden, and lectures from the Berlin University of Politics.

Soon afterwards, Bredow laid the foundation stone for the Haus Des Rundfunks the new Reichs-Rundfunk-Gesellschaft headquarters in the leafy suburbs of Western Berlin. Designed by Hans Poelzig, the building knit together fine acoustic qualities with faceted ceilings, non-parallel studio walls and absorbent vanes. The windowless Grosse Sendesaal, built into a double-volume first storey, could seat 800 people and a full orchestra. Even now, the building seems like a place forgotten by the passage of time; the reddish-black ceramic tile facade appears almost new rather than 90 years old. Surrounded by glazed red-brick columns, the vast lobby is overlooked by balconies reaching high above.

On a visit during the late 1930s, the American writer Jean Merrill du Cane described a vast 'semi-circular structure, where the front is stark and straight like a factory, but the rear is semi-circular in shape'. She was especially impressed by the continuous lifts, known as paternosters, which operated on an endless chain:

> The lifts are non-stop and consist of a succession of lift cages; there are no gates. As a cage comes up or down to your level you hop into it and jump out when it reaches the floor. If you get to the top of the building and forget to get out you are carried up and over the chain and find yourself coming down again. It is strange to see procession of black-coated announcers, uniformed engineers, typists, singers, and bandsmen, S.S. guards and party commissars rising and falling in these continuous lifts. [7]

2

RADIO REVOLUTION

With Hitler's appointment to High Office, old grievances against the RRG could be settled. Revenge measures were passed in quick step as Nazi Party lieutenants trampled over each other to pour scorn on the network branding it a corrupt 'Jewish influenced' threat to Germany. The zealot responsible for rabble-rousing, Joseph Goebbels, had led the tussle for airtime since 1928. Standing less than 5 feet tall, he proved to be a skilled bureaucrat with an insatiable appetite for work and boasted the most impressive academic résumé of all the Nazi hierarchy.

A son of Roman Catholics, Goebbels was born in 1897 and grew up in the Rhineland. Crippled by infantile paralysis, he dragged his deformed foot with a pronounced limp. However, his intelligence shone, leading to a local Catholic Association financing his scholarship at Heidelberg University, where he graduated as a Doctor of Philosophy. His thinking took a radical shift to anti-Church, anti-Jewish preaching when he fell under Hitler's spell in 1922. From then on, his oratory – rife with distorted ideas – elevated him to becoming a key figure in the Nazi orbit. But it was not until his appointment as Gauleiter of Berlin in 1926 that Goebbels discovered a wide outlet for his talents. He basked in success with the creation of *Der Angriff*, his own newspaper designed to sow the poisonous seeds of anti-Semitism and discontent, in which well nigh every edition was littered with bile-strewn articles. At one time, the paper had over 100 libel actions pending against it. 'It steamed up readers with an inexhaustible supply of invectives against liberals, democrats, the Weimar Republic and the Jews,' was the opinion of Frederick T. Birchall, the *New York Times* correspondent in Berlin.

From his tiny second-floor office in Hedemannstrasse, near the Anhalter railway station, Goebbels kept a sharp eye on the political world around him. He became a Nazi member of the Reichstag in 1928, a position that further elevated his notoriety. In addition, he took charge of Nazi propaganda, creating the 'Horst Wessel legend', making a noble hero out of a Brownshirt alley tout whose murder by Communists elevated him to a martyr of the Nazi faith. Goebbels refashioned an old Bavarian melody as 'the Horst Wessel Song', with the refrain: 'Our comrades killed by the Red Front march along with us.'

Steeped in a decade of tradition, RRG employees were understandably alarmed by the idea of sudden change when the Nazis shot to power. One can only imagine the whispered conversations taking place in the paternosters as newswires flashed bulletins of Hitler's appointment on that cold January afternoon in 1933.

Even before the news had filtered around the Haus Des Rundfunks, Hitler's new Interior Minister, Wilhelm Frick, was demanding coverage of the Nazis' first 'act of theatre'. He wanted live commentary from a torchlight parade later that evening. To enforce the demand, Eugen Hadamovsky, an assistant to Goebbels, dashed over to the radio studios in Charlottenburg: 'I burst in the hallway, opened the door that bore the sign "duty manager" and entered with my companion,' he later recalled, describing the event as the moment 'broadcasting revolution' erupted. 'I gave my name which had become embarrassingly well-known from my years of opposition. Then I demanded the immediate secondment of microphones, equipment, and personnel to the Reich Chancellery to carry out a national transmission of the evening parade.'[1]

A few hours later, Frick's broadcast was duly delivered. In the raw cold of winter, two blow-by-blow accounts of Nazis strutting by torchlight filled the airwaves that evening. Nazi journalists

Wulf Bley and Heinz von Lichberg climbed the outside steps to the chancellery roof to marvel at enthusiastic spectators jamming the streets. They described columns of Brownshirts, with torches aflame, goose-stepping through the Brandenburg Gate and along Unter den Linden, then onto the Wilhelmstrasse, where Hitler took the salute. Commentary was interspersed with comments from Herman Goring, by then president of the Reichstag, and Goebbels, who made a few brief remarks.[2]

US Consular official Robert Heingartner heard the broadcast at home in Frankfurt:

> The torchlight parade in Berlin last night turned out to be more of an innovation [ovation?] for Hitler than for Hindenburg to judge by the frantic cheering as the 15,000 national socialists were passing the Reich Chancellery where the 'Führer' stood at an open window to greet his followers. I listened to the cheering, singing and band music for perhaps half an hour and then closed the radio as I was afraid the uproar would waken Alex. The man at the microphone who described the scene said that such enthusiasm had not been experienced since the opening days of the war in 1914.[3]

There was no such excitement in the office of the RRG director, where Frick's demand for the torchlight broadcast prompted Hans Bredow to compose his letter of resignation. 'Herr Bredow is one of the most unpleasant phenomena in the broadcasting world,' the Nazi mouthpiece *Völkischer Beobachter* later gloated. 'His elimination under the new Reich government was a matter of course.'

In contrast to his later boasts of a glorious ascension by 'seizing power', Hitler had been elevated to the leadership through legally acceptable backroom bargaining. However, to enact reforms and cement power, the backing of the German people was essential. Thus, just a few days after his appointment, Hitler persuaded President Hindenburg to dissolve the Reichstag and call elections.

A few weeks later, Hitler was at the Sportpalast – the de facto Nazi grandstand – to stir up 10,000 enthusiastic followers and radio listeners. He wooed the German people with his 'Four Year Plan' and the slogan: 'With Hindenburg and Hitler for a

New Germany.' 'Give us four years and then judge us,' Hitler cried, amid frantic cheering, roars of 'Heil' and patriotic songs. Over the next 12 months, Hitler delivered 50 such broadcasts from rallies, meetings, and public gatherings.

The first half of 1933 was a period of never-ending drama. Just prior to Hitler winning the election on 5 March, the Reichstag fell victim to arson, an act Nazis claimed was engineered by the Communists. 'There is no doubt that a conspiracy has taken place here in some form,' Herman Goring told radio listeners, adding figurative fuel to the fire. Enlightenment on the blaze was still being pursued by the prosecutor. The incident was a pretext for Hitler to pass his Enabling Act, which gave him the power to bypass Parliament and rule by decree. At the same time, civil liberties and the freedom of the press were suspended. A soft-spoken young Dutchman, Martinus van der Lubbe, was accused of starting the fire and marched into a nationally broadcast show trial, where the drumbeat of anti-Communist propaganda was scripted by Goebbels and personally passed on to radio commentators to offer a daily torrent of well-rehearsed abuse against Bolshevism and hostile forces.

From this point onwards, until the last days of the Third Reich, media in Germany crossed a new frontier as it fell under the total command of Hitler's propagandists. Alongside Goebbels' appointment as Minister of Propaganda, Otto Dietrich became 'Reich Press Chief of the NSDAP', while Max Amann, the publisher of the *Vølkischer Beobachter* newspaper, was elevated to the post of 'Reichsleiter für die Presse'.

During his first months in office, Hitler appointed several hundred officials to senior positions, with Eugen Hadamovsky being one of them. As an ardent Nazi disciple and faithful protégé of Goebbels, Hadamovsky was perfectly suited to the role of RRG's 'Reich Programme Director', especially given his active service in the First World War, after which he had breezed through the University of Berlin and, during a colourful period, met both Hitler and Goebbels at Nazi gatherings.[4] Soon after, he took various jobs throughout Europe and North Africa, including working as a journalist, locksmith and contractor in Bilbao, before returning to Berlin to join *Der Angriff* in 1929, where he was mentored by Goebbels. Impressed with his student, Goebbels set Hadamovsky the task of editing *Der Deutsche Sender*, a journal featuring essays harassing broadcasters to give Nazis airtime.[5] From then on, he distinguished himself by devoting energy to engineering the kind of propaganda that would drive the Party forward.

Not long after his appointment as Minister of Propaganda, Goebbels cooed that broadcasting was totally in the hands of the State: 'We have put a stop to endlessly swinging this way or that; we have ensured that there will be uniform control.' As a senior minister, Goebbels liked to think of himself as a great leader, marshalling and directing his troops. At work he seldom raised his voice and never reprimanded staff in public. He didn't crack jokes but could be bitingly sarcastic and was an accomplished gossip (as was Hitler). 'He has a remarkably appealing personality, with a sense of humour and a keen brain,' was the impression left with British journalist Gareth Jones after he met Goebbels in February 1933. 'One feels at home with him immediately, for he is amusing and likeable.' Jones pondered that it was strange to think that 'this little man, who looks so Iberian, is a leader of the Nazi movement, which has as its basis the supremacy of the big, blond Nordic race'.[6] Disparaging comments on Goebbels' physical appearance were commonplace, especially within the pages of the Russian, American and British press.

In building the first fully fledged Reich Ministry of Public Enlightenment and Propaganda, Goebbels literally changed everything about the way news was created and delivered. Charged with 'the promotion of national, cultural and economic issues, and information for the public, at home and abroad', he created his empire from departments surrendered by the Finance, Foreign and Interior Ministries. This larger-than-life operation was installed at the Prinz-Karl-Palais, an old stucco and granite pile on Wilhelmstrasse, which reflected the character of its founder – the only modest thing about him being his height.

Known to staff as the 'ProMi', the ministry became the organisational centrepiece of the Nazi media apparatus. From the reception, a sweeping staircase with wrought-iron railings led to Goebbels' well-appointed office, which featured a fine mahogany-panelled drawing room from where the minister spoke to his radio audiences. In all, the 'ProMi' covered five key areas: broadcasting, propaganda, theatre, film and the press. The RRG radio system was split into four departments: director-general, administration, programmes, and engineering (excluding transmitters, which remained the responsibility of the Reichspost). At the same time, the 'ProMi' gained a toehold in the Dradag news agency – which it eventually absorbed to provide sanitised news on domestic and overseas broadcasts.

Goebbels also headed a new 'Reich Chamber of Culture'. Any artist, performer, producer or writer had to be a member. The Chamber was divided into individual departments – press, radio, film, theatre, music, visual arts and literature. In turn, the press and radio division belonged to the 'Reich Press Chamber', which, among other things, ensured publishers met the requirements placed on them by the Party and the State. The same chamber oversaw the professional association of journalists, presided over by Otto Dietrich.

From October 1933, entering the profession of journalism was linked to a multitude of conditions, such as being purely of Aryan descent, and having German nationality. Journalists working under National Socialism were no longer accountable to publishers, but to the State. This new situation promoted a Berlin wit to remark, 'If you want to act, sing, dance, broadcast, paint, draw, sculpt, write, or crack jokes... talk to Dr Goebbels.' To which someone acidly retorted, 'Or leave Germany.'

In his first speech to radio employees in the concert hall of the Haus Des Rundfunks, Goebbels delivered a simple message: Artistic freedom would be eliminated in favour of radio 'returning to the people'. This was music to Hadamovsky's ears, as he declared radio to be the 'species-specific' medium of National Socialism, which could give a 'world view of blood and soil, race, homeland and nation'.

For the first time in history we now have in radio a medium which enables us to mold nations of many millions by daily and hourly influence. Radio can have the same impact as newspapers, but is more up-to-date, more versatile, more profound, and more uplifting by virtue of its inherent artistic element.[7]

On 1 April, Deutschlandsender, the station with the greatest reach, became the principal network, ditching relays of educational talks from regional channels in favour of homespun content.

Goebbels envisioned Deutschlandsender working for the entire nation 'with first-class employees expressing the wishes and the will of the Reich government'. Output was to be 'versatile, rich, clear and radiant' and cover all areas of political and cultural life.[8] Deutschlandsender's controller, Otto Stoffregen, a former head of culture for the Berlin edition of the *Völkischer Beobachter*, saw his mission as being almost biblical. 'Under the guidance of Dr Goebbels, broadcasting under National Socialism is acquiring an even greater significance, just as the printing press did during the Reformation,' he wrote in *National-Funk*.[9] Listeners were promised realistic dramas, programmes focusing on community, opera and folk songs along with the 'rich treasures of German customs' and culture. Furthermore, Deutschlandsender would nurture young writers, and appeal to the working man. Amid this plethora of variety, the Führer would be portrayed as the nation's most valuable asset, along with talks on the Nazi way of life and the great mission of the German people. As the schedule from May Day 1933 shows, Deutschlandsender became the logical fulfilment of the Nazi radio conception:

10:15 Relay of the Youth Demonstration. Hymns by the Berlin Choral Society followed by an address from Dr Goebbels
11:00 Wind instrument Concert followed by Nazi marching, peasants and miners' songs
16:00 Symphony of Work by Herbert Windt, conducted by the composer
17:45 Musical Interlude
18:20 Radio Sequence
19:30 Government Report
20:00 Celebration of National Labour Day from Tempelhof, with a performance of 'Der Gott, Der Eisen wachsen liess'. Planting of

an oak tree in honour of Hitler to the accompaniment the Horst Wessel song. Inaugural speech by Dr Goebbels, followed by an address by Hitler. Tattoo and Massed choirs: 'Ich bete an die macht der Lieb', followed by fireworks.

22:00 Light music and Dance Music

Listeners noticed the sudden use of simpler common-day language, which could be understood by everyone. Newscasters began following a standard delivery, uniform pronunciation, and standardised inflection, while the scripts were written in sharp, dramatic, 'punchy language', with the announcers adjusting their delivery for the desired emotional responses.

It was also impossible to miss the huge burst of patriotic fervour and bombast injected into speeches and drama. Unsurprisingly, the changes – especially on the Deutschlandsender – prompted some public disquiet from irritated listeners. Some wrote rude and anonymous letters, others – from both the high and the humble – sent letters that were reasoned and properly signed. There is little doubt the audience was highly responsive at evaluating content presented on air. More importantly, a happy listenership was also a lucrative source of revenue, given the income from the monthly licence fees was funnelled into financing the Ministry of Propaganda.

To put matters right, Goebbels struck a balance by adding more popular music, reducing political output and 'elevating culture'. Furthermore, an extra 1,000,000 Marks were earmarked to improve programmes and the 'pecuniary situation of German artists'. Soon after, Goebbels declared radio must be a multifaceted, 'flexible means of expressing the desires, needs, longings and hopes of our time':

> We do not intend to use the broadcasting system only for our partisan purposes. We want to make room for entertainment, popular arts, games, humour, and music. Everything should include the theme of our great re-constructive work, or at least not stand in its way.[10]

From then on, for every hour of news, features and talks, about seven hours of music was transmitted.[11] For the most part listeners approved with the schedule tweaks, though some complained about repetitive playlists, a problem exacerbated by the banning of Jewish singers and composers from the airwaves. Mendelssohn, Offenbach, and Goldmark along with 'Jewish western music' on gramophone such as 'Ole Man River', 'Red Sails in the Sunset', 'Ten Pretty Girls' and 'Smoke Gets in Your Eyes' were prohibited. Given the increasing paucity of material available, one producer wryly remarked 'surely we are not so poverty-stricken that *Die Fledermaus* or the *Gypsy Baron* overture has to be performed once every day!'[12]

With his remarkable energy, Goebbels popularised radio by introducing the Volksempfänger, a budget Bakelite wireless launched at the Internationale Funkausstellung exhibition. Designed to make the medium accessible to every home, the set retailed at the remarkably low price of 76 Marks – the equivalent of two weeks' wages for a working man. The low cost was achieved by dispensing with imported components, the manufacturer's patent fee and using cheap cardboard for the back of the casing. A bonus, for the Nazis at least, was the unit received only local stations, thus preventing listening to distant foreign channels.

Despite the high sales, penetration of broadcasting into the lower social strata remained problematic throughout the mid-1930s. In 1934, over 21 per cent of listeners were civil servants; with workers, who made up 43 per cent of the total population, extremely underrepresented, forming just 5.7 per cent of the radio audience. Furthermore, there were irregularities in regional coverage. Even by 1937, there were 12.65 radios per 100 city dwellers, but only about five devices per 100 inhabitants in the countryside, who made up almost 43 per cent of the population.[13]

To address the problem, RRG initiated elaborate advertising campaigns designed to entice residents of the provinces and countryside. Hitler Youth brigades stuffed glossy brochures through letterboxes, and animated films on the subject were shown at community events. A 'try before you buy scheme' also turned out to be a successful gimmick. New Volksempfänger owners were advised to keep windows open during Hitler speeches 'so that neighbours without radio could hear'.[14] The push for new listeners went beyond the living room. Radio sets were installed in restaurants and shops, while authorities announced a scheme to place 6,000 loudspeaker pillars at bus stops, town squares, and railway platforms.

Such was the ubiquity of the Volksempfänger that artist Paul Mathias Padua immortalised it in his painting *The Führer Speaks*, which became the star exhibit at the Great German Art Exhibition in 1940. The work depicted three generations of the same family gathered under a picture of Hitler, listening to his broadcast 'fill their hearts with joy'.

Soon afterwards, a Labour Front communal wireless was released. Collective listening was deeply embraced by the Nazis, especially at the local level, where neighbours, friends and work colleagues could 'unify as one' to hear the same broadcast. In the workplace too, there was a sense of communal identity and social equality, especially in factories where managers and directors sat on the shop floor to listen with workers. Dr Eric W. Stoetzner, a former advertising manager for a Frankfurt newspaper, recalled an experience he had as president of an advertising club in southern Germany, which illustrated radio's great power: 'The club members were invited for a Friday twelve-o'clock luncheon meeting, to which they came from all parts of the country.' Stoetzner continued:

> We were just about to gather when, totally unexpectedly, an announcement came over the ether. The omnipresent Hitler was to speak over the radio at twelve o'clock. The effect was that of an earthquake. All means of communication were stopped. All labour ceased. Printing presses, big and small halted, for after the speech – who knew? – the world might look entirely different.

The plant workers and employees had to gather in an assembly hall and listen in as the 'folk's community'. The speech began to roar over all heads, the faces became masks, everybody put on an interested smile. After the speech was finished, the obligatory exclamations flowed: 'How inspiring! How wonderful!'[15]

Workers playing truant during important speeches faced punishment, as an employee at a Leipzig factory found out after being caught slipping out of a communal listening session. His case was brought before a Labour Court, which concluded:

> The group radio reception of a speech by the Führer is an occasion on which the sense of belonging to a great community of the people, on the part of every single business establishment and every single one of its leaders and followers, is brought home to the consciousness, not only symbolically and figuratively, but also actually and directly, through the physically perceived fact that millions are gathered around a single Führer and that all, without class distinctions, are members of the same community who have to march toward the same goal and not to quarrel among themselves.[16]

To ensure total coverage, the reach and range of every local transmitter was boosted to 100 kilowatts enabling them to saturate vast swathes of Germany and spill into neighbouring countries. Smaller apparatus at Breslau, Leipzig, Heilsberg and Langenberg was upgraded with 'anti-fading' aerials, while state-of-the-art units were installed at Stettin, Dresden and Konigsberg. At the same time, regional stations adopted characteristic interval signals – an early version of radio jingles – designed to make them easily recognisable to listeners. The Köln station used a merry peal of bells from its famous cathedral, while Berlin adopted the first eight notes of the song 'People to Arms'.

Another important instrument to create interest was provided by a proliferation of radio journals and magazines, including *Berlin hört und sieht, Dt. Radio-Illustrierte, Hier Berlin, Volksfunk, Funk-Woche, Hör mit mir, Europa Stunde, Der Deutsche Rundfunk, NS-Funk* and *Die Sürag*.

3

CLEANSING

The revolution, though well underway, was not complete. Still to come was the destruction of worker's rights and the independent judiciary combined with a concentrated effort to bury all memories of the Weimar Republic. Throughout the spring and summer of 1933, the Nazis made their presence felt as a significant force in daily life.

During the first half of the year, they banned trade unions, opened the first concentration camp at Dachau, held a one-day boycott of all Jewish-owned businesses, began persecuting Jehovah's Witnesses, excluded Jewish physicians from official insurance schemes and established the Gestapo secret police. On top of that, there were public book burnings and the enactment of a new law legalising eugenic sterilisation.

Over in Charlottenburg, old scores were settled at the RRG where the Nazis sought revenge on those who had kept them from the microphone. Hadamovsky spared no effort discrediting members of the former management, with its humiliation cemented in July when announcer Alfred Braun and four former managers were dragged from their beds, charged with corruption and carted off to a concentration camp. Braun's daughter Eta Amendt witnessed Gestapo men arrive in leather coats: 'They searched everything, even my nursery...'[1]

On hearing of the arrests, former RRG Director Hans Bredow telegraphed Herman Goring begging to be treated in the same way. 'I do not want to leave my former subordinates, who did such valuable service to German broadcasting, in the lurch,' he pleaded. In typical fashion, Goring duly obliged and Bredow too was arrested, and accused of appropriation of public funds. At trial in a courtroom in Moabit, Berlin's version of the Old Bailey, Braun was released, but he was left brittle and sought help at a Swiss sanatorium, while Bredow spent six months behind bars with his former subordinates.[2] As ubiquitous as he was, Goebbels kept his distance from being associated with the Bredow case. At the same time, he gave free reign to Hadamovsky to shake up the RRG to follow the party line, with waves of lay-offs taking place between March and June, which affected every layer of the network. Propaganda Ministry questionnaires distributed to RRG employees on 27 May asked respondents when they had become members of the NSDAP (Nazi Party), before or after 30 January, as well as whether and when they had served the SA (Sturmabteilung, also known as the Storm Troopers or Brownshirts), or Hitler Youth. Author Jochen Klepper, a producer at the Haus Des Rundfunks, was uniquely well positioned to observe the upheaval, recording in his diary on 8 March that the swastika had been hoisted above the station and, in another entry on 30 March, described his frustration at trying to produce a programme:

> The rehearsal had to be cancelled. The manuscript had not been photocopied because the company with which the station has worked so far is Jewish. The records I ordered were taken from me because either the company or the composer or the conductor is Jewish. I had to dismiss my most reliable announcer because he is Jewish. And by the way, the radio is almost like a National Socialist barracks: uniforms... uniforms of Party formations.[3]

Five days earlier, at a meeting with managers and regional station bosses at the Haus Des Rundfunks, Goebbels threatened, 'If you do not want to understand us or cannot understand us ... I think it would be appropriate if you left us. The radio will be cleansed, as the whole Prussian administration will be cleansed. I would be extremely grateful to you if you carry out this cleansing act yourself. But if you do not, then it will be done by us.'[4] Reforms based on Gleichschaltung (co-ordination) and the Führerprinzip (principle of leadership) were swift. Over the following weeks, 10 of the 11 regional broadcasting directors were replaced. The new men were awarded full powers to recruit fresh blood, while eradicating all Jewish, Social Democratic and Communist employees. To weed them out, RRG resorted to interrogations, denunciations, confiscation of personnel files, lay-offs, transfers, or reassignment on a lower salary. By June, 136 employees of 2,115 had been hounded out or taken into custody while nearly 100 senior officials faced charges of corruption or wrongdoing.

An early casualty of the RRG cull was Walter Schaeffer, a senior technician who, with his wife, was driven to suicide when he was dismissed for political reasons.

Herbert Antoine tried to fight his dismissal in the vain hope the law would protect him. This naive idea was slapped down when an SS courier hand-delivered the verdict, signed by Hadamovsky, citing the new 'Law for the Restoration of the Professional Civil Service' adopted on 11 April. Paragraph 4 stipulated that 'civil servants, who, after their previous political activity, cannot guarantee that they can wholeheartedly support the national state at any time, can be released'. Hadamovsky shot off a missive to Antoine advising that the 'continuing pay-out of the salary will take place according to the legal regulations of three months, therefore you are no longer entitled to additional benefits'.[5] With that, the matter was closed.

On 13 July, Hadamovsky tapped out a report on his accomplishments: 'Party comrade Dr Goebbels ordered me to purge the German radio of influence opposed to our cause. I can now report that the work has been done thoroughly.'

4

DRUNK ON CULTURE

Inspired and with growing authority, Goebbels set about further reforms of the radio system in early 1934 by redesignating local stations – once the proud voices of each district – as 'branch offices' under the title of Reichssender. Although retaining some autonomy, the regional news departments were absorbed into the Ministry of Propaganda.

Goebbels presented an elaborate assemblage representing every corner of Germany, headed by Reichssender Berlin transmitting on 841 kHz (formally Funk-Stunde), which promised to capture the 'essence of this city in which all the threads of the empire converge' with its wide-reaching 100 kilowatt signal. Station manager Otto Stoffregen[1] said through the news, through the talk shows, the 'life of the imperial capital with its great political, military, artistic and sporting events must be captured and conveyed to the listener'. Furthermore, the surrounding Brandenburg country with its forests, lakes, castles and villages would be represented. 'The Reichssender Berlin must report on this old historical ground. It has to bridge the gap between the city and the countryside.'

In its new incarnation as Reichssender Breslau, Schlesische Funkstunde on 950 kHz vowed to serve all paths of society and 'Silesian life in all its diversity'. It carried native dialect broadcasts along with programmes with a 'special obligation' towards ethnic Germans living beyond the borders of the Reich. 'Radio is often the only means of connection to the German mother population for countless German people living in South-eastern Europe,' the station noted. 'Reichssender Breslau covers the whole of South-eastern Europe, which is confirmed by the daily mailbags from Poland, Romania, Hungary, Yugoslavia, Greece and Turkey.'[2] On home soil, farmers, forest workers, miners, industrial workers, craftsmen, railwaymen and intellectuals, as well as 'the petty bourgeoisie', soldiers and men of the labour service were promised programmes they would find stimulating.

Down south, Reichssender München remained earnest and serious, given 'München was the capital of the Nazi movement. From here National Socialism began its triumphal march.' Accordingly, its first task was to 'beam the spirit of the National Socialist'. The second was to 'prove worthy of the name: City of German Art'.

Using five relay stations, Südwestdeutsche Rundfunkdienst morphed into Reichssender Frankfurt on 1195 kHz serving a vast landscape covering Kassel, Koblenz, Trier, and Freiburg. Station manager Hans-Otto Frikes spent extra energy on his centrepiece nightly broadcast: *Unser singende klingende Frankfurt*, a variety programme mixing operetta, native folk music and orchestral pieces – designed to divert listeners from their troubles. The Frankfurt station also had strong appeal abroad, given that its signal spilled into Switzerland, France, Luxembourg and Belgium, prompting a special nightly (midnight to 3 a.m.) broadcast aimed at foreign lands.

In the north, Reichssender Hamburg, the former Norddeutscher Rundfunk, attracted a larger, more diverse audience with a monster signal on 904 kHz, which spanned from the Dutch to the Polish border, north to Denmark, and southward into the Harz Mountains. Hamburg, Lübeck, Bremen and the ports of Kiel and Wilhelmshaven were all within earshot. 'Hamburg is today – more than ever before – the eternal gateway to the world,' controller Gustav Grupe gushed, adding, 'There is no profession that is not represented in our broadcast area.' Regional heritage was reflected with programmes in Low German, a West Germanic language spoken mainly in Northern Germany and north-east Holland. 'Low German is still the everyday language of millions of people. It is the language of the peasant, the sailor and the worker,' Grupe said. 'To all the many who still speak Low

German today, Reichssender Hamburg speaks to them in their language.' Sunday morning concerts from harbours and ports became a specialty attracting audiences far and wide.

Down south, Reichssender Köln took over Westdeutscher Rundfunk gliding out 'genuinely close-to-the-people broadcasting' under director Heinrich Glasmeier, a garrulous Rhinelander and future Director of the Reichs-Rundfunk-Gesellschaft. The channel excelled in the dissemination of political, economic and social programmes reflecting the life of the region.

There were few changes when Ostmarken Rundfunk morphed into Reichssender Königsberg. Covering a sparsely populated agricultural province, for many people it was their only connection to the outside world. Furthermore, as Controller Dr Alfred Lau explained, for tens of thousands of German people in the Baltic States and in Poland, broadcasting was the 'living spiritual connection' with their German homeland. 'The Königsberg station,' he added, 'is at their side at all times in their tough struggle to preserve their German identity.'

In the east, Reichssender Leipzig replaced Mitteldeutscher Rundfunk catering for its 'open-minded and receptive audience' which stretched throughout Saxony, Anhalt and Thuringia. Controller Carl Stueber promised he would 'always endeavour to do justice to this diversity' and adopted the slogan to 'preserve our roots, bring joy and relaxation and never forget the culture of our people'.

Like other regional networks, Reichssender Leipzig 'fulfilled its tasks' as a border broadcaster providing Sudeten Germans and Transylvanians with shows to 'bridge the gap between the Reich Germans and Germans abroad'. Since 1919 the Sudetenland, with its 3 million German inhabitants, became part of the newly founded Czechoslovakia. But when Hitler took power, these Sudeten Germans began demanding the right to autonomy more and more forcefully, much to the delight of the Nazis.

Meanwhile, over at Reichssender Stuttgart, late-night concerts in five languages drifted across much of Western Europe spreading the 'German soul culture', attracting vast audiences in the process.

Every evening at 19:00 (except Sundays), a uniform *Stunde der Nation* ran on all stations, including Deutschlandsender.

The programme normally consisted of a drama, talk, operatic performance or classical concert.

The individual Reichssender stations were quick to align themselves with local sports clubs and the Nationalsozialistischer Reichsbund für Leibesübungen (NSRL). 'True sport is a carrier of culture, which is politically determined according to our National Socialist view,' the *Handbuch des deutschen Rundfunks* stated. 'Broadcasting is one of the most important political instruments of our state, so sports radio also has a task of state political importance.' Saturday afternoons were reserved for a whole gamut of sporting coverage, which brought in a larger and more youthful audience. For example, over the course of just one Saturday in 1937, Reichssender Königsberg carried a skiing championship, Reichssender Köln had pitch-side commentary of a Germany–Holland game in Düsseldorf, while the German water polo championships in Hanover received the attention of Reichssender Hamburg. At the same time, Reichssender München was reporting from the German Rottach-Egern canoeing festival.

Education programming generally fared poorly in the new system. Even prior to the Nazi government, one school in every three was equipped with wireless with lessons heard by 2.5 million pupils and 65,000 teachers in 1932.[3] However, in the process of Nazification, the new Reich Minister of Science, Education and Culture, Bernhard Rust, was largely left to his own devices as he wheeled in leading Nazi thinkers before the microphone to discuss literature, humanities, the arts, sciences, music and history. Rust, a combative man with a tendency to rant, lived by the dictum that the whole function of education was to create a Nazi. His credibility suffered on several occasions when he rolled out new regulations and then repealed them almost immediately. Nazi ideology and distorted history were liberally spread among the schedules. Hans-Jürgen Meier, a schoolboy in rural Storkow, south-east of Berlin, lamented that windows to a colourful world of art, travel and literature were denied to students:

What do I remember from my school days? I was able to memorise the Horst Wessel song, which was sung at every opportunity. For dirty fingernails or lack of athleticism, there were beatings, because

Hitler wanted the German boys to be as 'hard as Krupp steel, nimble as weasels and tough as leather'.[4]

Schoolteachers often turned themselves into rag-and-bone men by collecting scraps from pupils, which their parents had been instructed to salvage from the dinner plate to be used in fertiliser, glue and explosives production. Germany excelled in the production of the ersatz and in the utilisation of waste materials. Every household was forbidden by law to destroy rags, cloth, anything made of copper, nickel, tin, aluminium, lead, iron and steel scraps, wastepaper, rabbit skins, bottles and bones.

During one radio lesson, children were taught America was discovered, not by Columbus, but by a German named Laef. To provide the proper background, a Professor Mueller took to the Deutschlandsender microphone saying, 'It is well known that America was discovered by Laef. We have evidence to substantiate this.'

On another occasion, teachers and pupils listened to engineer Hermann Sörgel outline his plan to create Atlantropa: a new continent would emerge by draining the Mediterranean, thus joining Europe to Africa. Sörgel insisted the moment had come when the vast undeveloped spaces of Africa had become the necessary economic complement to a crowded Europe if the 'white races' were to survive in the struggle for life against the ten times more numerous 'yellow races'. More than anything else, student Christel Hertenstein remembered school timetables were occasionally coordinated around radio broadcasting schedules:

> When I went to school in Köln, if Hitler was making a speech over the radio we all went to the auditorium and listened to it. We would then have to write an essay about the speech. Somehow or another I always got out of doing that. For one thing I didn't like to do it, and I have a suspicion that my teacher didn't mind whether I did it or not, because I always got out of it. I had some dumb excuse or another. She really didn't press it very hard.[5]

The influencing of adolescents by the media had an obvious and attractive appeal for the Nazi propagandists, thus, in addition to educational programmes, the Hitler Youth – working in concert with the National Socialist Teachers Association – took to the airwaves twice weekly with the *Young Generation Hour* and *Die Morgenfeiern der HJ* respectively. Both shows opened with trumpets, fanfares and high-decibel hymns. The cacophony aimed to deepen the world view and religious experience of the movement with songs dedicated to the Fatherland.[6] Audiences were enthralled with transmissions from special excursions featuring teenagers jumping into the deep end of swimming pools, leaping from buildings, scaling walls, crossing rivers, shooting rifles and boxing. Baldur von Schirach, the founder of the organisation, was a frequent contributor, where topics almost always had something to do with courage and readiness to die: 'You are nothing, your people are everything' was a regular theme.

At camps around the country there were 'other things that had to be mastered' by young recruits according to SS-Brigadeführer Karl Cerff, the man responsible for the Reichsjugendführung, the radio section of the Hitler Youth. For example, 'the erection and operation of the large loudspeaker systems required significant knowledge and experience'.[7] A special HJ Reichsfunkschule taught youngsters to rig speakers, fix antennas, balance sound and even help the elderly to tune their new Volksempfänger sets.

All Reichssender stations forged a close relationship with the KdF (Kraft durch Freude/Strength through Joy), a unit set up by the Nazis to promote 'employees' rights' and appease workers after the abolishment of Trade Unions in 1933.[8]

The organisation fell under the control of the German Labour Front (DAF) and enabled 14 million people to enjoy annual vacations at bargain prices. On paper, Strength through Joy aimed at improving the health of the population by encouraging running, hiking, swimming, and active family holidays. With millions of working people paying monthly dues, the organisation amassed a hefty fortune. There were trips to the Bavarian Alps by special trains, steamer excursions to Madeira and subsidised theatre tickets. By 1937, half a million youngsters were taking part in special sports courses such as sailing, fencing, and horse riding. On the Baltic island of Ruegen, workers were building a vast resort to accommodate 22,000 holidaymakers, while Hitler launched the *Wilhelm Gustloff* – the first Strength Through Joy vessel to cruise the Mediterranean and Norwegian Fjords with a cargo of 'deserving workers'. KdF leader Robert Ley insisted nothing characterised the trend of new Germany better than the fact that the worker was able to visit foreign countries as a 'representative of Germany and a messenger of goodwill'.

Ley launched the campaign 'Germany is singing again' during spring, treating listeners to a whirlwind of performances from amateur talents hidden within the workforce. Most Reichssender channels set up monthly showcases featuring this lay talent under the title *KdF Variety and Radio Parade* advertised under the rubric 'Art of the People'. Musical groups performed regular *KdF Song Book* concerts, amateur artists displayed their works, while music of all sorts wafted from factory and municipal buildings. A Reichssender Köln innovation saw the first unified factory sing-songs featuring folk songs broadcast from local workplaces, while other regional factories joined in at the same time.

There was no lack of lusty singing in crowded cafés and beerhouses either, where local 'turns' were recorded. KdF's radio unit churned out travel programmes, documentaries, monologues, theatrical productions, educational talks, sporting features, interviews, full-blooded operas and endless Beethoven, Brahms and Schubert recitals. The DAF insisted the working man could enjoy 'highbrow' culture, and arranged the *Music of Great Masters* project bringing 'outstanding works by famous composers' lunchtime factory concerts, performed by the leading artists and orchestras. The performances, DAF insisted, 'clearly abolished the prejudice that existed with "highbrow" and the perception of enjoyment which was reserved only for intellectuals ... that myth has finally been cleared up'.

The series was an unbelievable success. Participating artists unanimously reported the open-mindedness of audiences.[9]

While 'high culture' became more accessible, the distinction collapsed altogether on the airwaves as classical works were robustly represented alongside popular melodies, dance band crooners and warblers. During the day, silly, melancholy, propagandistic and sentimental gramophone records transported housewives far from domestic chores. The Nazi message was often entwined into lyrics: popular community, patriotism, nationalism and the demonisation of foes. The most popular 'radio artists' were Comedian Harmonists, Lilian Harvey, Willy Fritsch, Peter Igelhoff, Ilse Werner, Paul Godwin, Max Hansen and the Swede Zarah Leander, described by one music critic as a 'low-voiced charmer', who was similar in some ways to Greta Keller.

The jazz age failed to captivate the Nazis, with Hadamovsky banning the genre in 1934. 'I herewith pronounce final interdict on nigger jazz for the whole German wireless,' he told radio officials. 'Whatever other hardships the German people may have to endure under their present rigorous Government, they will be no longer condemned to suffer the torture of so-called jazz music.' Goebbels, on the other hand, colourfully described jazz as a 'product of primitives' and its proper place was in the museum of ethnology. The last word, it seems, went to the British conductor Sir Henry Coward who declared Hitler was worthy of the highest praise when he banished jazz, 'that is what should be done in Britain, for the sake of art, morality, and the Anglo-Saxon race'. Coward insisted jazz debased the taste not only for good music, both classical and light, but also induced in its fans a 'nervous twitching of the hands and body, and frivolous, inelegant manner'.[10]

In the immediate wake of the jazz ban, Hadamovsky also assured listeners they would no longer be subjected to 'Jewish-like' speech, not even when rendered with music, prompting *Volksfunk* to lay out a double-page spread under the headline 'From Jewish Broadcaster to People's Broadcaster'. The article glowed at the 'eradication of Jewish performers and thinkers from the airwaves', as the thoughts and voices of Fritz Rotter, Ernst Toller, Albert Einstein, Irene Ambrus and Alfred Kerr were consigned to the wilderness.

A snapshot of anti-Semitism on air can be gleaned from *Rulands-Eck*, a radio cabaret featuring a trio of Hamburg singers, relayed via various Reichssender stations, stuffed with variations on a common tune, namely anti-Semitic diatribes. They made comical reference to the anti-Jewish measures while, at the same time, tried to justify them. By this point, such actions were the least of the problems faced by the Jewish community, which had been ostracised, defamed and disenfranchised since the Nazi assumption of power.

5

THIS IS BERLIN

Berlin spoke to the world about German society and values through Deutsche Kurzwellensender (KWS) shortwave transmissions. Unlike other wavelengths, which carried only for a limited distance, shortwave spanned oceans and continents. For those Germans in remote information-starved corners of the world, it was the only connection to the Fatherland. By spinning a dial, a German farmer in Africa could keep up with the latest football scores, while remote mountain dwellers in the Alps needed never miss the latest utterances of the Führer.

Following the example of Russia and other European countries, Berlin also began an extensive schedule of shortwave broadcasts intended for listeners overseas by beaming across the Atlantic to Central and South America, southward over Africa, and to Asia, in daylight and darkness, with content trimmed to fit official Nazi policy concerns. Within 60 days of the Nazi regime taking power, KWS was pumping out a dazzling variety of items in German, English and Spanish to North and Central America from 01.00 to 03.15 daily.[1] By the end of the year, a full-scale invasion of the international ether flooded the airwaves from Berlin.

Station director Dr Kurt von Boeckmann opined that one of the most significant weaknesses of German governments before Hitler was they 'did not recognise the foreign policy implications of this new intellectual means of communication even though the technical requirements for its use already existed before 1933'.[2] One feature of the broadcasts was a series of regular relays from theatres, centres of amusement and scenes of various current events.

Political output was sweetened by the works of Mozart, Beethoven and Wagner, conducted by the Berlin Philharmonic Orchestra's Wilhelm Furtwangler – a man who became inseparably associated with shortwave service.

Another valuable purpose for this global voice was as a pioneer in denying the ill treatment of the Jews. Given the sensitivity of the subject, many news editorials devoted special attention to scoffing at overseas press reports concerning the plight of German Jews. It should also be noted especially on this point, Goebbels clearly differentiated between the strategic guidelines for domestic and international broadcasting, where contradictions in editorial policy were clearly evident.

Originally known as the new 'World Broadcasting Station', the first shortwave service burst onto the airwaves on 26 August 1929 with an eclectic assortment of offerings and a patchy signal. 'In the beginning, the music came in with some disturbance and was what I would call distorted,' a former Leipzig native living in Utica, north of New York, wrote. While another listener from Leadville, Colorado, fared better, noting the 'music was wonderfully clear and very loud'. With a slight increase in power, correspondence arrived from South America, Africa and some parts of Asia.

By Christmas 1929, signal quality had improved to the extent that 21 NBC stations in the USA relayed Wagner's opera *Tristan und Isolde* directly from Bayreuth. German language courses in the form of translated folk songs followed, along with regular relays from the nine regional stations.

But, even though technically the shortwave station was a success – and letters from obscure little towns around the globe were thrilling – the project garnered little interest from within Germany. Even Hans Bredow was generally unimpressed, instead waiting to see if enthusiasm would be maintained.

The real expansion began sometime in the spring of 1935 when the ground was broken for six long-distance shortwave transmitters at Zeesen, about 30 miles from Berlin. As the 200-foot towers rose above the countryside, it became known that they would be used to trumpet news to Germans living in Africa, Asia, Australia, the Far East and the Americas. 'The focus of the service is the fulfilment of the national and political obligation of the Reich towards Germans abroad,' Von Boeckmann declared.

> These millions of emigrants from earlier times have spread far and wide across the globe. Many of them have lost contact with their homeland, because this homeland had let them down.
>
> Because of the huge rise of the Reich under Adolf Hitler and its position as a major superpower in global politics, the Reich now offers protection and help to Germans abroad. The miracle of shortwave also means Adolf Hitler's Reich not only acts, it also speaks day and night in German and in many foreign languages.[3]

The KWS budget was increased from 100,000 RM to 2.68 million RM between 1933 and 1935, and later shot up again and again.[4] With such investment, programme variety was rich and spanned just about every cultural field. *From the German Heart* was a platform for works of German poetry with interpretive and introductory words. In between commentaries and talks, regular 15-minute programmes included concerts from the Philharmonic Orchestra and Berlin State Orchestra. Under the title *European Portraits*, teacher Willi Schäferdiek produced a series of biographical radio plays on Goethe, Schiller, Beethoven, Shakespeare, da Vinci, Michelangelo, Cellini and Cervantes. For his report on 'broadcast propaganda', journalist Mark Potter tuned into Berlin during the summer of 1935 where he heard music and song, sandwiched with 'news from the German point of view', and of information concerning German and Nazi activities which the 'Reich consider it desirable that the English speaking world should know':

> The information concerned the German plans to combat unemployment by putting men on the land, draining marshes and converting them into agricultural land, and so on. On three

different shortwaves the Germans regularly broadcast in English, so as to cover the greater portion of the world.[5]

The Party organisation for Germans abroad presented regularly scheduled features such as *Germans All over the World* and *Socialism and Germans Abroad* to cement expatriate loyalty to the Fatherland. Operetta performances, choral music and organ performances were relayed from Deutschlandsender and Reichssender stations. 'Again and again it is confirmed by foreigners that there are permanent regular audiences. The desires of members of other nations to be able to hear the German broadcasts in their own language are also increasing,' Von Boeckmann surmised. Elsewhere on the schedules, well-known authors were used to write depictions of German landscapes, including Peter Huchel who wrote about Brandenburg. Oda Schäfer composed an essay on Silesia, Alfons Paquet on the Taunus, Jakob Kneip on the Hunsrü and Johannes Kirschweng on the Saarland.

> As often as they want, our comrades-in-arms overseas, wherever they may roam, hear the voice of Germany. It tells them everything they need to know about the Reich and brings relaxation and joy through German music and poetry and lets them participate in the great national events, just as the comrade back home does. Programme-wise, there is hardly any difference between the home services and the offerings transmitted to those in the Brazilian jungle, African bush or on Asian plantations. On this basis, there is no longer any inhibition of space and time for the German global community. [6]

Although Nazism never found much appeal in America, the RRG shortwave service managed to attract considerable groups of listeners after it first wafted over American shores. Von Boeckmann busily pointed out the arrival of 'uninterrupted flood of letters, gifts and donations in cash' from all over the world, which he considered the most moving part of his work. Indeed, the RRG correspondence files from the period are stuffed with glowing praise from afar. 'I wish to compliment the staff for the high-grade quality of the programmes. The music is gorgeous – real artists and accomplished musicians – characteristic of the German people. Every day the programme is different, no two of them just alike, which makes them all the more enjoyable,' a listener from Sedalia, Missouri, gushed. 'Another thing, your announcements are so polite and dignified; it radiates real culture and makes one feel and appreciates a real true friendship.' The letter continued:

> Last Sunday, mother was ill in bed in another room from the receiver and she enjoyed your programme so much and particularly the phrase at the close, 'We wish you a very pleasant Sunday'. She is better now and up and around again. Your little acts of courtesy and pleasant good wishes do not go unnoticed, I assure you. Hope you will continue to announce in this pleasant way. It is unique und so interesting. Your diction is perfect – your manner polished – your English as perfect as your German. DJB [the call sign] is our 'pet' foreign station.

A listener from Syracuse opined that KWS announcers were 'the most polite, thorough, considerate I have ever heard from a foreign or domestic transmitter', while a fan in Toronto had no doubt the station was 'helping to promote better understanding between Germany and her friends across the Atlantic'. While for many outsiders it was revolting to hear as the Nazis petulantly deconstructed Jewish society, for others, though, it was entirely an internal matter:

> Your announcer in my estimation is perfection both in diction and even his voice is very polite, (it is too bad a few of us all too ready to condemn Americans) could not listen to the German side of the view, perhaps then they would not be so ready to take sides in what in my estimation is a German question of policy. I want you to know that I am an American, a veteran of the World War, who now realises that if I had known what it was all about I would have never been there.

Investment in the service to America was considerable. When author Bertram de Colonna was given a guided tour of the KWS he was lucky enough to find American expatriates rehearsing for the broadcast of their Thanksgiving ceremony:

> The Pastor and choir of the American church were taking part. It is always a strange sight to see a singer in front of the microphone dressed in an old jacket more comfy than smart and to ponder over the impression his song may be making in far-off New Zealand and distant San Francisco. We later heard the real broadcast, after the rehearsals.[7]

Around the same time, the columnist from the British *Wireless Whispers* column painted the KWS in glowing colours after enjoying a folk music concert emanating from Berlin. 'How delightful it was to hear the choir of children singing with their elders – a rarity in the case of British broadcasts,' he commented admiringly. 'It is interesting to hear how much the authorities in Berlin are in touch with people who speak English in our Colonies, and how the listeners are encouraged not only to tune to the German stations, but to write.'[8] According to Von Boeckmann, the most effective proof of 'real contact' with foreign audiences came with the introduction and success of a German language course, which began initially as an experiment for American listeners, but proved so popular they became a permanent institution.

6

THE OLYMPIC DREAM

In trying to wire up an entire mountain, RRG engineers took on a challenge worthy of an Olympic athlete during the autumn and winter of 1935 as they feverishly prepared for the Winter Olympics. At the Bavarian resort of Garmisch-Partenkirchen technicians laid the groundwork for an event widely viewed as the dress rehearsal for the upcoming summer games in Berlin.[1] As the first major international competition to be held on home soil since the First World War, the events in Bavaria were considered historic.

As arrangements got underway to host 80,000 spectators, 1,000 entrants from 28 nations prepared for an event bigger than any previous games, sparking intense international media interest. When a member of the Propaganda Ministry was appointed to the Winter Olympic Committee, a correspondent from the *New York Times* remarked the Olympics were 'essentially a propaganda undertaking by the German government'.

Broadcasting operations centred on a special wooden 'Olympic Station' hut from where, according to the chief engineer, reporters' rooms were fitted with soundproof walls to prevent any hindrance from extraneous noises:

Lighting and heating was provided, and this latter prevented the formation of ice on the windows. Every announcer's box was fitted with a telephone. Thus the radio reporter had a direct connection to the engineer who could switch the telephone connection into long-distance lines. The central switchboard was there. All relay and communication lines could be switched from there. The house also contained the recording apparatus.[2]

The enormous scale of broadcasting the event required pioneering spirit, with the laying of cables alone taking more than half a year. At the same time, microphone points for reporters were fixed so every broadcaster was afforded the best possible view of skiers, skaters, bobsledders and curlers at venues spread over 5 miles. Although the panorama topped by Germany's highest peak, the Zugspitze, provided a stunning backdrop, RRG technicians faced a multitude of 'special difficulties' arising from the high-alpine character of the district:

> It must be considered that portable equipment which was only installed shortly before a broadcast was required as well as permanent apparatus. The apparatus for relaying the Slalom had to be taken up into the mountains late at night so that the technical equipment would be ready for the start early next day. It was not always possible to transport the apparatus with motor-cars. It was, therefore, necessary to use sleighs drawn by horses or oxen. Often the engineers had to carry the apparatus required for the relays up into the mountains themselves.[3]

Outside Broadcast Manager Horst Cleinow oversaw a special service with a staff of reporters providing commentaries in four languages placed at the disposal of the Kurzwellensender. Some reporters required direct relays, while others were eager to make recordings for later transmission. 'It was only partly possible to make arrangements beforehand as most of the sports events relied on the results of the preliminary contests before they could be fixed,' Von Boeckmann remembered. In his highly detailed written account of the Games, Von Boeckmann noted as well as battling the intense cold and shifting weather patterns, keeping transmission schedules elastic was a major worry: 'Distant connections from Garmisch-Partenkirchen to the relaying stations in Europe, North and South America as well as Asia had always to be available'.

As a listener, Von Boeckmann favoured the live relays, which, he thought, gave a sense of immediacy, allowing listeners to become participant observers in the events they heard. In all, 287 programmes in 14 languages were beamed from Garmisch-Partenkirchen, leading IOC president Henri Comte de Baillet-Latour to express his 'intense satisfaction' in a personal letter to Eugen Hadamovsky:

> I should like to take advantage of this opportunity to express my best wishes for the success of the broadcasting organisation at the coming games in the summer. This task will be, for your corporation, even more difficult and strenuous than the first.[4]

With the countdown to the Summer Olympics, Goebbels presided over the switch-on of six new shortwave transmitters at Zeesen which, he promised, would 'carry propaganda for the new Germany of Adolf Hitler, and to disperse so far as is possible the remnants of the untruthful and distorted concepts prevalent abroad about us'.[5]

Regions which were specially covered included India, China, Australia, New Zealand, Siam, South and Central America and South Africa. By this point the shortwaves were becoming increasingly congested with stations from America, Australia, the Dutch East Indies and Russia, something like 45 altogether, being receivable at any hour of the day or night. 'Shortwave has definitely come to stay, and that there will be big run on sets of this character there is no doubt,' was the verdict of the syndicated British *Wireless Whispers* column.[6]

The Summer Games catapulted Germany into the focus of the world as hundreds of thousands of tourists descended on Berlin's Olympic Stadium, built to hold 106,000 spectators. Designed by architect Werner March, the arena – flanked by 136 vast limestone pillars on the outer wall – lived up to its aspiration as a national landmark.

The RRG organisational effort was much larger than at Garmisch-Partenkirchen, given that the commentary points were integrated at the track and field arena, swimming stadium, hockey pitch, equestrian stadium, tennis courts and the open-air theatre.

Moreover, other challenges facing commentators had been overcome, especially at the rowing regattas in Berlin's Grunau district where a mini shortwave transmitter was fitted to a boat enabling reporters to transmit live – and moving – commentary from the water.[7] The evolving nature of these tests discovered microphones placed above the lake caught the ambiance of splashing and yelling oarsmen, adding extra sparkle.[8]

An entire page of the *Völkischer Beobachter* was devoted to news that engineers had rigged up 350 microphones and equipment for 100 reporters, 30 of whom could broadcast live, while the remaining 70 were able to record reports to 16-inch aluminium electric transcription records.[9] A journalist for the *Northern Whig* toured special cabins built into the wall of the stadium which commanded a clear view of all the events, 'and special recording apparatus was also provided so the commentaries could be used other than at the particular times the events took place'.

To aid foreign radio reporters, an 'Olympic Passport' ensured access gratis to all points of the contest; furthermore, *Die deutsche Rundfunkaussprache* guidebook helped with the correct pronunciation of the names of 6,000 competitors. More than anything else, many reporters remember being loaned Olympiakoffers, the first battery-powered portable radio. Priced at 156 RM with tubes and batteries, the green mock-leather device was advertised as a 'receiver for travel, weekends and sport'.

The build-up began on 20 July, when the Olympic flame left Ancient Olympia in Greece to begin its journey to Berlin. Over the next weeks, the excitement built as the torch passed from runner to runner across seven countries. By the end of July, the journey had been elevated to the daily news highlight on Deutschlandsender. Apart from the sports angle, propaganda was designed to creatively engage audiences along the lines of a 'cultural spectacular' using the Strength through Joy organisation, the Hitler Youth, and the League of German Maidens.

Punctuated by gigantic swastikas and grids of light enveloping the stadium, the big day arrived. The opening ceremony on 1 August was witnessed by 1,800 journalists from 60 countries.[10]

This kind of shared international experience was an entirely new phenomenon. Never before in human history had such a mass of humanity from across the globe been joined together. As the world listened, thousands of faithful Nazis, some with tears in their eyes, roared with approval as the torch bearer jogged into the arena. 'Hitler's arrival, signalled by a trumpet solo from the huge towers that form the Marathon gateway to the stadium, was taken up by a hundred-piece symphony orchestra, which burst into "Deutschland Uber Alles" and the "Horst Wessel Lied",' a correspondent of the *Herald Tribune* reported admiringly. The German athletes received a rapturous reception from the crowds, as did squads representing Finland, the United Kingdom, Norway and the USA.

During the parade of athletes, Richard Strauss, one of the leading composers of the late Romantic era, conducted a chorus of 1,000 men and women singing the Olympic hymn. The public couldn't avoid the blare from tinny speakers hanging from trees across the city relaying Reichssender Berlin's special coverage of the sporting events and festivities. Berlin police complained the loudspeakers broadcasting results along 'Festival Street', which ran from the City Hall in the east to the Olympic Stadium in the west, 'had a negative effect on the control of traffic, since truck drivers stopped their vehicles at the loudspeakers in order to hear the results of the Olympics. The behaviour hindered the movement of traffic.'

RRG arranged a dizzying list of special performances using dance orchestras, the radio symphony and chamber music groups over the 16-day schedule. Against this festival background, the official task of Reichssender Berlin was as follows:

1. The 'Olympic-Radio-Quick-Service' to announce immediately Olympic victory and shortly afterwards the official result.
2. At the end of each full hour during the contests, the most important results of the last hour were to be announced.
3. The Finals of the different games were to be transmitted directly from the points of contest.
4. Attention was to be drawn to the most important events in the midday, evening and late-evening bulletins.
5. Eye-witness descriptions of the daily contests were to be broadcast during the night-concerts from midnight till 02:00 in five languages.

As the days wore on, Paul Winter's 'Fanfare' – used to open and close radio reports – became the classic example of a modern earworm. 'The first Fanfare is an awakening call to contest, to the gathering and concentration of all one's energies,' Winter explained. 'The second is a sort of crowning of victory and the pouring forth of the Olympic idea over the whole of life.' The apparatus by which this earworm emitted was described in the book *Olympia Weltsender* as a 'luminous sound-generating device that reproduces the tune of the fanfare'.

Perhaps unsurprisingly, Deutschlandsender sat at the core of home coverage. From two offices deep in the bowels of the stadium, the station orchestrated coverage not just for their own listeners, but for every individual Reichssender (except Berlin) around the clock. Controller Otto Stoffregen would never forget the 'going and coming of messengers, the uninterrupted ringing of the telephones, the noise of the typewriters and the systematic confusion of orders and directions... it often reminded me of the atmosphere in the staff command during a battle'. Guidelines for commentaries on domestic radio stipulated reporting should neither overemphasise nor underplay German victories. Rather, it was instructed, 'they should reflect a just recognition of all countries'.

In a tiny room squeezed between the restaurant and storage area, transcribers followed the work of the foreign reporters by intercutting snippets of commentaries into a daily dossier. A surviving script shows the excitement of the Japanese commentator Shinroku Tanomogi informing his native country by shortwave of Kitei Son's victory in the marathon:

> One hears the applause in the stadium. Son is at the head. Son is
>   the first. Son is the first!
> There are a hundred metres till the winning line.
> Son appears at the Marathon gate.
> Our Son will soon reach the winning line.
> Japan is in the first place.
> Son is the first, Son is the first, Son is the first.
> There are only 50 metres till the winning line.
> Only 40 metres. Only 20 metres, 20 metres, 10 metres.

Son has reached the winning line.
Our Japan, the Marathon victor. Our Japan has gained the
Olympic victory long wished for.

Coverage of the Games was one of the early successes of the growing
television service, which beamed low-definition pictures to public
viewing rooms across Berlin.[11] To begin with, architect Werner
March was unhappy with the prospect of television coverage,
fearful the bulky equipment would damage his stadium. Only after
a personal intervention from Goebbels did he allow cameras into the
arena. In addition to placing a huge Telefunken Ikonoskop camera –
known as the 'television cannon' due to its 2.2-metre length –
under Hitler's VIP box, two other cameras, one from Fernseh AG
and another from the Reichspost, were situated at the swimming
pool and Marathon Gate. At the same time, the Reichspost parked
a new television truck at the stadium to experiment with time-
delayed transmission. While no footage survives of the original TV
broadcast, a copy of the opening transmission script does exist:

> Achtung! Achtung! Here is the Paul Nipkow Berlin TV station
> with sound on the 7.06 metre wave and with pictures on the 6.77
> metre wave with a special Olympic broadcast. We will start the
> Summer Olympics with a film broadcast of the 'Preparations for
> the Olympic Games' and will then switch to the May Field to
> provide you with a mood report.

To give athletes a flavour of the excitement, TV sets were also
placed in the 'Hindenburg House' at the Olympic village where
competitors, according to a security guard interviewed by the
television service, watched the proceedings with interest:

> **Interviewer:** Have you ever actually been inside the television
> parlour here?
> **Guard:** I've been here before and there's always a big crowd in the
> television parlour.
> **Interviewer:** And the foreign athletes too?
> **Guard:** Yes, sir. All the foreign athletes enjoy taking a look at this
> television.

Back at the stadium, the invincible American athlete Jesse Owens was busy stealing the show by winning four gold medals. 'They are tripping like thoroughbred horses,' the TV commentator of the 100-metre sprint declared overexcitedly, 'two blacks against four whites. Europe against the United States... the fight begins!' Then, Owens stormed to victory receiving a wild ovation. 'White mankind should be ashamed,' Goebbels grumbled.

The scale and ambition, not to mention the audio clarity of the production was incomparable to anything the RRG had ever produced. There was not one slip, miscue or delay during the entire 16-day event. Furthermore, the Games gave a huge boost to listening figures with the industry journal *Der Radio-Händler* recording 91,940 'people's radio' sets had been sold in the last quarter of 1936.[12]

Revelling in the moment, Hadamovsky ordered an initial print run of 20,000 copies of *Olympia Weltsender*, a lavishly illustrated 128-page book detailing the mammoth accomplishments of the RRG. 'Radio itself,' he wrote in the introduction, 'was linked up high above all frontiers, mountains and oceans directly with the Olympic arena':

> We could thus in imagination expand the vast space of the arena, with its more than one hundred thousand seats, into a gigantic forum in which all the peoples of the earth were participators and listeners at the Olympic Games. So does Radio serve perfectly the peaceful union of nations, and is proved a most powerful instrument of peace.
>
> More swiftly than that Greek youth, more than two millennia and a half ago, after his breathless run brought to his Athenian fellow-citizens the tidings of victory at Marathon, has the voice of the Radio announced to you, in your very homes, the dramatic course of the Olympic Games and the victory of your team.[13]

For his part, Goebbels found time to scribble a few lines in the same edition underneath a black and white portrait, depicting him gazing toward the reader, with the Swastika flag proudly draped behind.

The German wireless has particularly through its transmissions from the Olympic Games contributed in strengthening the bonds of friendship between the nations.[14]

The investments made at the Kurzwellensender for the Olympics left it splendidly equipped to transmit news items in five languages – German, English, Dutch, Portuguese and Spanish. It also gained a legion of new fans including Fritz Kuhn and his German-American League, a New York-based Fascist organisation run on Nazi lines. The group warmly welcomed the RRG's growing influence and enthusiastically distributed programme materials far and wide.

In a further expansion, RRG aimed new programmes at the British Empire – India, South Africa and Australia – on nine different frequencies in German, English, and other languages. Fresh offerings included *Old Dominion* for Canada; *Hallo, East Africa*, for Tanganyika territory; and a special broadcast for Cape Town, *Hallo South-West Africa*, which, as a listener noted, opened with genuine 'Teutonic coyness':

Hullo, dear friends and listeners in South Africa! This is the German shortwave station calling you. Here are our best wishes for very fine entertainment and tip-top reception.

Over on the domestic services, Hadamovsky, still basking in Olympic glory, rolled out a schedule weighted with a range of 'socially worthy' programmes. Under the dual banner *Joy and Community*, and *Joy in the Plant and at Home*, the new slate began with a concert from a Reichsbahn repair shop in Munich, followed by a plethora of shows from Tempelhof airport, an Autobahn construction site, a coal mine in the Ruhr, Hamburg docks and a herring fishery plant. In addition to the arbitrary sing-song, programmes detailed how factories and works across the country had been inspected to see there was nothing detrimental to the health of the workers. Employees told how they were benefiting from 10,000 new canteens, sports pitches, swimming pools and modern washrooms. Much publicity was awarded to a 'model factory' in Leipzig which scrapped the howling of sirens for a large church bell to summon staff to and from work. 'This bell expresses the Germans' idea that daily work is the sublimest prayer,' the local KdF leader explained. 'The bell adds to the beauty of work.'

In another offering, broadcaster Max Barthel hosted a series of 'holiday postcards' in *Mit KdF nach Madeira* recorded during a six-day cruise from Bremerhaven to the Mediterranean. On the same theme, Reichssender Hamburg transmitted from Lübeck Bay and the island of Rügen where work continued on the vast KdF holiday resort at Prora with 10,000 sea-view rooms in eight six-storey blocks. Architect Clemens Klotz designed every block with its own cafeteria, which could serve up to 2,500 people per meal, divided into several sittings at breakfast, lunch, and dinner.

At Christmas, the first *Winterhilfswerk* concert spreading holiday cheer took to the airwaves, hosted by Heinz Goedecke, aided by the Luftwaffe Orchestra. The show collected donations for seven successive Sundays, helped by volunteers calling out their well-worn slogan: 'None shall starve or freeze'. American journalist Harry Flannery later recalled how he nurtured a particular hate for the scheme:

> I had been in a subway when a lusty German workman came in with his red can, made a speech at the end of the car, and then set out to shake the box under each nose. I was once in a night club when a collector accosted me. I was polite at first.
>
> 'Nein, danke' I said, 'no, thank you,' in German.
>
> He appealed again.
>
> '*Nein, danke,*' I said, louder this time.
>
> He continued to beg.
>
> 'I don't want any,' I cried in English.
>
> The man looked at me with his mouth open in surprise. He left.

Among other changes, Hadamovsky introduced a weekly programme on world literature, as well as farming analysis and interviews. Culture was exported physically when the Berlin Philharmonic Orchestra arrived in London for a performance of *The Ring* during Coronation week, which was broadcast on both Deutschlandsender and the BBC. The programme formed part of a new series of special 'evening leisure hours' featuring top-class conductors and soloists.

Deutschlandflug, a spectacular celebration of the Air Force, provided excitement with a special concert live from Rangsdorf airport, while motor racing from the AVUS racetrack – a few hundred metres from the Haus Des Rundfunks – attracted scores of listeners. Between the races, the music corps of the Wachtruppe Berlin belted out popular melodies.

Of all the memos churned out by Hadamovsky, a one-page telegram to Goebbels on 1 January 1937 was his proudest. In it, he announced there were approximately 8.9 million radio listeners in Germany, double the figure for 1 January 1933. Furthermore, 1936 had seen listeners increase by three times the number for any year before Hitler came to power, and the increase was twice as large as that in England. And, on top of that, 2 million of the new listeners had purchased people's receivers, the special cut-priced sets.

These achievements were loudly broadcast during the great meeting between broadcasters and retailers at the Internationale Funkausstellung, where Goebbels initiated a war against radio interference to stamp out buzzes, howling, whistles and electrical humming – a problem common with mediumwave and longwave reception, especially in apartment blocks. To put matters right, he said, more money would be invested in a Wireless Investigation Bureau to provide a free service dealing with the suppression of interference. Listeners could report problems to the postman, which would then be processed by engineering troubleshooters. During painstaking 'on the spot' inspections, pipes, vacuum cleaners, hairdryers, and devices incorporating small electric motors, telephone lines and anything that could cause interference were checked. At the same time, a new transmitting system at Herzberg using a 337-metre tower and power of 150kW was put into operation for Deutschlandsender, which was later increased to 200kW giving the station a vast footprint across Germany, Holland, Austria and Hungary.

It wasn't long afterwards that Goebbels instructed an increase in the quota of 'serious and high-quality' music on Deutschlandsender. 'That will,' he said, 'be expressed above all in the transmission of German symphony concerts and opera performances.' 'Above all,' he added, 'Deutschlandsender should be a reflection of German artistic, intellectual and political life.' Accordingly, Otto Stoffregen arranged more performances from the music festivals in Bayreuth and Salzburg and additional broadcasts from provincial operas and concerts. The effort caused considerable headaches as in many cases local theatres were too small for live broadcasting equipment. 'Apart from very few theatres,' Stoffregen complained, 'the question of the suitability of many concert halls and theatres for broadcasting purposes remains a problem. It should, therefore, be advisable to think about the needs of broadcasting when planning new or renovating theatres and concert halls.' There were other discussions too, including a debate raging about the merits of recording:

> An infinitely important problem for broadcasting is the question: direct transmission or broadcast on wax record? The views are different, and it is usually the case that theatre directors and conductors want live transmission, while the radio expert prefers it the other way. Stage managers and conductors can give no valid reason for their demand. On the other hand, the radio operator has a number of serious arguments for the transmission of wax, especially since this does not result in a loss of quality.[15]

German papers were quick to point out that between September 1938 and March 1939, Deutschlandsender transmitted 13 live Philharmonic performances (seven conducted by Furtwangler), featuring the music of Brahms, Rossini, Mozart, Handel, and Bruckner, while between September and October 1938, 16 symphony concerts were broadcast live from Vienna, Munich, Stuttgart, Leipzig, and the main concert hall at the Haus Des Rundfunks.

7

THE TELEVISION MIRACLE

On a cold, dreary afternoon in September 1937, pioneering viewers in Berlin gazed open-mouthed as images of a huge swastika looming up behind Nuremberg castle beamed onto tiny glass screens before them. 'We heard and saw what was going on in Nuremberg at the same moment that these things were taking place,' the *Berliner Tageblatt* gushed, reporting the very first live telecast of the Nazi Party Congress. 'Not a minute, not a second, not even the thousandth part of a second was lost...'[1]

To make this technical milestone possible, TV cameras used at the Olympics were shipped south to the vast Zeppelin Meadow parade ground on the outskirts of Nuremberg. From there, proceedings of the Nazi rally could be relayed to television rooms back in Berlin, along with speeches and man-on-the-street interviews. In typical style, the Women's Labour Service opened the programming parading side-by-side with 50,000 suntanned men from the DAF.

'As if in a dream, television enthusiasts sat in front of the receivers in Berlin and experienced what happened in Nuremberg in the same second,' controller of the Paul Nipkow station Hans-Jürgen Nierentz told reporters. 'They saw the leader, they heard his words, they saw the marching formations...'

For the Nazis, television presented a world of possibilities when it emerged from the experimental stage to becoming a practical reality with its debut at the Berlin Radio Exhibition in 1935. The station was named in honour of Paul Nipkow, a pioneer who demonstrated first wired-image transmission in 1928. From 1933 onwards, Nipkow was lauded by the National Socialists as the 'inventor of television' in blatant disregard for the achievements of other Germans such as the Jewish physicist Siegmund Loewe and scientist Manfred von Ardenne.

Keen to develop TV technology, RRG embarked on an ambitious plan to put a regular service on air, a move boosted by a television policy decree signed by Hitler, which supported its parallel development in military applications:

> The further development of television makes [it] urgently necessary to unite in one [body] the responsibilities of the various government authorities concerned. In view of the special importance of television as regards the provision of safety in flying and as regards national air defence, I order competence in the sphere of television is transferred to the Reich's Minister for Air, who will exercise control in consultation with the Reich's Minister of Posts.

It was along these lines the first-ever trial TV experiment between two cities – 125 miles apart – linked Berlin and Leipzig. Soon after, technicians at the Tempelhof scientific laboratories managed to transmit a signal reaching a distance of 250 miles, 'an almost incomprehensible miracle' according to Eugen Hadamovsky.

Before RRG began transmissions from Berlin-Witzleben, an ultra-shortwave antenna was hoisted atop their new studios on Rognitzstrasse, not far from the Haus Des Rundfunks. While programme production fell to the Propaganda Ministry, broadcasting frequencies were assigned by the Aviation Ministry.

By the summer of 1935, Nipkow TV was televising films practically every day, although with a signal range of just 5 miles. At the start of the early transmissions, the announcer – usually a popular actress or singer – welcomed viewers in typical Nazi style: 'Attention, attention! This is TV station Paul Nipkow. We greet all our comrades-in-arms in the television rooms of Greater Berlin with the German greeting: "Heil Hitler!"'[2]

Special 'television theatres' invited crowds to gather in front of tiny screens to watch free of charge. The first of these rooms opened on 9 April, at the Postal Museum, using two television sets and seating for 40 people. Reporting the event, the *Daily Telegraph*'s correspondent in Berlin noted the idea was to allow the public to 'form an idea as to the practical possibilities of television and thus give the German broadcasting authorities an opportunity of judging its probable extension'. On three days of the week, the public were authorised to 'look-in' without charge and to express their opinion of the reception.[3]

Although the first test was described by viewers as 'satisfactory', the low-definition picture was so poor at first some visitors depended on the audio commentary to understand what they were 'watching'. Later, TV parlours with room for almost 300 people, and kitted out with larger screens, opened across the city.

For the most part, schedules were punctuated with feature films, cookery tips, gymnastics, musical recitals, magic tricks, jugglers, and a reservoir of propaganda. Most of the live acts were done simply by inviting the cast of popular shows and cabarets to recreate their stage performances for the cameras at the studios on Rognitzstrasse. Occasionally, variety shows – especially those with a higher budget – were simulcast on Deutschlandsender.[4]

In addition to live material, UFA films such as *Die Lokomotivenbraut* and road safety features like *Achtung, Rotes Licht* were added to the schedules. At one point, an early version of *Crimestoppers* detailed the exploits of local villains and asked the public for their help in catching them.[5] An edition transmitted on 7 November 1938 appealed for information regarding the murder of a taxi driver who had been shot dead. A coat left behind by the perpetrator was shown and, despite the grainy postcard-size picture, a witness came forward.[6] On another occasion, a special television documentary, *The Brides of Hitler's Men*, gave a glimpse into life at a special bridal school at Schwanenwerder in south-western Berlin. Young women were obliged to produce a certificate from one of the 'brides' schools' before they could marry. At the school, women were instructed in household work, their duties as mothers and wives, and National Socialist ideas.

Led by manufacturers eager to put their new TVs on sale, television took pride of place at the 1937 Internationale Funkausstellung exhibition, where Fernseh Telefunken and Reichspost dominated proceedings. Other manufacturers too set out their stalls to provide for what they thought would prove to be a good market. 'The exhibition, which seems to grow larger each year, sprawls through eight vast halls,' a British journalist observed. 'Television fills the whole of one hall.' That year had seen Germany adopt a 441-line and 50 pictures-a-second system, a standard slightly higher than the 405-line definition of the BBC. One of the highlights of the Internationale Funkausstellung included:

... big-screen demonstrations of television. One screen measures 6ft. by 8ft. Another, giving some of the best big-screen pictures I have seen, measures 3ft. by 5ft, the only drawback being a certain lack of illumination.

The Volksfunk schedule for August 1937 reveals the entertainment on offer:

20:00: Blende Auf! Kurt Balke with a cheerful weekly report assisted by Werner Gille.
20.10: Picture reports (topical photographs and newsreels)
20.27: Melodies with Paul Lincke, featuring Friedel Schuster, Luise Stösel, Kati Rauch, Kurt Miihlhardt. On the grand piano: Waldemar v. Vultde.
21:22 Feature Film (with sound): *Liebe und die erste Eisenbahn* (UFA).
21:52 Closedown

The television service moved to the Deutschlandhaus on Adolf Hitler Platz in late 1937, given the building was more 'optically and acoustically suitable for television broadcasting'. Covering 300 square metres, the studio was originally designed as a café, with a ring-shaped floor plan, allowing sets and backdrops to be built all around the circular wall. Wherever the artists moved, the technicians and their special Fernseh AG cameras – three of them in the middle of the floor, plus the microphone – could effortlessly pan between different sets with a swivel to capture the action. The new structure allowed the regular staging of live plays, usually with six to ten actors and a medium-sized orchestra. The productions were 'not much more than radio plays in vision, which could have been comfortably followed with closed eyes' according to a critic from the *TFT* magazine.

British cabaret artists William Aherne and his sister Gladys, who claimed to be the only performers ever to have been 'televised' in two countries, were full of admiration for the Deutschlandhaus. Although impressed with the BBC, the pair insisted the German studio facilities were much better than their British counterpart. 'There is more room to move about. The studios, dressing rooms, cooling systems, etc., are all very elaborate and superior to those at Alexandra Palace.'

8

THE ROAD TO WAR

The world was genuinely shaken by the news that Germany had occupied Austria on 13 March. When Hitler's troops marched into Vienna, it became the biggest story of 1938, consuming more type space than any other event that year. 'Austria now part of the German Reich' read the *Sheffield Independent* headline. The *Daily Mail* put out extra editions and rushed them to the news stands. 'Austria Absorbed in German Reich' was the six-point headline in *The Scotsman*.

Within hours of crossing the border, Nazi agents occupied police stations, transport hubs and government offices as jubilant locals threw flowers at Wehrmacht troops on the streets, evoking images of liberation. Listening to events back home, Germans rubbed their eyes with disbelief at the suddenness of the Anschluss.[1]

The campaign in Austria marked the first period of extended news coverage in RRG's history, heralding the moment when live outside broadcasting came of age, and changed the speed at which news travelled in Germany. 'These occasions were riveting, they were moments in history and people could share them live, this of course was very exciting,' notes radio historian Wolfgang Bauernfeind.

On the morning of the occupation, the German High Command and the Ministry of Foreign Affairs unleashed their band of propagandists on the RAVAG Österreichische Radio-Verkehrs[2] at 06.45. The first Nazi programme on Radio Vienna (which would later be rebranded Reichssender Wien) opened with the words 'Greetings from National Socialist Austria', followed by the Horst Wessel song and a quote from *Mein Kampf*.[3] In contrast, at 10.50, a lecture on 'The woman in the National Socialist state' was followed by a warning to occupying Nazi troops against confiscations, requisitions or making arrests without the express orders of their superiors. Another bulletin advised depositors that bank withdrawals could be made only for special payments that 'must be justified'. As this was going on, Wehrmacht engineers hooked up stations in Innsbruck and Salzburg to Reichssender München, while Dornbirn Radio began relaying Reichssender Stuttgart, and channels in Linz, Graz and Klagenfurt were connected to Vienna. 'Day after day, millions of Germans have sat at their radio sets listening with varying degrees of thrills and admiration, to reports of the dynamic manner in which the Führer was changing the map of Europe with one gigantic daring coup,' the *Observer* noted.[4]

A silvery morning light shone on Adolf Hitler when he arrived in Vienna to the thunderous screams of 'Ein Volk, ein Reich, ein Führer!' on 14 March. On the radio, commentators described mass formations of marching members of the SS, Wehrmacht and Hitler Youth as thousands of supporters surged along the famous Ring, waving tiny paper swastika flags. That day, offices and factories across the country had been shuttered to allow workers a chance to celebrate. Throughout the evening, reporters marched with torchlight processions and spoke to delirious citizens gathered outside the Imperial Hotel, waiting for a glimpse of their new leader. Given its historic nature, the event was covered with a personal radio commentary by Hadamovsky, who stood alongside as Hitler reincorporated his homeland into the Reich. Interestingly, while the press paid tribute to the Austrian situation with hundreds of articles, the Berlin Nipkow television station seemingly ignored events, with the exception of showing *Bauernhochzeit in Kärnten*, a short UFA film about a peasant wedding in the Austrian state of Carinthia.

By the time the hangover had worn off, a massive wave of arrests had cleared Hitler's political opponents out of the way, while measures were adopted against the Jewish population. By 10 April, Germans and Austrians were ordered to the polls to ratify the Anschluss and 'elect' a new Reichstag. During several talks on the 'National Plebiscite and Greater German Reichstag', Interior Minister Dr Frick explained 'Full Jews' were not permitted to vote. Citizens were required to answer 'Yes' or 'No' to two questions:

1. Do you agree with reunion of Austria with Germany which was carried out on 13 March?
2. Do you approve the list (of candidates for the Reichstag) of our Führer, Adolf Hitler?

It was hardly surprising when the Nazis gained an overwhelming majority to both questions.

Just a fortnight after the absorption of Austria, Germany's march toward war continued when Berlin laid claim to the Sudetenland – sparking an emergency meeting of Hitler, Mussolini, Chamberlain and the French leader Daladier. The gathering resulted in the so-called 'Munich agreement', which required Czechoslovakia to vacate the Sudeten regions. While Chamberlain – brandishing the agreement and 'predicting peace in our time' – believed he had saved the day, Hitler saw the deal as one further step in the war he was planning to secure Lebensraum in the East.

Unsurprisingly, Hitler's popularity at home boosted his willingness to take further risks, including hatching a plan to occupy the rest of Czechoslovakia. True to form, Goebbels whipped up propaganda designed to build up war hysteria, leading to the Slovakian parliament declaring its independence from Prague on 14 March 1939. At the same time German troops occupied Bohemia and Moravia, which, according to the official communiqué, was to 'assure the safety of the life and property' of all inhabitants. A few days later, the seizure of Brno Radio ended one of the most creative channels in Europe, famed for pioneering Esperanto language operas, plays (including Shakespeare), talks and news, many of which were relayed globally.[5]

There could be no doubt, however, that things had changed in Brno when well-known fascist Dr Karl Schwabe – the newly appointed police president – took to the airwaves to appeal for all Germans to help keep order and to welcome troops. The Brno station was renamed 'Volksdeutscher Sender Brünn', with programmes in both German and Czech – its first major broadcast came with Foreign Minister Joachim von Ribbentrop's speech from Prague where he delivered Hitler's proclamation declaring the territory a 'German protectorate'.[6]

Rolf Wenzel, the Nazi official responsible for radio in the Bohemian–Moravian region, insisted existing Czech radio could 'still work and develop with full freedom' after the protectorate had been established. 'Its administration is quite independent,' he claimed.

No changes have been made in the radio company itself or in its relationship to the authorities of the Czech government. Czech broadcasting has a free hand when it comes to programming. They can exchange programmes with foreign channels, send their reporters abroad to broadcast from other countries, and do whatever they see fit. On the German side, everything that could be perceived by the Czechs as coercion or injustice has been avoided in the field of broadcasting. [7]

By this point, the Anschluss, coupled with Italian adventures in Abyssinia, Hitler's reoccupation of the Rhineland, and the Munich crisis, had spurred the BBC to launch their own propaganda effort against Germany under the supervision of the Foreign Office. Transmissions were ramped up after the occupation of Bohemia and Moravia and by early 1939, the BBC was transmitting a five-minute news bulletin in German on the Regional programme at 22.45 each weekday as well as via shortwave on the Overseas Service.

Soon after, the sound of Bow Bells – the interval signal of the BBC German broadcasts – was changed to the soft ticking of a clock, after requests from hundreds of listeners that the sound of the bells could attract the attention of ear-wigging neighbours. Over the course of the next 12 months, the BBC's European output in German and French would increase by 9,000 hours.

Back in Germany, the RRG prepared for a hectic April, firstly with an outside broadcast of Hitler launching the battleship *Von Tirpitz* in Wilhelmshaven, an event which marked one of the major Nazi ceremonial occasions that year. A few weeks later, the entire state media apparatus created a mixture of excitement and high anxiety for the 'momentous occasion' of Hitler's 50th birthday, a national holiday. For weeks, listeners had been urged to buy special stamps issued in honour of the occasion, as well as a jubilee edition of *Mein Kampf*, bound in dark blue leather with gilt edges and lettering.

Hadamovsky had ironed out preparations with microscopic attention. A dozen commentators, 10 broadcasting trucks and hundreds of technicians were mobilised, along with two television units, which had boosted its range with a second transmitter placed on the top of the Karstadt department store in the east of the city. TV programmes had also been extended from 5 p.m. to 10 p.m. daily while the public had been promised the new 'Einhefts-Fernsehempfänger E1' television set as the counterpart of the 'people's radio' was on the way. Plans were also underway to build two mountaintop TV transmitters – one on the Brocken (where a five-storey building had been constructed on the summit) and the other on the Feldberg, near Frankfurt – enabling TV to reach a quarter of the population.[8]

On 10 April 1939, Hitler woke up to a musical serenade performed by Leibstandarte Adolf Hitler in the Reich Chancellery garden, which was also being beamed to every breakfast table across the country. It followed a 'wireless link-up', when Hitler Youth organisations in all parts of the world sent greetings. Running commentary commenced at 10.15, as Hitler's open-top Mercedes swept out of the chancellery gates and past lines of adoring crowds. From a podium overlooking the Technical University, Hitler stood upright acknowledging ecstatic sightseers waving their hats and cheering. He saluted – arm stretched – with restrained dignity. For radio commentators, this felt like the beginning of Germany's golden age as they described columns of goose-stepping soldiers, tanks, multiple-rocket launchers and artillery vehicles rolling past.

During the 5-hour parade, Goebbels' heart fluttered at the 'brilliant image of German power and strength... Hitler was feted by the people like no other mortal man has ever been celebrated.' The streets began to empty quickly once the parade was over, but for shortwave listeners, the 'storms of applause' could be heard from New York to Johannesburg well into the night. While commentators painted the event in glowing colours, Spike Hughes of the *Daily Herald* scowled he had rarely heard anything so 'pathetically dull as the German broadcasts on Hitler's birthday'.

> It almost seems as though when a German is faced with the job describing something truthfully, he dries up. For three hours, German stations had the music of military bands playing and the sound of tanks and bombers and marching soldiers. 'Such-and-such a regiment is now passing the Führer and Oberbefehlsthaber,' said the commentator. Then there was a gap of five minutes in the 'commentary' and the formula was repeated. My! It was dreary.[9]

Even before his 50th birthday celebrations, Hitler had revealed plans to military top brass for an imminent attack on Poland.[10] Once finalised, peaceful propaganda gave way to jingoism and violent themes, including 'threats from Jewry' and bolshevism. Jumped-up accusations claiming Germans living in Poland had been subjected to brutal abuse were followed by hints that Warsaw was preparing to attack Germany. For Poles, the German radio sounded like tuning into an alternate universe as accusations were being made publicly that would have been unthinkable six months before. The station at Gleiwitz (which fell under the supervision of Reichssender Breslau) whipped up a campaign in the form of the *Silesian Hour*, featuring a stream of charges accusing the Poles of maltreating Germans. To stir tensions further, the native German population in Poland were encouraged to boycott Polish shops and services.

When the British expressed support for Poland, Goebbels launched a two-pronged radio assault on both London and Warsaw. In his theatre of propaganda, anti-British rhetoric promptly switched to a more confrontational tone on the daily English commentary beamed via Reichssender Köln and Reichssender Hamburg.[11] A second front of anti-British propaganda in Afrikaans targeted British Africa and succeeded in sufficiently provoking the Chamberlain government. The African service transmitted in German, English, Portuguese, Afrikaans and French, with 58.6 per cent of their output being news and politics. London newspapers were quick in pointing out that a great deal of damage was being done to 'British prestige and Imperial unity by Nazi radio propaganda', particularly in the more scattered Afrikaner homesteads. 'Quotations from English newspapers are used in a most unscrupulous manner,' a British journalist complained in the story 'Falsehoods Broadcast to South Africa', published in the regional press:

> Thus, some misguided person may have written a letter to the Press urging, say, the return of the former Colonies to Germany as a peace gesture, which the editor in fairness has printed for what it may be worth, leaving it to the intelligence of his readers to assess its true value. Statements are quoted from this letter in the Nazi broadcasts, however, not as the views of an individual reader but as the settled policy of the newspaper.[12]

The problem was compounded by the fact that the BBC broadcast in Afrikaans for only 10 minutes on a Sunday afternoon. The impressive signal strength from Zeesen was also praised in comparison with the weak and patchy reception of competing stations from Europe, including the BBC. 'I have no hesitation in saying that Berlin has the world's finest broadcasting,' wrote a listener from Harding in Natal. 'I congratulate you and your engineers on your wonderful work.' A British listener also was prompted to note, 'I am a Britisher – but fair play, you come over the air clearer than Daventry.'[13]

As the weeks passed, Goebbels seemed suitably satisfied with his anti-British agitation. Even though these first efforts were fairly amateurish, listeners in Africa embraced them, a fact reflected in the vast amounts of mail received from the region. 'Together with many of my fellow Afrikaners (Boars the British called our fathers) I have quite a soft spot for Germany and I am very glad of the privilege to be able to listen to your broadcasts,' a listener wrote from Bloemfontein in the Orange Free State province of the Union of South Africa. 'We are following

Chancellor Hitler's doings with interest and are glad of the news at the end of your programme every night. It is interesting to look at any question from both sides.'[14]

Typically, transmissions opened with a short programme featuring light music, followed by news and features. Dr Erich Holm, a Volksdeutscher from South Africa, worked as head commentator and produced series including *Ethnic Democracy of Africans* and *Men Shape the Nation* to appeal to Boers. Ever cheerful and optimistic, he used a well-trodden route of enticing listeners with songs and poems in Afrikaans. This rather simple formula seemed to work. However, while commentaries and talks about Europe were easily made, comment on actual events in South Africa proved tougher, as news sources were scant. Editors relied on information from Ribbentrop's Foreign Office (which was patchy) and when news was impossible to obtain, African-zone workers resorted to an oft rolled-out story about meat scarcity in Johannesburg (a common affair, caused by drought).

While the British poured scorn on the African broadcasts, they were impressed by their unstuffy production and effectiveness. This discomfort was exposed when a British news report, citing the South African press and obviously intended for the eyes of Goebbels, made a cutting claim: 'Holm is of Jewish blood, being the grandson of a rabbi. It is maintained his claim to speak on behalf of Afrikaners is wholly unjustified,' the Press Association Foreign Special desk reported.[15]

Back in Europe, agitation of the Poles and British was temporarily paused on 23 August when Germany secured the neutrality of the Soviet Union with the signing of the Molotov–Ribbentrop pact, which cleared the way for Hitler to march towards the Second World War. The non-aggression deal saw Berlin and Moscow agree not to go to war and carve up the conquered East between them. It also ensured Soviet non-intervention for any German invasion of Poland.

9

POLAND

Poland is what editors nowadays would call a 'holy shit' story –
where the public awaited every bulletin with eager anticipation.
As naval and military forces were mobilised during the last
days of August, air-raid precautions became commonplace
across Germany. At the Haus Des Rundfunks, the small team
of civilian guards and caretakers not only learned how to use
ammunition but also drilled and paraded on the pavement on the
Masurenallee alongside the SS unit.

As this was happening, Berlin began jamming Radio Warsaw
making it impossible for its receipt in the outside world. And
then, on Thursday 31 August 1939 – the last day of the old
world – German troops prepared to move. At 05.48 the following
morning, the duty editor at the Haus Des Rundfunks took a sharp
intake of breath when a crucial telex from Hitler's office – Ref
8004-ddd bln – arrived: 'We kindly ask you to make the following
announcements at 06:00, 08:00 and 10:00':

> The Polish State has refused the peaceful settlement of relations
> which I desired, and has appealed to arms. Germans in Poland
> are persecuted with bloody terror and driven from their houses.
> A series of violations of the frontier, intolerable to a great Power,
> prove that Poland is no longer willing to respect the frontier of the
> Reich. In order to put an end to this lunacy, I have no other choice

than to meet force with force from now on. The German Army will fight the battle for the honour and the vital rights of re-born Germany with hard determination. I expect that every soldier, mindful of the great traditions of eternal German soldiery, will ever remain conscious that he is a representative of the National-Socialist Greater Germany. Long live our people and our Reich!'

Listening to the broadcast in a village close to the Dutch border, schoolmaster Ludwig Sager knew this was the stuff of history. 'The people are calm and collected,' he noted, his nerves frayed to a frazzle. 'The mothers are worried about news from their sons at the front.' By midday, the Haus Des Rundfunks canteen was packed, the air thick with tense anticipation and no little amount fear. That same evening, the first daily army radio report addressing the military situation – known as Wehrmachtbericht (WB) – was passed to the duty announcer. From then on, WB bulletins, which were often repetitive, but reassuring – became the main source of military news available to the public. The news cycle began before sunrise, when RRG newsreaders heard the ping of telex, and ended sometime in the early hours, with editors preparing stories on the latest revelations from the front lines. 'We lapped up the daily special reports and became intoxicated with the successes of the German army and the genius of the leadership of these soldiers,' recalled teenager Werner Mork, who sensed the urgency and energy in every broadcast. 'This war was very different than the one from 1914–1918, also for us civilians!'

For many Germans, the invasion was a noble struggle against Polish aggression – it was a widely shared opinion given the population had been duped into believing it was a 'defensive action' in response to Polish soldiers attacking a German transmitter at Gliwice. In fact, SS troops wearing Polish uniforms had staged the incident. Before the day had ended, both France and Britain demanded the withdrawal of German soldiers from Polish territory within 48 hours, but, an unruffled Führer, basking in his new glory, let the ultimatum fizzle out.

By the Saturday – a day after the invasion – Hitler was holding military reports inches from his nose, flicking over the pages at the rate of two a minute. The documents – presented in large type due to his appalling eyesight – detailed how Polish airports and fighter planes had been destroyed as defences crumbled. At the peak of its armed might and with little to stand in their way, German troops ploughed up the Polish countryside, mauling everything they encountered.

Until this point, the Reich chancellery had been imbued with an atmosphere of celebration but the mood changed swiftly on Sunday 3 September at 12.15 Berlin time, when British Prime Minister Neville Chamberlain – honouring his promise to stand by Poland – made a stunning broadcast:

> This morning, the British Ambassador in Berlin handed the German Government a final Note stating that, unless we heard from them by 11 o'clock that they were prepared at once to withdraw their troops from Poland, a state of war would exist between us. I have to tell you now that no such undertaking has been received, and that consequently, this country is at war with Germany.

Rushing out onto the streets of Berlin, an American radio reporter observed 'neither bitterness nor enthusiasm'. There were no demonstrations at the gates of the British and French Embassies, and 'the sentries posted there had nothing to do'. That evening, a visitor to blacked-out Berlin described a 'lost city at the bottom of the sea'. Street lamps showed only tiny green flames on amber mantels, while buses and trams crawled slowly with a single, ghoulish blue light. The blackout's impact would be profound, with harsh punishments meted out for crimes committed under the veil of darkness. Under such conditions, prostitution thrived as sex workers haunted the city's freezing streets. 'Even the old girls, the wrinkled ones, stood on corners with their ugly features safely hidden in the darkness and shone their flashlights on their legs in invitation,' an observer noted. The cover of darkness would also give sex pests ample protection to stalk, molest or make inappropriate advances.

Such delicate subjects were seldom broached on the State broadcasting network, where the mood music was just right for extended bouts of flamboyance, leading to military analysts representing the three services becoming unlikely celebrities. General Quade, the Luftwaffe's spokesman, presented *Our Air Force*, Rear Admiral Friedrich Lutzow gave talks on naval operations, while Colonel Kurt Hesse spoke on behalf of the Army.[2] On the home front, nine daily news bulletins, with the first presented at 05.30 and the last at midnight, also kept the population informed. Newscasts frequently ended with an appeal, a government warning, or a 'special announcement'. Despite the information overload, an American journalist noted life in Berlin was still quite normal: 'The operas, the theatres, the movies are all open and jammed.'

Soon afterwards, to more applause, Wehrmacht Propaganda Companies (PK) began providing a vast amount of material for radio, newspapers and magazines. The deployment of the PK was a novelty in the history of conflict. For the first time, war correspondents acted as soldiers within military formations – a form of deployment that initially had no equivalent on the Allied side at the beginning of the war.[3] The Ministry of Propaganda was able to issue instructions to the PK; it also had a say on the selection of personnel. Major General Hasso von Wedel, who commanded Propaganda Troops, recalled the Wehrmacht came to terms with the Ministry of Propaganda in ideological and strategic terms. 'The PK man is in no way a conventional reporter, but a soldier,' Goebbels explained. 'Beside the pistol and the hand grenade, he carries other weapons with him: the film camera, the pencil and the notepad.' In turn, 'PK' became a term synonymous with quality reporting and journalism. PK teams flew on planes, rode in tanks and reported from submarines, making it possible to convey the conflict with unprecedented intensity and topicality. The units quickly gained a quasi-monopoly in German front-line reporting, with their numbers increasing sharply as the action expanded to include more and more theatres of war. 'He was trained among the troops and he lived among soldiers. He knows their style of life because it forms his own being,' Goebbels declared. 'He speaks the language, thinks the way they think and feels their feelings.'[4] PK work from all fronts – film, sound, photos, texts, paintings, and drawings – were present in all National Socialist media, especially in the press, on the radio and in the weekly cinema newsreels. Units included well-known journalists, cameramen, photographers, and painters. As soldiers, these journalists were command recipients, obliged to obey military orders.

Through their exciting dispatches, young PK reporters helped introduce a new word to the lexicon: Blitzkrieg – Hitler's fresh brand of terror. Poland's position had been hopeless from the outset and within just two weeks, a large part of the numerically and technically inferior army was encircled and taken prisoner, leaving a state of almost 8 million inhabitants to be annexed by Germany.

With the opening of the Polish campaign, Hitler provided one of the clearest signs that Goebbels' star was no longer in ascendancy as his endless philandering – usually with impressionable young actresses – had caused considerable embarrassment. Thus, Hitler's displeasure was made clear when he subordinated the entire overseas propaganda effort to the Foreign Office on 1 September. The Propaganda Ministry, which had hitherto been responsible, reluctantly gave way but only for a short time. It didn't take long for Goebbels to sulkily launch a tug-of-war for influence against Von Ribbentrop, who, he reckoned, had bought his name, married his money and swindled his way into office. Such acid and biting sarcasm earned Goebbels many enemies, not least among them economist Hjalmar Schacht, who itched to strike the 'little minister' down but refrained from doing so 'because he could not hit a cripple'.

Meanwhile, as the Polish campaign continued, Hans Krieg, a director in the Propaganda Ministry, followed a fighting unit tasked with occupying Polish radio stations where he witnessed the 'destructive rage of the Poles' and the 'monumental achievements' of the German Army in fixing wrecked transmitters. Krieg was on hand to oversee the Nazification of stations in Lodz, Warsaw and Krakow, and took part in the opening of 'General Government Broadcasting Corporation' in Katowice which became the RRG headquarters given that the city boasted an orchestra, a singing club, a chamber concert hall and a lecture room. Radio Warsaw's longwave transmitter was reassigned for use by the Swedish- and Russian-language services of the RRG, while new stations in Poland, aided by PK reporters, began feeding content to Reichssender stations. Special features on the activities of the Deutsches Rotes Kreuz in the Polish campaign, and interviews from mobile hospitals made up an entire series. Writing in the radio journal *Welt Rundfunk*, journalist Kurt Wagenfuhr opined that events in Poland had seen dramatic changes 'never recorded since the establishment of broadcasting organisations'.

> The previous military developments in Europe – and outside of this continent (Spanish civil war, Italian–Abyssinian campaign, Japanese/Chinese war) – as well as a number of political high tension and crisis periods in 1938 and 1939, prompted substantial and extensive changes in broadcasting. However, the impact was not as 'great' or as drastic as it was in September 1939.

During a meeting with Goebbels, Hans Frank, the newly installed Nazi governor of Poland, outlined his future vision for communicating with his new subjects: 'It will be essential to provide the Poles with certain news by means of powerful loudspeakers,' he declared, adding, 'The Poles are not to be allowed wireless sets; they are to be left with only those newspapers which provide news and nothing else – there is to be no press which might express any opinions (...) the Poles are to be completely deprived of the opportunities of listening to the radio.'[5]

After the defeat of Poland, parts occupied by the Wehrmacht were incorporated into the German Reich as the districts of Wartheland and Danzig, West Prussia, while the rest of the country was designated as under the General Government and placed under a German civilian administration, which organised its economic exploitation and the forced transport of hundreds of thousands of Poles for labour in Germany.

For most Germans, the first few months of the war had seemed rather distant and although the speedy defeat of the Poles – along with British and French reluctance to intervene – had boosted morale on the home front, life had become considerably duller. The pleasures of peacetime radio listening, such as to international sporting events, comedy and even weather forecasts, had become a distant memory as orders were bellowed on the airwaves from dawn to dusk. As well as receiving a welter of pamphlets on rationing, housewives were subjected to radio campaigns on fuel economy and household management. Meat, fats, butter, cheese, milk, sugar and jam were put on ration, as were bread and eggs. Then, the rationing of textiles was introduced, prompting an American reporter to quip, 'Germans are saying even if they do survive the war, they will end up in a lunatic asylum as a result of the rationing system.' In a bid to make life easier, Gertrud Scholtz-Klink – the head of the Nazi Women's League (and once described by Hitler as the 'perfect Nazi woman') – took to the air to issue her 'Ten Commandments' for shopping during wartime:

1. The shopping housewife shall not lose her temper if the article she wants doesn't happen to be in stock at the moment.
2. She shall not claim for herself more than others are receiving.
3. She will not attempt to get into the good books of the shopkeeper.
4. She shall not start racing from store to store to grab things she never bought in peacetime.
5. She shall not leave her shopping until the last moment just before closing time.
6. She will have due consideration for professional and working women and the little time they have for shopping.
7. She will show a greater understanding of the need for a closing time at 7pm.
8. The shopkeeper should be good humoured until the very last moment.
9. He will not show his personal sympathies and antipathies too plainly.
10. To both shopkeepers and customers, the following, however, applies – always keep calm and never lose your temper, even when difficulties are encountered.

A decree against so-called public enemies, or 'National Pests', was enacted two days after the outbreak of war, which, in the vaguest terms sought to deal with those who exploited wartime conditions to carry out crimes, such as robbery, arson, looting, or anti-social behaviour. In practical terms, the decree cleared the way for judges to impose long jail terms or the death penalty more freely.

Another important order concerned radio listening. While Goebbels couldn't stop foreign radio waves drifting into the Reich, he could make listening to enemy channels a crime, which he did as soon as war broke out.

The prohibition came as a bitter blow for many armchair travellers given to enjoying overseas programmes. So-called 'knob-fiddling' to listen to the whole world to hear many points of view and languages had long been a popular pastime, spawning countless amateur radio appreciation societies. Hilversum, the Dutch station, had long been a favourite choice, along with the BBC, Radio Luxembourg, Radio Strasbourg and Swiss radio. Once the prohibition was in force, the public were warned listening to banned broadcasts, whether enemy or neutral, was a crime of the highest order. There was a sinister tailpiece to the directive:

> Those disregarding the decree must be isolated or else rendered harmless as quickly as possible. They represent such a serious danger that no penalty is too high for them. In order to remove the last doubts it must be repeated that is not only forbidden to listen to the radio stations of enemy countries, but also to those of neutral countries.[6]

The BBC was considered the most dangerous enemy of domestic propaganda, given that it reached Germany on a variety of high-powered medium, long, and shortwave transmitters.

Foreign journalists working in Berlin were exempt from the law as long as the 'privilege' was not abused. Under the heading of 'Abuses', foreign correspondents were warned turning the loudspeaker on to full strength, permitting German employees to listen in, or indiscriminately spreading the information heard on overseas broadcasts, would be considered unacceptable. Furthermore, correspondents were cautioned to tune in only to those broadcasts which had a direct bearing on their journalistic activity.

10

GERMANY CALLING

By late 1939, RRG's foreign-language services were outgrowing their position as a simple department. Bulletins in Swedish, French, English, Spanish and Polish were beamed via the mediumwave transmitters of various Reichssender stations in addition to the shortwaves of the KWS. The English service, known as England-Redaktion, evolved and expanded so quickly that it seems decisions were made before they could be planned for, let alone carried out.

Throughout the Polish campaign, announcers had managed to botch one story after another, as they tripped up over unpronounceable words prompting the installation of Eduard Dietze as a 'language corrector' and 'pronunciations coach'. As the son of a Scottish mother and a German father, he spoke perfect English and German. A former colleague remembered he had a keen sense of his own worth: 'He was very idealistic and strict and respected sincerity and truthfulness. His great fault was that he was very proud of himself.' Dietze forged a position in the years immediately before the war as a radio broadcaster covering a wide variety of sports before becoming Deutschlandsender's preferred presenter for major commentaries such as the Oxford and Cambridge Boat Race, and the World Economic Conference in London and Wimbledon.

On top of RRG work, he was familiar to BBC listeners after providing reportage on the Hindenburg funeral, a boxing bout between Max Schmeling and Steve Hamas, and the Saar plebiscite. He also commentated at the 1936 Olympics for NBC in the United States. Now, with the country at war, he was kept busy as overseas audiences gained an insatiable appetite for news from Germany.

Over in London, Sefton Delmer, a Jewish-English journalist of Australian heritage, who headed the German-language section at the BBC, was a frequent listener. He later opined that even though the British prepared for war at the last minute, the England-Redaktion was worse equipped regarding the 'provision of English-speaking announcers, news writers and commentators than the BBC was for their equivalent in German'. William Joyce, the man destined to be the star performer on the England-Redaktion, was a case in point. 'They had not even organised in advance the recruiting to the Berlin team of William Joyce. His appearance was entirely fortuitous,' Delmer recounted.[1]

Joyce clocked in for duty at the KWS just a week prior to the outbreak of war. Having felt increasingly uneasy in London where fascists were being rounded up, this razor-slashed ex-Mosleyite stuffed his world into a suitcase and fled with his wife Margaret to Berlin to avoid internment.

William was born in New York in 1906 to Irish parents. The Joyces returned to their native Ireland in 1911, where William grew up in Galway during the period of the Anglo–Irish war. After receiving threats accusing them of being pro-British, the family upped sticks to the mainland in 1921. During his time as a British Union of Fascists (BUF) lieutenant, Joyce co-ordinated propaganda for its leader Oswald Mosley and cultivated its anti-Semitic flavour. During a meeting at a little café near Manchester Cathedral, he was slashed with a razor by a group of communists, which left him with a long, disfiguring scar on his cheek. He revelled in the silly theatricals of fascism where he could give the same salutations as the Nazis, wear similar uniforms, chant slogans and mete out brutal treatment to opponents. 'I don't regard the Jews as a class but only as a privileged misfortune,' Joyce told a crowd during one of his early speeches at a BUF assembly in Chiswick. 'The flower, or weed, of Israel shall never grow in ground fertilised by British blood.'[2] Having watched Joyce perform in northern England, newspaperman Tom Wielding dismissed him as an overbearing snob and 'arrogant braggart', with the 'unpleasant characteristics of a bully, with perhaps one exception; he was not afraid of personal danger'. For such a man, Nazi Germany held plenty of attractions. Once installed in Berlin, Joyce busied himself reading news and commentaries for the England-Redaktion, presenting his first broadcast on 18 September, a fortnight after war was declared. CBS reporter William Shirer described Joyce as a 'heavily built man of 5 feet 9 inches, with Irish eyes that twinkle. He speaks a fair German. He has a titanic hatred for Jews and an equally titanic one for capitalists.'

Accounts suggest the England-Redaktion was staffed by a 'grumpy band of misfits', all eking out a living delivering propaganda aimed at Britain. Unlike Joyce – who was destined for international fame – his co-workers, including Wolff Mittler and Norman Baillie-Stewart, an old ex-Seaforth Highlander with a spiky personality, would rarely trouble history books.[3] Baillie-Stewart had gained some minor notoriety after being caught passing military secrets to a German woman in 1933, leading to his court-martial and a five-year stretch in the Tower of London. From then on, he came to be known as the 'Officer in the Tower'. After his release in 1937, he vanished from public view before eventually resurfacing in Berlin just a fortnight before Joyce.

At the England-Redaktion, Baillie-Stewart read the news between gulps of whiskey from a golden hip flask. Accounts suggest he spent his happiest moments unpicking his co-workers and highlighting badly written 'nauseating scripts'. William Shirer believed Ballie-Stewart's Scottish nature was 'too unbending' for officials at the RRG and ProMi. On one occasion, an editor presented him with an appallingly written script which stated that 'a torpedo struck the machines and kettles of the boat', leaving Baillie-Stewart in a state of total despair. Another time, listeners were informed the Luftwaffe had caused damage in south-west London 'particularly in the suburb of Random', leading to the RAF cheekily pointing out, 'This obviously implies that the Germans have been dropping their bombs at random. Apparently, the inspired Nazi wireless has no idea that no such suburb as Random exists in London.'

For his part, Mittler held forth in an accent that was one part German to four parts Bertie Wooster. At just 21 years old, he had been a hardcore radio enthusiast, but displayed a severe distaste for politics and went weak-kneed at the increasingly violent material he was obliged to read.

Beyond Joyce, Dietze, Mittler and a few others, the RRG never seriously attempted to develop or improve the English-language services, unlike the BBC's German service, which was busily expanding into a vast organisation. Viewed in this light, it was unsurprising when Joyce won praise from his superiors and began actively writing his own broadcast material. To his mind, no theme was hackneyed if treated with his genius and originality, which it seemed, suited the average listener back in Britain looking for something saucy to tickle the palate.

The British press soon tuned in but being clueless as to the identity of the mystery announcer, Fleet Street nicknamed the voice 'Lord Haw-Haw', due to its distinctive nasal, upper-crust drawl. According to Baillie-Stewart, the moniker actually had three owners: 'The first Lord Haw-Haw of the Berlin Rundfunk was not William Joyce or myself, but the handsome, 6 feet 2 inches tall, Wolff Mittler, a man with both snobbish manners and an aristocratic voice.'[4]

In any case, it didn't take long for Joyce's style to prove a distinct departure from the staid performance of his co-workers. Within a few months of arriving, Joyce had truly made himself at home, and while he fooled with fascism and radio politics, Margaret – noted for her beauty and high-spirited charm – kept busy shopping, watching the latest flicks at the UFA cinema at Zoologischer Garten, and widening her horizons with boys on home leave.

That winter, the RGG covered every new horror, success and outrage. There was dismay when President Roosevelt ordered the US Customs Agency implement the Neutrality Act of 1939, allowing cash-and-carry purchases of weapons to non-belligerent nations, such as Sweden. Soon after, celebration followed when a German submarine sank the British battleship HMS *Royal Oak* in Scapa Flow with the loss of 833 sailors, while extensive airtime was afforded to Moscow's attack on Finland, starting the war in late November.

For both reporters and listeners overwhelmed by the pace of developments, Christmas brought a semblance of normality back to the airwaves. As cathedrals rang in the Holy Night, festive requests sent by pupils to their former headmaster serving on the Western Front were broadcast from Reichssender Vienna, while a Hitler Youth battalion greeted comrades in Berlin. A long and wearying list of other dedications was punctuated with musical items paid for by donations from factory girls and a branch of the Bund Deutscher Mädel (League of German Girls).

Unsterblicher Walzer – one of the bigger box office hits of 1939 – was showing across the Reich during Christmas week. It told the story of the Strauss family, interspersed with folksy sentimental music. Like radio, film production had endured a turbulent decade. UFA, Terra Film, Tobis, Bavaria Film, Wien-Film, and Berlin-Film – all staffed by a carefully groomed Aryan workforce – doled out a potpourri of comedies, musicals, melodramas, war flicks, and romances. Both Hitler and Goebbels were enthusiastic film buffs; surprisingly, both men were devoted fans of Greta Garbo and Micky Mouse.

Having lost no time in marching onto film sets in 1933, an immediate measure for the Nazis was to create 'departmental cells' overseeing every phase of production from finance to distribution. In this weighted system, each proposed project needed the approval of each cell. For example, a 'scenario cell' – the Reichsfilmdramaturg – censored storylines, which were thoroughly examined to conform to Nazi thinking. The 'casting cell' became the area of the greatest disputes and hold-ups, as no actor could reach the screen unless they proved they were of Aryan decent back to their great-grandparents. The casting department delved into the genealogical history of every actor, actress, producer and director, establishing a formidable filing system comparable only to the elaborate fingerprint records of a major police force. This led to a good many Jewish performers and technicians packing up. As the purge gathered pace, Jewish matinee idols Gitta Alpár, Elizabeth Bergner, Rosie von Barsony, Franciska Gaal and Maria Matray were squeezed out of a living.

Joyce was also on the air, but instead of bleating festive cheer, his lightly malicious banter focused on the BBC, which, he said, based its news reports on belief, not on knowledge. 'German wireless is different,' he said. 'We do not announce any success unless we are certain of it.' Then, with grim intoning, he declared he couldn't wish the British public a happy Christmas knowing what terrible punishment awaited England at the hands of the Führer.

The general feeling at the Haus Des Rundfunks was the propaganda was being made cheaply, quickly, and to great effect. With the British public having been served up high comedy, low gossip, and outlandish threats, the London-based EKCO radio company cashed-in by advertising full-range battery and electric models on which purchasers could 'hear Lord Haw-Haw at his best'. His celebrity had also prompted the British public to send sacks of Christmas cards and letters addressed to 'Lord Haw-Haw, Berlin'. Every one was incinerated by the Post Office.

II

1940

Winter brought a blast of bone-numbing arctic air, which plunged Germany deeper into the bitter cold, a situation worsened by fuel shortages and power cuts. Compounding the misery, rail links between Berlin and Copenhagen halted and the Baltic froze solid, which ended deliveries of bacon, eggs and fresh butter. 'Everyone is grumbling. Nothing like continual cold to lower your morale,' grumped CBS journalist William Shirer from his centrally heated suite at the Adlon Hotel. A common complaint was that coal could only be purchased by conniving, cajoling and bribery. Wood fuel was forbidden, and electric heaters were virtually impossible to obtain. Shirer's associate Harry Flannery spent New Year's Eve at the Cafe Wein on the fashionable Kürfurstendamm, but was left unimpressed: 'The numbers played that night were such poor arrangements that they sounded as if they had been made by someone who wrote them down as he listened to orchestras from the United States over a badly distorted shortwave.'

During his New Year's Eve radio address, Hitler provided a foretaste of the travails to come by calling on the services of the Almighty 'who in the past has clearly taken us under his protection'. An hour later, Goebbels, speaking with unusual candour, confirmed prolonged uncertainty and continued war when he declared citizens would 'have to earn victory, not only those men the front lines, but also those at home'. Taken together, the comments underscored the challenges faced by German people at the beginning of 1940.

The New Year brought a series of changes on both Deutschlandsender and Reichssender stations accelerated by chaotic schedule disruptions since the outbreak of war, which had been widely criticised by listeners. To compound difficulties, a chronic manpower shortage was forcing RRG to operate with just 25 per cent of its 5,091 male employees. By autumn 1940, over 80 per cent of broadcasters and editors, and almost a third of technicians, would be called up to serve in the propaganda companies of the Wehrmacht or on foreign radio services.[1]

For Hadamovsky, anxious about the state of his network, there was a renewed sense of mission. Obstacles aside, he managed to lay the central planks of a new 'prime time' line-up spearheaded by the news magazine *Aus dem Zeitgeschehen* at 18.00, supplemented by regional bulletins. Thereafter, front-line reports – including on-the-scene coverage – aired at 19.00 on Reichssender stations, interspersed with local variations. For example, news of deployment of Bavarian troops would be covered through the Reichssender Munich, while naval stories usually featured on Reichssender Hamburg.

As usual the breathless pace of war events featured in the front-line dispatches, which aired nationally, with the most exciting editions repeated on Sundays. As a rule, more homely items followed in the evening; comedy and music were well adjusted to the sensitivities of war. Since many young men were on active service, programmes avoided formerly popular topics such as dating, holidays and family planning.

A more serious new programme, *Kameradschaftsdienst*, filled the airwaves nightly with 'important personal messages' from the homeland to the front.[2] News of illnesses and deaths were strictly forbidden but other announcements could be sent by telegram and, in particularly urgent cases, telephoned to the RRG, but only with the permission of the police. Given its importance, *Kameradschaftsdienst* was supported by the Wehrmacht High Command, Police and Arbeitsdienst. *Volksfunk* noted,

Every German woman, every mother, and every father, who have something important to tell their husband or son at the Front can use the programme. The radio waves carry their wishes and messages to the bunkers in the West, to the occupying forces of the East, into the aerodromes and onto our navy out at sea. A message that might have taken days to arrive can now be transmitted in this way within a short time.[3]

Kameradschaftsdienst was undoubtedly an idea cultivated by Hadamovsky, who had returned from Poland as the commander of a propaganda squad. During his exploits, he learned there was 'nothing as important in war than the close connection between the front and home'. He expanded this idea in his book *Blitzmarsch auf Warsaw*, detailing the entire Polish campaign.

Those lucky enough to be home on Sunday afternoons enjoyed the *Wunschkonzert für die Wehrmacht*, a variety show belting out beloved hits and requests for the military. From the start, its genial announcer Heinz Goedecke – a master of nimble comic timing – tailored his on-air persona as a champion of army morale, winning hearts by informing troops at the Front of the arrival of additions to their families. 'The number of twins and even triplets announced is astonishing,' a listener observed. The show was performed live in the concert hall at Haus Des Rundfunks and featured a high-wattage cast including Marika Rökk, Heinz Rühmann, Rosita Serrano and the light supple voice of Zarah Leander. The locations of military units were never disclosed during the transmission, which was usually approved by Goebbels three days before broadcast. *Wunschkonzert für die Wehrmacht* became an institution, earning Goedecke the War Merit Cross and a legion of fans, many tuning in from abroad, as a letter from a fan in Sweden attests:

In search of news from Germany, we found the request concert for the first time. Since then, we have become devoted listeners. We no longer need political news, because there is nothing that could give us a more vivid picture of the mood in Germany! It is an everlasting, indelible impression. A great people become one family. They are brothers and sisters who love each other warmly.

In a letter to Goedecke marking the 50th edition of the *Wunschkonzert*, Wilhelm Keitel, Chief of the Armed Forces High

Command, noted, 'These concerts have become an increasingly important link between the German people and their soldiers.' Furthermore, he expressed the hope they would continue to play their part in the 'unbreakable unity of the German people'.[4] In a spin-off book, *Wir beginnen das Wunschkonzert für die Wehrmacht,* Goedecke wrote of request letters 'piling up as high as mountains' along the corridors of the Haus Des Rundfunks.[5]

Popular entertainer Kurt Krüger-Lorenzen hosted *Ankerspill,* another show which rose to national prominence playing a homespun blend of sea shanties and sketches. Krüger-Lorenzen's mellow voice became recognisable to a generation of Kriegsmarine, always opening with the 'La Paloma' fanfare blended with the sound of crashing waves. Mariners on home leave were occasionally paraded in front of the microphone to sing, dance and strum guitars. Another well-loved offering, *Blinkfeuer Heimat,* also brightened the lot of sailors. Like the audience, the acts – including singers, magicians and comedians – all came from the ranks of the navy.

Hadamovsky introduced more 'political talks' and anti-British radio dramas, including Rehberg's *Cape Town* and Kuhnert's *Dr Mackenzie's Mission.* Add to that works by Günter Eich, who churned out over 160 radio plays including the virulently anti-English *Rebellion in der Goldstadt* which spun the yarn of South African miners downing tools to protest the pittance they received from the 'swinish capitalist' British owner, Lord Pembroke.[6]

Elsewhere, a typical day started with news at 05.00 followed by *Morgenmusik,* a mixture of melodies aimed at farmers and shift workers. At 06.10, Ilse Möbius and Inge Schmitz – both athletes noted for their superb enunciation and enthusiasm – presented vigorous exercises on *Gymnastik*, alongside pianist Abo Münstermann who provided musical accompaniment.[7]

Next up, *Kunterbunt* featured light music interspersed with tips for cooking and housekeeping, after which the lunchtime news bulletin at 14.00 weaved in official announcements, a High Command Communiqué, detailed reports from all military services and even the occasional Italian communiqué. There were also appeals for the Winter Relief Fund or the German Red Cross, as well as air-raid precaution instructions and local Nazi party announcements.

Programmes aimed at women, children and adolescents followed, which often included talks on needlecraft, child welfare and first-aid. Occasionally, topics focused on privations in daily life, such as the shortage of soap which, in an age before deodorant, could be unbearable. Reporter Howard K. Smith remembered the stench of unclean clothes and pungent body odour was enough to literally drive some commuters off the trains: 'In summer it is asphyxiating ... dozens of people, whose bodies and stomachs are not strong anyhow, faint in them every day. Sometimes you just have to get out at some station halfway to your destination to take a breath of fresh air between trains.'

The smells can't have been much sweeter in factories around the capital from where Reichssender Berlin began twice-weekly broadcasts produced with the German Labour Front and Strength through Joy, 'proving to the world again and again that even in war, cultural enthusiasm and the joy of music are present in the German people'.

Throughout January, radio commentaries focused on the strength of the domestic economy and its immunity from the British blockade. In fairness, there were some good reasons to initially steer the coverage in this direction, given one of the first manifestations of physical warfare came with an extensive British naval blockade targeting German imports and exports in reprisal for numerous incidents at sea, such as the sinking of the *Athenia* and the *Simon Bolivar* by the German Navy.

To begin with, the British action had little effect on food supplies, but it did sap the flow of oil required to keep the Wehrmacht running, while at the same time hindering whale oil supplies, a key ingredient for margarine production. One area where the blockade did prove catastrophic was for the once-booming German shipping industry. With the outbreak of war, passenger liners ran the gauntlet to reach home ports such as Hamburg and Bremerhaven or sought sanctuary in neutral harbours.

In the face of this economic assault, Germany threatened to hit back with a 'steel ring' of submarines and mines around the United Kingdom 'through which even a rowing boat could not pass'. With that in mind, 'British weakness', 'the rottenness of social life' and 'British brutality and unscrupulousness' provided the backbone of attacks on the enemy that winter. According to a British War Cabinet assessment on German propaganda, special emphasis was given to an alleged shortage of shipping tonnage, the supposed growth of inflation and rationing.[8]

At the same time, Goebbels ramped up attacks on France, using an increasing pro-Communist flavour. For example, focus on the allowances paid to soldiers' wives was held up to scorn – 'only the rich have anything in France' – while the theme of Britain exploiting France remained constant. The main items of German radio commentaries were, in order of their importance:

1. France is politically subordinated to Great Britain.
2. It was said since the presence of British troops in the Front line could no longer be denied, the new contingents 'arrive in small numbers and do no fighting'.
3. It is repeated that the preoccupation of the 'Tommy' (slang for British soldier) was French women rather than with German soldiers.

Joyce also dipped his toe into agitation against the French, announcing on Reichssender Hamburg on 2 January that an epidemic of typhoid fever had broken out in Paris, where 'more than 100 people have already died'. Furthermore, he confided, the French press had so far not mentioned a word of the epidemic, 'in order to avoid a panic'.

Meanwhile, the punishing winter, which had produced record snowfall and seen temperatures drop to their lowest level in 114 years, dragged on. In several cases, the bitter cold turned dangerous, even deadly. During a snowstorm sweeping across Saxony, a passenger train smashed into a bus killing 12 people – highlighting the deterioration of the railways, which at the expense of passenger services, had transformed into the logistical backbone of the Wehrmacht. According to CBS reporter Harry Flannery, the pleasures of rail travel had become a distant memory. He angrily noted that a journey from Köln to Berlin took nine and a half hours 'for a trip that took five hours before the war'. Like many foreign correspondents in Berlin, Flannery was a busy man. At the outbreak of war, all three major US networks – National Broadcasting Company (NBC), Columbia Broadcasting System (CBS) and

Mutual Broadcasting System (MBS) – had representatives in the German capital. Flannery, and NBC's Dr Max, was able to continue filing reports. His scripts, as well as all others from foreign correspondents, were required to be submitted 'in good time' and in triplicate for censorship by the Wehrmacht, Ministry of Foreign Affairs and Press Department. Censors, according to the notes of Goebbels' daily conferences, were ordered to pay attention to 'the person of the speaker to make sure a harmless text is not made to produce the opposite effect by a mocking delivery'.

That spring, under the government slogan 'Every hectare must be exploited,' Deutschlandsender focused attention on farming in the occupied territories. 'New farming villages in new Germany' painted a rosy picture of young settlers lured onto usurped farms in Poland and Czechoslovakia, where land, timbered houses, cattle, seeds, feed, fertilizer and equipment was provided from the Reichsnährstand – interest-free until 1942. For the settler to achieve something 'he must be able to rely entirely on his wife', the programme advised. 'It is particularly important that he has a loyal comrade in her who is strong and hardworking.'

Surprisingly, as this was happening, the home services were also transmitting a steady torrent of appeals to persuade women to replace their menfolk in the workforce, as the labour shortage had grown acute. Dwindling manpower in the farming sector was compounded by a multitude of problems. Given the bitter winter, corn was badly laid while widespread potato disease and an invasion of black and yellow striped Colorado beetles from France led to a grim harvest forecast.

Hoping to fashion a remedy to the labour squeeze, the Ministry of Agriculture guaranteed they 'could make any female absorb enough about agriculture to run a farm' in six lessons – a claim which was completely at odds with reality. However, given Agriculture Minister Walther Darré's excruciating observations often focused on mysticism and race, and other mumbo-jumbo, it wasn't entirely surprising. 'Bread,' he once explained during a radio talk, was 'a sacred concept. In it, the spirit lives from the source of culture and the primordial power of our race.' His broadcasts often featured on *Zeitgeschehen* where items about chemically prepared substitutes such as artificial chicken, eggs, and yeast became a frequent topic. Listeners learned how the ever-expanding army was nourished with synthetic products including powdered apples, cheese, jams, tomatoes, and imitation spinach.

Fortunately, as part of the government's preparations for the long-anticipated war, local radio stations had been infused with agricultural content throughout the thirties. A snapshot of the volume of farming programming can be gleaned from the spring 1937 schedules, when Reichssender Hamburg arranged a lecture on 'pig breeding and husbandry on a proprietary basis', while *Riesenkartoffelernte auch im nächsten Jahr?* from Reichssender Berlin focused on the type and quality of seeds needed for a good potato harvest. In the north, Reichssender Konigsberg championed a campaign on kitchen waste, animal feed and recycling. A few years earlier, the landmark series *German Nation on German Soil* aimed at 'reintegrating urban man's soul in the life of the land' by projecting a cyclical presentation of the rural year in four transmissions. These comprised,

A *Rustic Day in Winter* (Reichssender Leipzig), *Song and Spring Sowing* (Reichssender Munich), *Swabian Summer* (Reichssender Stuttgart) and *Autumn Festival* (Reichssender Frankfurt). Furthermore, additional shows focused on *Soldiers and farmers on Markische soil* (Reichssender Berlin), while farm servants and maids, sailors and artisans were the focus of a Reichssender Köln production. The series finale: *The Ages of Man* took the form of a three-part series on the farmer's circle of life: birth, marriage, and death.[9]

During the spring of 1940, Goebbels began demanding journalists be more inventive and think harder rather than 'waiting for material to turn up'. The exception, it seems, was the English-language service where William Joyce gleaned his best ammunition – usually concerning rationing, bombing and grumbling – from the pages of the *Daily Express*, a purveyor of the kind of item suited to the task. In short, grist for the Haw-Haw mill came by mixing official German government fodder with subtle and sophisticated distortions of English newspaper stories and BBC news. Writing the nightly broadcasts became a task in which Joyce indulged with utter relish. In the absence of substance, he created a smorgasbord of entertainment, composed using his derisive Nazi lexicon of 'Jewish agitators' and 'antisocial elements'. The 'common touch' was exactly what Goebbels wanted, nothing highbrow. Foreign broadcasts, he told staff, must 'unleash anger', and not just touch the intellect of a few. Armed with English slang and understanding of the British mentality, Joyce succeeded in getting under the skin of many listeners. When rationing began in Britain, he asserted that Germans were so well fed 'it was difficult' to use up their food quota. Furthermore, he said there were no 'unemployed outcasts' in Germany, unlike in England:

> I would like you to contrast the friendly and sympathetic attitude of the party members of National Socialist welfare with the methods of public assistance offered in England. You would be very sorry that you ever condemned National Socialism.[10]

Then, he painted a pathetic picture of evacuated English children 'going about in freezing weather with insufficient shoes and clothes'. On another occasion, imaginations ran riot when he 'disclosed' the British Women's Auxiliary Corps were armed with 'stout umbrellas' instead of rifles. Soon after, he passed on the unhappy – and entirely fictional story – of a British nurse sentenced to four years penal servitude for receiving a postcard recommending she tune into German broadcasts.

Nonsensical rumours about his every utterance abounded across Britain. Haw-Haw was supposed to have spoken about town hall clocks being half-an-hour slow and having detailed knowledge of local munitions factories, but of course, he never said anything of the kind, as the *Daily Herald's* W. N. Ewer complained:

> There is another story going about just now which is certainly being spread deliberately in the hope of causing alarm. In Didcot, for example, it is put about that 'last night the German wireless said that Didcot is going to be the first town bombed.' I have had that story (always from somebody whose brother-in-law actually heard it, or something of the kind) from at least a dozen different places. Of course, when you get hold of the brother-in-law, he says no, he didn't actually hear the German wireless himself: it was a man up at the golf club whose sister heard it.

And nothing of the sort has ever been said about Didcot or anywhere else since the war began. That goes for another variant, too; that Lord Haw-Haw has said, 'Hullo, you Puddleton people. We know your town hall clock stopped this evening at 5 o'clock.' Or, 'Hullo, you workers at the Puddlecombe aircraft works. Pity they ran out of bitter at the Dog and Duck on Sunday.' All complete lies.[11]

Far from ignoring this obvious menace, the London press – overwhelmed by the sheer volume of outrageous material – hung on to his every dubious word, propelling his fame skyward. A report compiled by the BBC concluded the blackout, along with the novelty of hearing the enemy, played a part in his success:

> ... the desire to hear both sides, the insatiable appetite for news and the desire to be in the swim have all played their part in building up Hamburg's audience and holding it. The entertainment value of the broadcasts, their concentration on undeniable evils in this country, their news sense, their presentation, and the publicity they have received in this country, together with the momentum of the habit of listening to them, have all contributed towards their establishment as a familiar feature of the social landscape.[12]

Basking in such acclaim, the Irish renegade also achieved celebrity status at the Haus Des Rundfunks where friends remembered an intelligent, polite, dreamy romantic, who loved books and rarely caused problems, whist enemies, on the other hand, recalled a cranky workaholic with too much time for drink. It wasn't as if Joyce cared what others thought, as he enjoyed himself immensely playing the 'voice of Germany', while cannily preserving his legacy by curating an archive of scripts in his beautifully decorated apartment at Kastanienallee on a leafy street near the studios. There, Joyce wrote *Twilight Over England*, a book he hoped would prove a fitting successor to *Mein Kampf*. In it, he extolled 'absolute belief in National Socialism and conviction of Hitler's superhuman heroism'. Joyce also wrote about his long-standing attachment to Germany:

> Perhaps the attraction was due to the German blood which flowed in the veins of some of my ancestors. It was no doubt helped by

my veneration for the genius of men like Wagner and Goethe. Perchance my studies in Germanic Philology did much to make me aware of racial bonds that time and money have obscured. Whatever the reason may be, I grew up with that mystical attraction which has ended by my making Germany my permanent home. My hopes of being able to play some part of a definite kind, however small, in this struggle have been realised, thanks to the wonderful kindness and trust with which I, as a stranger, was greeted. It would be impossible for me to close this preface without adding that my wife has been of inestimable help to me.[13]

A British critic slammed this widely forgotten book as 'a diatribe against Britain and the British people' which contained a jumbled collection of distortions 'that could only have been the product of a mind that lived on hate'. Accounts suggest *Twilight Over England* was sketched out at the Funk-Eck café and the Press Club on the Leipzigerplatz where Joyce spent most evenings with Margaret. At the latter, hot meals were served all day and members could take a bath and get a haircut. There was a fully stocked bar, writing room and a 'news corridor' where papers from all over the Reich were set out on tables or pegged to hooks. Francis Stuart, an announcer with the Irland-Redaktion, remembered Joyce being 'treated quite regally',[14] as did former RRG employee Richard Baier, who never forgot Joyce lunching at the studio canteen. 'That's where I usually saw him. He was always sitting on his own with a book or scribbling away.' A Swedish editor gave a similar account, noting Joyce usually had 'one or more bottles of wine in front of him, but rarely looked happy'. Stuart also heard Joyce received rations 'only diplomats got'. 'We got very meagre rations. I think he was highly thought of.'[15]

For pocket money, Margaret shared her husband's shameful complicity by occasionally giving talks on 'women's issues', when not mooning at soldiers or engaging in romances with Wehrmacht officers. She had proved an apt as well as a willing pupil at the RRG, and an eager convert to the Nazi message.

Over in London, experts were divided on whether the best defence against Haw-Haw was ridicule or reply. As the scholar of Philosophy at Edinburgh University W. A. Sinclair put it, the 'Haw-Haw technique' was divided into three categories – 'unskilled lying, semi-skilled lying and highly skilled lying'. Sinclair explained 'unskilled lying consisted in making plain, simple statements which aren't true at all', while 'semi-skilled lying' was composed of conflicting statements, part true and part false. 'Highly skilled lying,' he said, was when Haw-Haw made statements which were true but used to convey a wrong impression:

> I don't think that many people are actually deceived by the mixture of truth with falsehood, but nearly everybody is irritated and disturbed. We feel there is something wrong somewhere and yet we can't always disentangle the truth from the falsehood.[16]

Had W. A. Sinclair heard German domestic radio, he would have been left equally horrified at the outrageous claims. On one occasion, a Deutschlandsender announcer asserted the British public felt 'the urge to raise their courage by resorting to drink'. 'Never,' he said, 'were so many drunken people seen in London as now.'[17] Furthermore, horses unfit for army service had been slaughtered to 'replenish England's rapidly dwindling meat stocks'. The following evening, news that butter had become so scarce in England was wistfully delivered, with the disclosure King George was compelled to spread margarine on his toast.

Anti-British rhetoric was also spread evenly across the printed press. *Volksfunk*, a popular weekly listings journal similar to the *Radio Times*, often featured it. 'The people who are the poorest in their own music and have the most venerable folk songs are the English,' columnist August Schmitt asserted. 'The only truly beautiful and genuine folk songs in the English tongue are from Ireland and Scotland.' In a similar vein, *Die Surag* replaced peppy lifestyle features with high-volume 'exclusives' about the destructive power of German submarine torpedoes against British shipping.[18]

12

GRUMBLES

For many, the blackout – or Verdunkelung – was a menace instead of a protection. Unlit streets and a spike in crime prompted more people than ever to stay home, behind locked doors with the radio for company. Therefore, it came as a great disappointment to Eugen Hadamovsky to learn his new schedules weren't to everyone's taste.

Within a few months of being rolled out, the Ministry of Propaganda was batting off public requests that popular musical items should be featured instead, especially in the evening hours, which were dominated by talks and news. The Ministry, however, said it was 'not in the position to comply with these requests':

> The German wireless has a mission to perform within the borders of the Reich as well as abroad. It also has to present to the world the German viewpoint in its foreign language programme. For this part of the programme the evening hours are the most important. Thus the wireless programme will remain the same as it has been.[1]

Since the outbreak of war, all manner of folk passed on their opinions about RRG output, with the most contentious subject being foreign languages interrupting German-language shows on home service Reichssender stations (English on Hamburg, French on Stuttgart and Swedish on Koningsberg). Government Minister

Hans Schaudinn acknowledged listener frustration, 'especially when a nice concert is abruptly cut and followed by ten or fifteen minutes of foreign language news'.[2] He also admitted very few listeners were able to understand these broadcasts, 'especially if they are in languages such as Swedish, Romanian, Serbo-Croat, Hungarian or Greek'. An editorial in *Volksfunk* took up the issue:

> You have the choice to switch off and thus miss the beginning of the next programme or patiently endure the foreign-sounding words. In the enemy countries themselves, it was quite impossible to hear an objective voice. Today things have changed. Our extensive broadcasts penetrate all countries, meaning they all can hear Germany. In order not only to reach the German-speaking people among them, German radio addresses the individual countries at certain hours in their own language. Listeners in Sweden or Greece or in Turkey knows that at any time he has to turn on the German transmitter in Königsberg or Wroclaw if he wants to know how Berlin assesses a situation, as German reports correspond to the truth. This also forces those newspapers of these countries, which are unscrupulous in accepting English lies, to be a little more cautious.[3]

Foreign Language on Domestic Transmitters, 1940

Bulgarian: Leipzig: 19:45, 20:40 and 22:45.

Danish: Bremen: 19:35.

English: Hamburg and Bremen: 10:15, 14:15, 17:15, 20:15, 21:15, 23:15 and 0:15.

French: Frankfurt, Köln, Saarbrücken, Stuttgart, Leipzig: 08:00, 12:45, 14:15 (Stuttg.), 17:15, 20:15, 21:15, 22:15, 23:15 and 00:15.

Greek: Breslau: 20:10.

Dutch: Bremen: 13:00, 18:40, 20:30 and 23:00.

Irish: Bremen (Sundays): 21:40.

Italian: München: 19:45, 21:15, 22:15, 23:15 and 00:15.

Lithuanian: Königsberg: 7:15, 11:30, 19:30 and 22:40.

Norwegian: Bremen (Sundays): 20:50.

Rumanian: Vienna: 17:45, 19:00 and 22:45.

Swedish: Königsberg: 22:20.

Serb-Croat: Breslau: 17:45, 19:45 and 23.00.
Slovenian: Graz: 17:45, 19:00 and 22:45.
Spanish: Stuttgart: 23:45.
Turkish: Lodsch: 19:00 and 20:15.
Hungarian: Bohemia: 17:30, 19:00 and 22:15.

During March, Hitler held talks with the Italian leader Benito Mussolini at Brenner Pass in the Alps, where the latter was informed Germany was preparing to attack the west. At the same time, Goebbels began softening up France for invasion with a heavy dose of vitriol courtesy of Reichssender stations in Stuttgart, Frankfurt, Köln, Saarbrücken and Leipzig. From Stuttgart, agitation created by Paul Ferdonnet and André Obrecht proved so effective that the pair were proclaimed traitors and sentenced to death in absentia by a Paris tribunal. Obrecht, using material written by Ferdonnet, sapped French Army morale by disclosing sensitive information supplied by fifth column informers. He accurately disclosed where French units would be billeted, causing a wave of hatred in France and forcing his mother and daughter, both then living in Paris, to seek refuge in a convent.

A French listener confessed she often tuned in to the 'Traitor of Stuttgart' out of curiosity. 'As for my husband,' she revealed, 'he gets irritated and shouts: "Shut up or I'll smash the wireless!"'

Author Edward Tangye Lean was also a keen listener. He described Ferdonnet (it was, in fact, Obrecht) as a first-class speaker 'who drove home his simple, unvarying points with force and conviction'. Lean argued many Frenchmen thought him better than anything to be heard on their own stations: 'Certainly, he was incomparably superior to the English Lord Haw-Haw, and his personality seems to have spread over the other talks and the news editing.'

In addition to the Stuttgart agitation, two 'freedom stations' supposedly transmitting from 'somewhere in France' sprang onto the airwaves designed to undermine confidence in the local population. Until this point, Goebbels had sought to frame propaganda based on the concept of not hiding its origin or nature, through official channels like Reichssender and the Deutsche

Kurzwellensender. The 'black propaganda' effort was led by Goebbels' little-known aide Adolf Raskin, from his perch in the Haus Des Rundfunks, where, with Walter Kamm and Erich Hetzler, he cultivated the shady Büro Concordia to produce subversive radio propaganda, stir up defeatism, strife and dissension.

The 39-year-old Raskin – a dead ringer for the mobster Al Capone – had gained his stripes running the Saarkampfzentrale, a propaganda agitation unit helping to ensure the return of the Saarland during the 1935 plebiscite. A posting to Vienna followed, where he was charged with liquidating Austrian Radio (RAVAG) and forming Reichssender Wien. By early 1940, Raskin had devised a blueprint for a roster of fake freedom stations aimed in the beginning at France but soon to include Britain and the Arab world. Day-to-day operations were overseen by Hetzler, a former economist and official of the Foreign Ministry who had also worked as a personal translator to Ribbentrop then as an assistant to Harald Dietrich, the head of censorship at the Ministry of Propaganda.

With France clearly in Hitler's sights, communists were recruited to write content, while advice was provided by SS-Intelligence official Walter Friedrich Schellenberg, who helped to 'create the greatest possible confusion among our enemies, especially the French'. The first station, Les Voix de la Paix (The Voice of Peace), had been blurting out sporadic transmissions since Christmas 1939, promoting panic with false and scurrilous reports, peppered with 'apocalyptic portraits' of war. In an effort to irritate French soldiers, Goebbels fabricated the highly salacious *Diary of an English Prisoner of War*, describing the amorous exploits of an Englishman in Paris. Other efforts to sow despondency claimed the government intended to flee Paris and France had been betrayed by Britain. Announcers warned of the possibility of a run on the banks and accused Jewish refugees of being German spies and fifth columnists, while members of these imaginary 'fifth columnist' groups received nonsensical instructions:

> Soldiers who are still in towns not occupied by the Germans should make sure that the name of everyone opposed to our movement is reported to the chiefs of groups. Anyone pretending to act for

our movement but unable to produce our official identification card should be handed over to the chief of the group. All chiefs of groups have constantly to be on the alert and ready to execute Order No. 202d as soon as instructions are given.

Horrified listeners were left feeling they had eavesdropped on secret wireless traffic. Schellenberg recalled how 'news' on these sham stations was based partly on material from French agents and on 'idiosyncratic but highly effective ideas'. In one case, he recounted, it was possible to direct the flow of French refugees fleeing the north and a little later from the Paris area in the direction the Germans desired. 'This gave German troops the freedom of movement they wanted, while the routes taken by the French armies were considerably blocked.'

For its part, Radio Humanité, another Concordia French-language effort, urged listeners to evade military service and hold demonstrations in the name of peace. The name Radio Humanité was inspired, given the Communist Party in France had been banned following the Molotov–Ribbentrop pact, as had their newspaper, *L'Humanité*, providing the Germans with a golden opportunity to masquerade as genuine French communists. Scripts were written in Berlin by German editors, including Ernst Torgler, a communist who had been charged with arson and treason in connection with the Reichstag fire but later acquitted because of a lack of evidence against him. His words were read by several announcers, including Josef Haafs, Anna Jankowski and movie actor Theodor Thony, a bit player in *The Gypsy Baron*, *Serenade* and *Schneider Wibbel*.

To facilitate the Concordia project, studios were knocked together at the Villa Concordia (also known as Villa die Grosse) opposite the Haus Des Rundfunks at Soorstrasse 33 but later moved to the Olympic Stadium. The effort was supported financially by the Propaganda Ministry but fell under the jurisdiction of the Foreign Office, which exerted full control regarding policy. RRG covered day-to-day running costs, ploughing in 22,000 Marks a month on wages for broadcasters and their accommodation. Every morning at 10 o'clock, a joint meeting of officials of the Propaganda Ministry and the Foreign

Office was held to decide general principles to be adopted in material for each day's broadcasts.

Certainly the object of Goebbels' deepest, most profoundly felt hatred was Britain. So, inspired by his successful agitation against France, German radio commentators adopted an icier tone toward England during March. From then on, a stream of violent threats aided by a new battle hymn, *Bombs on England*, saturated the airwaves. Sung by the choir of an artillery patrol, the brassy number contained the lyrics:

> We challenge the British Lion to last out a decisive battle.
> We shall name the Day of Judgment and the fall of an Empire.
> This will be our proudest day.

Each verse ended with the words, *Bomben – Bomben – Bomben uber Engelland*, and a realistic swish and crashing drum bang. Sure enough, the song was playing when the first Luftwaffe bombs scattered over Scapa Flow, Brig o'Waithe, Stenness and Orkney on 14 March. The following evening, the German public howled with delight as Lieutenant Philipps, who took part in the Scapa raid, told reporter Lothar Hartmann about his exploits in a special front-line report.[4] A few days later, a communiqué on Deutschlandsender declared, 'From now on Germany is determined to wage a war against England as such a war must be waged hard and inexorable.'

From the spring of 1940, music was at the forefront of all patriotic activities, especially during charity drives and soldier welfare campaigns. Singers and stars fanned out through every state in the country, addressing rallies, signing autographs and performing for the troops. On 26 March, Germany introduced summer time in anticipation of energy savings, which ran continuously until November 1942. With the lighter nights, RRG was busily relaying everything from local bands to Italian opera singers who screeched their way around the country. The Littoria Orchestra – the permanent Italian Radio Symphony under the direction of Giuseppe Savgnone – sweated through a series of broadcasts and Strength through Joy (KdF) events. *Romeo and Juliet* by Heinrich Sutermeister premiered at the

Staatsoper in Dresden and *Palla de' Mozzi* attracted crowds to the Deutsches Opernhaus in Berlin. Ticket returns revealed Wagner was the most popular composer, followed by Verdi, Puccini, Mozart, and Rossini.

There was a great ovation from war workers at the annual Bayreuth festival which featured Wagner's Ring operas – *Das Rheingold, Die Waikuere, Siegfried* and *Gotterdaemmerung* – performed exclusively for the benefit of radio and Strength through Joy audiences. The KdF radio crew always received a tremendous reception during tours and by early 1940, had clocked up 247 transmissions since hostilities began. Like ENSA in Britain, KdF arranged live entertainment for troops and munitions workers with singers, dancers, a ventriloquist, conjurer and mobile radio unit whizzing around airfields, naval ports, and camp canteens to perform. Songs, humorous sallies and comedians were their specialty but unlike ENSA, the liberal use of smutty or political gags was curtailed. As for female performers, they, under the circumstances, were allowed to show a 'generous amount' of flesh on stage. According to the records of Goebbels' daily conferences, instructions were issued to 'raise the standard' of KdF shows from 1 April, due to concerns they were degenerating into a 'veritable funfair'.

To keep the German war machine running, natural resources needed to be constantly available. Neutral Norway, with its strategic location and access to important resources, such as iron ore, became a prized target of both the German and British navies. For the Germans, resources could be easily shipped along a maritime supply line to Hamburg from numerous ports nestled along the Norwegian coast.

With that in mind, the British gave notice to the Norwegian government in Oslo on 8 April reserving the right to 'take such measures as they may think necessary to prevent Germany from obtaining resources or facilities in Norway' by denying them the use of their territorial waters. While the response to this missive was uneasy in Norway, it generated a full-blown furore in Berlin.

Furthermore, the Royal Navy announced it had rendered Norwegian waters dangerous to navigation by laying mines, and 'vessels entering did so at their peril'. That night, the Swedish-language news on Reichssender Königsberg contained an immediate response from Berlin:

> With ice-cold calmness, Germany is confronted by the English abuse against the neutral Nordic countries. This desperate English operation is unmistakably an expression of weakness and nervousness. [...] With a last effort, England unconditionally tries to expand the theatre of war all the way to the Nordic countries. Thus, Germany awaits with the greatest interest the reaction of the Nordic countries, especially Norway; regarding the English mine-laying action on the Norwegian coast.[5]

Even at this dangerous moment, few people imagined that less than 24 hours later, German troops would trample over Denmark and Norway in the first combined land, sea and air operation in history. The peaceful spring atmosphere in Berlin was shattered with another brief, but dramatic, High Command bulletin on Deutschlandsender:

> In order to oppose the British attack on the neutrality of Denmark and Norway, the Wehrmacht has taken over the armed protection of these states.

That night, William Joyce was on air trotting out the news in English to a stunned world:

> The Supreme Command of the German Defence Forces announces the operation to occupy Denmark and the Norwegian coast has proceeded according to plan today. On marching into – and landing – on Danish territory, no incidents occurred anywhere. No significant resistance was offered along the coast of Norway, except near Oslo. Resistance there was broken during the afternoon and Oslo itself was occupied. The German minister for Norway, Dr Bräuer, received representatives of the Norwegian press today and informed them of a new appeal that is addressed to the Norwegian government. It runs as follows: 'In recalling this morning's appeal, I wish, once again, to draw the attention of the Norwegian government to the fact that any resistance to Germany's action will be completely senseless and would only lead to an aggravation of Norway's position.'

After reading the official news, Joyce shifted into propaganda mode for his *Views on the News* monologue:

> Germany has no quarrels with Denmark or Norway but Germany has carefully studied the maritime history of Great Britain. She remembers Copenhagen in 1807. She remembers the seizing of Malta and Gibraltar. She remembers the bombardment of Alexandria in 1882 and she has not forgotten that England and France were making preparations to occupy the Balearic Islands during the Spanish civil war – that attempt was frustrated by Italian watchfulness. Germany has for months been observant and aligned to the danger which threatens all strategical points in northern Europe that might serve naval or air force bases for Great Britain and France in their war of destruction against Germany.

While conquering Norway proved difficult, the assault on Denmark took just seven hours, becoming the shortest campaign of the war. Old rules of journalism no longer applied as PK reporters – patched through telephone hook-ups to Berlin – delivered reports through the first bombardment. 'Those who had the opportunity,' *Volksfunk* observed, 'did not stop listening to the radio so as to miss nothing. These historical days beamed out of loudspeakers from morning to night.' Running commentaries peppered with witness accounts dominated the airwaves, as did the flurry of special announcements, known as *Sondermeldung*:

> On Tuesday morning, German troops and armoured forces crossed the German–Danish border at Flensburg and Tønder...

> At dawn, German troops landed in the Little Belt near Middelfart...

> Copenhagen fell before dawn without a fight...

> The landing of German troops has succeeded in all places from Oslo to Narvik...

Despite their small numbers, the Norwegians put up a dogged defence – forcing the Germans into countless fierce encounters. As the fighting raged *Volksfunk* devoted a four-page spread to the 'breath-taking pace of this surprising, but necessary action'. Over the coming weeks, the Wehrmacht occupied Oslo, Bergen, Trondheim, and Narvik. While there was some pro-invasion celebration in Germany, it wasn't unanimous. For Goebbels, explaining this unprovoked attack against an 'Aryan brother people' provided an immense headache, says Niclas Sennerteg, author of *Tyskland talar*, a history of the RRG Swedish-language service. 'The radio propaganda to Sweden, therefore, became very ambivalent,' he says. 'The depiction of the German military superiority and the claim Germany saved the Scandinavians from "plutocratic slavery" became the main ingredients of the broadcasts until the much larger offensive in Western Europe stole all attention.' For the most part, the public in Sweden were left bewildered.

Soon after the occupation, Norwegians were ordered to surrender all radio receivers, but the newly created 'Ministry of Culture and Popular Enlightenment' continued to bankroll Radio Oslo, despite only Nazis and German soldiers being in a position to listen to it. That situation made the station useless to the new regime, given its inability to spread propaganda among the general public.

The excitement from the Norway campaign had barely died down when the RRG laid on grand gestures for Hitler's birthday. As in previous years, events ran from 05.00 till midnight. The day opened with the performance of a children's choir in Bielefeld, followed by workers from the Krupp steel factory belting out a musical serenade, and classical concerts from Vienna, Dresden and Berlin:

05.00 Werken und Fruhkonzert Spielleute und der Musikzug der SA. Standart 'Feldherrnhalle'
06.00 'Wach auf! es nahet gen den Tag' Chor aus Richard Wagners 'Meister singer von Nürnberg'. Der Chor und das Orchester der Staatsoper Berlin, Leitung: Generalintendant Staatsrat Heinz Tietjen. 'Freiheit und Vaterland' Stats schauspieler Friedrich Kayssler, spricht Worte von Ernst Moritz Arndt.

06.10 Grosskonzert der Wehrmacht Es spielen Musikkorps des Heeres, der Kriegsmarine und der Luftwaffe

08.00 Festliche Morgenmusik GF Händel Friedrich der Große – Johann Sebastian Bach Das Große Orchester des Reichssenders Hamburg. Leitung: Oreste Piccardi

09.00 Braunau Deutsche Jugend in der Heimat des Führers –

09.30 Sang und klang aus deutscher Landschaft

11.30 Der Bielefelder Kinderchor Leitung: Friedrich Oberschelp

12.00 Werkkonzert ans den Friedrich-Krupp-Werken

13.00 Konzert aus der Hauptstadt der Bewegung Mitglieder des Bayrischen Staatstheaters und das Bayrische Staatsorchesler, Leitung: Intendant Prof. Clemens Krauss

14.10 'Auch kleine Dinge können uns entzücken' Kammermusik und Lieder Mitwirkende: Erna Berger, Sopran – Walther Ludwig, Tenor – Wilhelm Strienz, Bass, Hubert Giese, Klavier – Karl Steiner, Violine – Adolf Steiner, Cello.

15.00 Gruß aus Wien Beschwingte Weisen

17.10 Das Kaiser-Quartett von Jos. Haydn Es spielt das Dresdner Streichquartett

17.40 Die Regensburger Domspatzen singen, Leitung: Domkapellmeister Professor Dr. Th. Schreins

18.00 Das MusikKorps SS – Leibstandarte Adolf Hitler

18.30 Aus dem Zeitgeschehen, Frontberichte

20.15 Die Berliner Philharmoniker spielen

22.15 Frontberichte –

22.30 Unterhaltende Abendmusik Es spielen: Das Grosse Orchester des Reichssender Berlin. Leitung: Hans Roshaud und Barnabas von Geczy

23.30 Der große Zapfenstreich Musikkorps und Spielleute der Wehrmacht, Leitung: Professor Hermann Schmidt

00.10 Nachtkonzert

01.00 Closedown

13

HITLER'S WINNING STREAK

Flags flew, crowds cheered and balloons ascended skyward when the 'phoney war' abruptly ended at dawn on 10 May as German mechanised columns overran Belgium, Luxembourg and the Netherlands. That day, tears ran down the cheeks of many listeners as a military pipe band struck the *France Fanfare* before the *Sondermeldung*. According to Goebbels, a British and French strike against Germany had been imminent: 'This Allied attack would be carried out through Dutch and Belgian territory.'

Journalist P. Koch was invited to the Haus Des Rundfunks to experience the thrill of a *Sondermeldung* announcement being tapped through. 'Organisation is everything here,' he observed. 'And when a *Sondermeldung* arrives, activity begins':

> A telephone rings and a few moments later the duty officer, the line manager, the transmitter engineers, the technicians and the newsreaders swing into action. After about ten minutes, the special message is ready for broadcast. A telex machine has begun to tap out: 'The High Command of the Wehrmacht announces...'

Koch was drawn to a map with 'strange lines in all colours', denoting foreign languages and radio transmission times. 'Here you can see exactly which German station is currently broadcasting. The wireless service has to decide if the special message is so important that it is transmitted immediately or delayed.' To top it off, there was a question: Should the message open with a fanfare? More often than not, the task of delivering *Sondermeldung* fell to four men, who, in turn, became the best-known voices in Germany. They were Chief Announcer Dr Hermann Rau, RRG spokesman Elmer Bantz, presenter Hans Goedecke (of *Wunschkonzert für die Wehrmacht* fame) and journalist Hellmuth Vietor.

With the opening of the campaigning in the West, listeners to local Reichssender stations received a rude awakening when a new *Einheitsprogramm* trimmed local output in favour of a simulcast Reichssender Berlin (from then billed as Gross Deutscher Rundfunks or Reichsprogramm). Listeners to Reichssender Hamburg and Reichssender Köln, both of which had established a large and loyal following, mourned their demise. Although a few regional programmes remained on air, the Reichssenders became a de facto second national network. According to *Volksfunk*, the changes were 'significantly influenced by the beginning of operations in the West' and a need for tighter programme control: 'Radio must be prepared every hour for the transmission of important news from the theatre of war.' Other tweaks meant it was 'completely impossible' for English or French pop music to be included in programmes, 'but it is just as unthinkable that today we only burden our hard-working and fighting folk with classical, tragic or heroic music'.

With the invasion of the Low Countries, plans for the occupation of Dutch radio along with stations in Belgium and Luxembourg swung into action. In fact, transcripts from Goebbels' daily conferences noted on 13 May, 'The radio is to make immediate recordings of the announcements by Brussels and Hilversum radios, so the voices of the regular speakers can be used if necessary, if in some special circumstances, we put ourselves on these enemy wavelengths.'

When Wehrmacht trucks finally turned up at the radio studios in Hilversum, they were armed with enough pre-recorded programmes (in Dutch) to last two weeks.[1] The first on-air directive, it seems, was a decree that Dutch time would be placed on the same footing as Berlin time.[2] Then, rather than using threats of violence, the Germans opted to let the Dutch presenters continue as usual, but without playing music from British, French or Jewish composers.

US Army intelligence noted one of the cleverest policies the Nazis employed was of restoring a country's broadcasting service to its normal presentation shortly after the cessation of military operations. 'The voices of the native announcers, the same broadcast schedules, the unexpected absence of German influence on the surface of broadcasting, combine to reassure the population and calm their fears about the occupying enemy.'[3] In Holland, 'the public recognised the familiar voices of the old announcers and were greatly reassured, and many concluded that things were not going to be so bad after all,' a former presenter recalled.[4]

However, there were some changes. Dutch Nazi Max Blokzijl, who had earned his Nazi stripes contributing fervently fascist articles to pro-Hitler newspapers under an assumed name, was installed as a senior announcer and commentator. Possibly the most indiscreet broadcaster, Blokzijl quickly earned the sobriquet 'Moaning Max' because of his constant complaints about the activities of Dutch patriots. In the first week of his new job, Blokzijl rattled off a flurry of directives, which among other exhortations forbade buying 'more food than is indispensable for one day'. Then, the purchase of clothing and woollen goods was restricted to a minimum as 'stocks of these materials have dropped to a very low level and no fresh supplies can be expected for any definite period'. Other directives, which covered six columns of A4 print, included the following:

* Anyone found in possession of firearms without a licence issued by the German military authorities would be shot on the spot.
* Petrol and oil in Holland were reserved for the German military.
* Reich Treasury Certificates would be introduced as legal tender in Holland.
* Ambulances and hearses could only be obtained under certain conditions.

To begin with, existing Dutch broadcasters – AVRO, KRO, NCRV, VARA, and VPRO – continued operations under supervision until Dr T. Goedewaagen took the helm at the newly created 'Department of People's Enlightenment and Fine Arts', and later established De Nederlandsche Omroep, a single national network, which gained fame for producing Paulus de Ruiter's outrageous anti-Semitic cabaret show *Zondagmiddagcabaret*.

As May rolled on, Hitler had reason to be grateful to his warriors as they pushed the British Expeditionary Force to beat a hasty retreat through France. 'Back from the steel thrust of the German war machine comes the BEF,' reported the *Pathe Gazette* newsreel as thousands of Allied troops made a successful home run from the port of Dunkirk. 'Words of mine can never convey fully the scene that faced us,' recalled Harry Hargreaves, a British sailor charged with picking up stragglers near Cherbourg. 'As far as the eye could see was a graveyard of vehicles of every kind. Bren gun carriers, troop transports, supply vehicles, ambulances, motorbikes, canteen trucks, army coloured automobiles, even bicycles.' The Admiralty had called on the public to help with the evacuation, broadcasting an appeal over the BBC on 14 May:

> The Admiralty have made an order requesting all owners of self-propelled pleasure craft between 30ft and 100ft in length to send all particulars to the Admiralty within 14 days from today if they have not already been offered or requisitioned.

Between 27 May and 4 June, more than 320,000 men made it home during Operation Dynamo on board small ships, private yachts, and fishing boats – transforming the disaster into a victory of sorts. Churchill hailed the action as a 'miracle of deliverance' which enabled the Allies to continue fighting.

Back in Germany, Deutschlandsender trumpeted every success using accounts crackling with immediacy from the heat of battle. Reporter H. von Kobilinski accompanied a PK company to discover how thrilling front-line despatches were produced. Each day, he monitored the mechanics of these fine, 'almost sculptured real-life accounts of the war'. Accepting enormous personal risk, Kobilinski hitched a ride across flat farmland during the Dutch campaign, squeezed on board a camouflaged PK pick-up known as a 'U-Wagen' manned by a driver, reporter, and audio technician.

Intoxicated by his task, Kobilinski explained in such conditions profound bonds of friendship were formed. 'When these men with the microphone speak, every citizen knows what's going on along the front line – in the East and in the West.' As the campaign rolled on, Kobilinski witnessed reinforcements open a massive ground offensive. 'The reporter,' he observed, 'always needed an impeccable view of the action. He can only give listeners a gripping performance if he is in the middle of it.' Technically, the process of field reporting was simple but cumbersome. In most cases, long cables hooked the microphone to the recorder (sometimes for hundreds of metres) and a beep from the pick-up horn gave a cue for the reporter to begin speaking. Back in the 'U-Wagen', wax discs spun on the cutting machine, capturing the action. 'This type of embedded reporting was one of the inventions of the Nazis – there was no illusion, they were there. They had a front-row seat and that is what listeners heard,' says Wolfgang Bauernfeind, author of the official history of the Haus Des Rundfunks. 'The whole idea could be exceedingly dangerous but the concept was brand new and listeners appreciated hearing these reports.'

Several well-known RRG personnel were killed during the campaigns in Poland, Scandinavia, and the West. Hans Spelsberg, who had covered the Sudeten crisis and the march into Poland, went missing in Norway, as did engineer Werner Bartsch from the Deutsche Kurzwellensender. Fred Ohlsen-Öhlschläger found a soldier's death in Holland while reporting for Deutschlandsender, while Willi Kluge, a reporter known for his coverage from Warsaw, was killed in Belgium. Arno Hellmis, a celebrated sports correspondent on Reichssender Berlin, was fatally wounded on the front line in France.

Heinrich Glasmeier, the Director General of the RRG, remembered the British retreat from Dunkirk was portrayed as a humiliating defeat. He would never forget a specially composed 'France song' blaring across German airwaves denoting the Maginot line had fallen. 'Almost a week later, the whole military and the entire nation were singing it.'[5] On 27 May, Calais was in German hands, as Deutschlandsender reported:

> What did not succeed in the Great War has succeeded now. At that time Foch said: 'Whoever holds Calais has the key to the door of England and France.'

> ... Duff Cooper, who boasts of knowing French as well as a born Frenchman, went before the microphone last night to give the French the supreme pleasure of hearing him. He now insists on his wish for peace, but the peace he has in mind is to be enjoyed by England, while others are to fight and be pushed into misfortune.[6]

As German troops continued to trample toward Paris, Büro Concordia escalated their activities to sow discord among locals. As noted by Edward Tangye Lean, RRG, via Reichssender Stuttgart and the Concordia stations, had already built up a large audience of listeners: 'The weapon was already in contact with its objective.'

On 10 June, the loudest sabre rattling came from La Voix de la Paix, which claimed to have 'never published false news', before announcing,

> All Paris is threatened with poisoning because fifth columnists have succeeded in poisoning several reservoirs of drinking water. ... Is Paris to be another Warsaw, or is it to be a Brussels? We must save Paris as Brussels was saved. Must we see our capital destroyed, Notre Dame, Sainte Chapelle, the Louvre in ruins, and the blood of our women and children flowing along the pavements? [7]

At the same time, Radio-Humanité aggravated panic among susceptible listeners by begging them to flee, while transmitting fake 'coded messages' to imaginary cells, as well as warnings of a fifth column stalking the countryside.[8]

When Paris fell on 14 June, a Deutschlandsender announcer caustically remarked, 'the pursuit has been carried out at such speed that the French simply cannot understand the sudden appearance of German troops. They have taken them for English soldiers. They thought the English had come to the assistance of the French!'[9]

Fred Kaltenbach, a commentator for the RRG US Zone, provided colourful 'on the spot' coverage from the French capital. In his broadcast to America, he described 'Italian fashionable women making their purchases as unconcernedly as though no German soldier was within miles of Paris':

It was apparent that Parisians were agreeably surprised by the manners of the German soldiers. German authorities in France are doing what they can to help the refugees. A proprietor who lived in Paris for 40 years said the French collapse came as no surprise to him. The breakdown of the French people was evident before the war. The French had taken their liberty too lightly. A woman in the street blamed the British for letting their ally down.

Back in Germany, Berliners celebrated the conquest amid a frenzy of cheering, singing and shouting. Dorothea Günther, a 22-year-old resident, never forgot processions and delirious joy that day:

Hitler was glorified more than ever as the 'final victory' seemed within reach. How could there ever be doubters? The German army moved into Paris. There French perfumes, lingerie and other Parisian chic sold out. The victory parade that swept through the Brandenburg Gate in Berlin was simply bombastic. Dunkirk was hailed by the Nazi press as the victorious end of the greatest battle ever.[10]

When the campaign ended – and in some cases during the fighting – German intelligence attempted to ensure captured French radio stations could be reactivated. 'In their hasty retreat the French destroyed some studios,' *Volksfunk* reported. 'In this futile destructive rage, destruction was conducted not only with hammers and rifle butts, but also with bullets. Other equipment was torn out and scattered on the floor.' *Volksfunk* continued:

Gasoline was then poured over valuable equipment and set alight. At Pontoise in the north-western suburbs of Paris, a total of 14 short and long-wave transmitters were destroyed. Even the transmission towers were blown up, while others teetered near collapse.

After 'strenuous and indefatigable work', the situation was under control as many studios were repaired and put back on air within a month. Of all of the stations which fell into Nazi hands, nothing was more precious than Radio Paris. It was an expensive one too – employing 1,000 staff maintained by an annual budget of 1 million Marks. Sitting under the shadow of the Eiffel Tower, the Renaissance-style studios were set on the Rue François-Ier, in a plush residential quarter. A visitor once remarked, 'The lugubriousness and artistry of the studios is foreshadowed by the richness of the vestibule, from which sweeps a wide staircase, heavily carpeted in wine colour and relieved by gold fittings.'

Like operations in Hilversum, Radio Paris wore a mask of normality as it churned out music on records, including symphony concerts and biweekly operas. Pierre Hiegel, the star presenter, spun mainly French composers such as Ravel, Debussy and Fauré while shunning pieces by Germans, which, given intelligence reports that showed when German music was broadcast listeners generally tuned out, was just as well. Only *Au Rythme des Temps*, a show adapting well-known songs into pro-Nazi or anti-Allied slogans, displayed a propaganda twist.

14

BRITAIN

Eventually, life at the Propaganda Ministry established a pattern. Every weekday morning divisional managers would be joined by Goebbels to discuss war developments. A large map in the conference room showing the vast expanse of German military operations was usually the starting point for these meetings. Green pins were used to indicate the location of troops in Europe, the East and Scandinavia. As the war progressed, ProMi employees were often so overwhelmed by the vast amount of information coming in from all fronts, it became difficult to keep track.

With the fall of Paris that summer, Britain was alive to the expectation of a German invasion. Angst was increased when Goebbels deployed the full strength of his international propaganda to send a single message: Britain is next.

From this point onwards, the BBC Overseas Intelligence unit began tapping out a daily dossier on German propaganda. Ernst H. Gombrich, the Austrian-born art historian, worked as a monitor at Evesham. One of his tasks was listening to Reichssender Hamburg from where Joyce was leading the vanguard of the threatened foray onto his home soil:

> The great offensive against France has been brought to a victorious conclusion. The French have laid down arms and throughout the world, people wonder when the final act – the offensive against British soil – would come.

Gombrich remembered priority being given to preparing reports from Deutschlandsender and the difficulties involved: 'The reception was often poor, and the task we monitors were faced with, to translate or summarise what we heard under time pressures was anything but easy.'

That summer, Joyce spoke of a declining Britain in the throes of death where businesses had 'come to a standstill' under Churchill, the 'corrupt dictator' of England:

> The great exodus from Britain is well underway. The rich and the affluent are removing themselves and their valuables as fast as they can. Great stretches of the coastline have been evacuated to a depth of 20-miles. Hastily improvised defences are being erected. And the defeat of France within six weeks after the entry of German troops into Belgium and Holland is the most eloquent testimony of what Germany can do in modern warfare. It needs no stressing.

When not broadcasting, Joyce took a personal hand in preparing the English aspect of the Concordia project by touring prisoner of war camps recruiting would-be broadcasters with the promise of better rations. Eventually, more than two-thirds of Concordia's staff consisted of British fascists sympathetic to the Fatherland and POWs. Among others, William Griffiths, a Welsh Guardsman, remembered meeting Joyce at a POW camp:

> Joyce told us we had nothing to worry about, the work was quite easy, and that if we used our heads we would fall in with the German plans. We told Joyce we did not want to do this work and he replied that things would not be easy with us if we refused to do the work, and that if we refused we would be sent to a concentration camp and there would be no hope of us returning to an ordinary prisoner of war camp.

By the time the French campaign had passed into history, four new Concordia stations purporting to be broadcasting from inside the British Isles started churning out a toxic brew of fear and paranoia. However, the difference between the French stations and the poorly co-ordinated and uninspiring effort aimed at the United Kingdom was considerable.

The most ambitious channel, The New British Broadcasting Station (NBBS), played the British national anthem at the beginning and end of each transmission and hectored listeners with warnings of a Nazi fifth column organisation undermining the Churchill government.

Another effort, The Christian Peace Station – a replica of the Voix de la Paix – camouflaged itself as an apostle for peace:

> Get the word 'Peace' everywhere. Write it on the pavements, chalk it on the walls. Give slogans a rest and concentrate on the word 'Peace', write it on slips of paper, put it in envelopes and send it to your MP. This is our biggest campaign—peace before winter. Plaster the word everywhere.

On one occasion it accused every woman working in the armaments industry as committing a crime against God:

> Women of Britain, we appeal to you to put an end to this horrid war. No cause, however just, can be fought for with the wicked methods of war. We must admit frankly that we have done wrong in going to war. We must humble ourselves and pray for forgiveness. And then and not until then will God listen to our prayers. War is not Christianity. God's will is peace.[1]

Transmissions usually wrapped up with hymns and a prayer. From the very same studio, the *Workers' Challenge* star performer was a Cockney-speaking German who addressed British workers using language, according to a listener, 'that would shame a Billingsgate porter'. Arthur Chapple, a NAAFI worker recruited by Joyce, made his debut on the station playing a malcontent 'northerner' talking from 'a working man's point of view'. Joyce encouraged his protégé to 'ham up' a thick Yorkshire accent. 'Can anybody be fooled by t'Jewish – plutocratic agitating lies?' Chapple asked listeners.

North Somerset Yeoman Signalman William Alfred Colledge was assigned to *Workers' Challenge* where Margaret Joyce coached him to deliver newscasts, which, as it happened, wasn't successful.

> After a long course of instruction I was finally rejected as unsuitable (…) I was sent for at a later date by Hetzler who dictated a British-German war report. He asked me to punctuate it and to alter it in the best way that I thought fit. This I did and roughly speaking I did this sort of work on-and-off for about a year. I was known as the 'War Report Man'.[2]

Colledge remembered that except for Joyce, nobody at *Workers' Challenge* was able to compose or speak their own material, as everything was 'subjected to Hetzler's dictation, correction and re-correction'. He considered anti-communism was best promoted through *Workers' Challenge*. 'It was, however, Communism exaggerated and revealed in all its foul-mouthness, which should be sufficient deterrent to anyone with common sense':

> Incidentally, no one was ever allowed to speak directly into a microphone. All talks were recorded and checked at the time of recording by a trusted German and ordered to stop if a slip was made. It was rumoured that two Russians were shot for having either coughed or hesitated or somehow given a signal before certain words.[3]

Of all the Concordia stations, nothing outshone Radio Caledonia – the 'Voice of Scotland' – which crackled over the glens to the strains of 'Auld Lang Syne'. It was, without doubt, the clumsiest effort imaginable. A BBC monitor noted the announcer had a 'slight Scottish accent' but was generally incoherent – as was the content, which also included items about hunger, the Fatherland, capitalism, the working man and so on. Scottish workers were badgered to 'throw down their tools and stop fighting the capitalists' war'. It maintained relations between England and Scotland were 'at breaking point', citing Scots returning from London bringing reports of violent unrest. Furthermore, it asserted Scottish people would not only prefer but would also feel much safer 'if our native soil were defended by our own Scottish lads. England's dictator, however, without consulting us, has sent our men all over the globe and replaced them with Czechs, Poles, and heaven knows what'. The sharpest words were always reserved for Churchill:

> We are opposed to that corrupt politician, Winston Churchill. We have always advocated a separate peace in Scotland. Many people have asked us if this will imply that we wish a complete separation from England. That is not suggested for one moment. We hope it will be possible for Britain to secure peace, but in any case, we must get it for Scotland. Our geographical position makes it possible. If we get peace and England does not, it will mean a new Government for Scotland.[4]

Then there was the promise to Scots farmers of a series of talks on agriculture: 'A prosperous farming industry is the first essential for a prosperous Scotland,' the announcer declared. 'We understand many of our most enthusiastic listeners are connected with agriculture, and that they appreciate our efforts on behalf of Scottish farming.'

A journalist listening in Glasgow observed 'not once since the war began has Radio Caledonia been able to understand Scotland's part in our island life and activity'. Edward F. Balloch from the *Aberdeen Evening Express* was equally appalled:

> I wish I could reproduce in full the rubbish which the Nazi radio station, Radio Caledonia, is pouring out for the benefit of the Scots! The whole of the broadcast is sheer bathos. There are sickening references to the 'Bonnie Scotland' which the Nazis will build up if they get the chance. There is an appeal to Scots to have nothing to do with Mr Churchill and to 'protect your own lovely hills and glens'.[5]

While there is no satisfactory statistics or surveys concerning the effectiveness of these stations, their jumbled messages and erratic tone won few supporters. 'These fake German stations crop up like mushrooms on a certain wavelength, blither and blather for some time, then entirely disappear,' a listener noted, while the gossip writer of the *Yorkshire Evening Post* cracked that German authorities had 'at last become convinced that their official broadcasts in English are either boring or ridiculous'.

In the Fatherland, after the thrill of non-stop successes, the excitement continued in July with the beginning of the Battle of Britain – a sequence of air encounters, which, much to the annoyance of Berlin, did nothing to lessen British confidence in the worth of their Royal Air Force. As German fliers desperately tried to 'soften up' their target for invasion, raids on Britain became practically continuous. This, though, was still a two-way street, as the RAF hit back at several locations across Germany, including Hamburg docks. For a nation that had been winning battles everywhere, the bombing came as a shocking wake-up call.

By September, the Royal Air Force had denied the Luftwaffe air superiority over the skies of England. An RRG bulletin that month described 'disastrous conditions' in London leading to the government evacuating and the royal family fleeing to Canada. The spectre of a German landing was beefed up, along with reports of an overwrought public gathering every morning to meet astrologers seeking enlightenment on England's fate. As this was going on, Hitler had already secretly postponed the invasion of Britain 'until further notice'.

For all their tough talk, the Concordia stations and Joyce failed to prevent the growing number of RAF's raids, which were rapidly sobering up a population hitherto drunk on victory. In way of distraction, the propaganda rolled on with the threat England would 'become the last battlefield as the British Empire approached its natural end'. Fantasies were repeated over and over again. 'Food,' it was reported, was so scarce, that Englishmen were joining the army 'in the hope of at least getting a square meal'. Then there was the tale of a soldier caught sleeping on sentry duty because hunger prevented him from standing up. A bulletin monitored from the Bremen transmitter claimed England was transferring German Prisoners of War to ships anchored along the English coast 'ostensibly to expose these ships to attacks by German planes'.[6]

With huge swathes of the Continent under occupation, journalist Herbert Urban asserted 1940 had seen Germany become the dominant player in European broadcasting. In an article for *Volksfunk*, he noted that Reich-controlled stations across the Continent were 'vital for the upkeep of Germanity'. By factoring in the elimination of anti-German influences in Denmark, Norway, the Netherlands and Belgium, Urban reckoned 'Germany now controls all of the broadcasting in central Europe, which, a couple of years ago would have been deemed absolutely impossible. Radio Germany,' he cooed, 'is just as hard to beat as Germany itself!'

That autumn, 40-year-old Hans Fritzsche established himself as something of a national radio institution. Known for his unflappable delivery and well-structured arguments, this clean-shaven, lantern-jawed journalist would guide listeners through triumphs and tragedies alike, always opening his talks with the words, 'Hier spricht Hans Fritzsche!'

Having studied economics and philosophy, Fritzsche got a job in print journalism with the Hugenberg Press in the 1920s before becoming Director of the *Drahtloser Dienst*. Goebbels successfully recruited him as deputy to Alfred Berndt, the creator of the 'Desert Fox' myth during the North Africa campaign.

Once behind the microphone, Fritzsche often pushed beyond his allocated 10-minute segment – the variety and range of his work was astonishing. In one notable performance, following an RAF raid, he abandoned mincing words with the threat: 'For every bomb dropped on Berlin, ten will be dropped on London!'[7] To make matters worse, the attacks began disrupting radio operations of all long and mediumwave transmitters, which were forced to shut down between 23.00 and 03.00 to prevent British pilots using them as directional beacons. From then onwards, such interruptions plagued the network until the end of the war.

Despite the setbacks, the Luftwaffe continued to prowl over the skies of England. On 4 October, PK correspondents Heinz Laubenthal and Hans Kriegler – armed with recording equipment and throat microphones – joined the Luftwaffe on a raid over

London to witness the thrilling spectacle of 'bombs of the heaviest calibre' raining down on London.

> On the right side of us, we see flak shots flare-up closer and closer to Dunkirk. That can only be German flak because that's where our competitors are at work. We have now reached the English coast. Above us is a glorious starry sky and below us a small layer of haze, in which the beam of the anti-aircraft spotlights breaks through. In front of us lies the narrow crescent of the moon.

Revelling in the success of other air raids of Britain, Luftwaffe flying ace Major Adolph Galland was invited to Deutschlandsender to deliver a personal talk. 'The Englishman is an obstinate opponent,' he explained. 'But he now has a great many young, ill-trained pilots among its ranks.' He giggled when asked if he had flown over London:

> Yes! The day before yesterday, twice! It is like any other big city, surrounded by strong haze, but from this haze come the landmarks.

Around the same time, Deutschlandsender claimed Marshal Goring piloted a plane over London, where he was 'impressed by the effects of the Luftwaffe bombing attacks'.

In November, Adolf Raskin, the driving force behind Büro Concordia, was killed in a plane crash. Just half-an-hour after departing Berlin for Sofia, the Lufthansa four-engine Junkers Ju 90 he was travelling on began lurching violently up and down before smashing to earth, killing 5 crew and 23 passengers. Raskin had planned to explore the possibilities of creating a clandestine station aimed at Greece. A few weeks later, newsreel cameras captured the requisite speeches and tributes at a memorial service in the concert hall of the Haus Des Rundfunks. Luminaries included RRG director Heinrich Glasmeier, who described Raskin as a 'radio man, a human and a National Socialist', while Goebbels provided the emotional high point when he placed a War Merit Cross First Class medal on Raskin's casket. American journalist Harry Flannery was watching the spectacle from the back of the theatre:

The radio symphony orchestra of 150 pieces was on the stage, with evergreens and ferns on both sides and to the rear. Dr Raskin's casket was centred in front of the stage, with banks of flowers, topped with red roses, on each side. Two of Hitler's tall, blond elite troopers stood at attention on each side of the casket, with numerous wreaths from Hitler and other Nazi leaders along the full front of the stage. At the rear of the hall, a robed choir sang special Nazi numbers arranged so that they sounded like Gregorian chants.

For its part, *Volksfunk* mourned Raskin as the 'most significant, versatile and successful expert' in the broadcasting industry.

With Christmas on the way, revellers could have hardly avoided the increasingly depressed mood in Berlin. On 21 December, any festive spirit disappeared when a heavy raid killed 53 people and destroyed the first truly important building in Berlin, the cathedral at the Lustgarten – the setting for the annual May Day parades.

Over at the Haus Des Rundfunks, engineer Dr Ludwig Heck pulled off a master stroke on Christmas Eve with one of the most remarkable accomplishments to emerge from the Reichs-Rundfunk-Gesellschaft. Over a period of 90 minutes, the *Deutsche Weihnacht 1940* treated listeners to an extraordinarily smooth set of 40 'live-links' between the front and home.[8] Opening with Erich Heyn's schmaltzy melody 'Heimat Deine Sterne' with the accompaniment of bells from a garrison church in Postdam, announcer Werner Plucker declared, 'The German Christmas is now on air, beaming from the Arctic Circle to the far South, from the Atlantic to the Eastern territories.' Record-tweaking relays gave wing to voices as soldiers in Narvik and their relatives in Graz opened proceedings, followed by a link to a reconnaissance plane over the North Sea, a navy destroyer in the Atlantic, a volunteer company in Italian East Africa and a military mission in Romania. Ernst Himmler, the youngest brother of Gestapo Chief Heinrich, worked as an engineer on the project, which Goebbels envisioned as a 'common experience', designed to leave an imprint on 90 million people.

Since joining the RRG in 1933, Himmler had worked on the transmission of major events, including the Nuremberg party congress and the Olympic Games. While he was in his element, dealing with like-minded men over details of engineering and communications, it was not until the Western campaigns that RRG had a fair opportunity to judge his ability when he secured the construction of radio connections between Berlin and Wehrmacht troops at the Front. 'Of course I met Ernst Himmler in the Haus Des Rundfunks and as head of the overall broadcasting technology during his work later on,' former announcer Richard Baier recalled. 'I remember he always wore a white coat over his suit to cover the "Golden Party Badge of the NSDAP" attached to his suit lapel. In character, he was the opposite of his brother Heinrich.'[9]

15

FAREWELL AMERICA

Cheery songs on the radio could not alter the growing sense of morbid gloom sweeping across a landscape of taped windows, blackouts and air-raid bunkers. For the grumblers, and there were plenty of them, griping and moaning was conducted in hushed tones.

As the New Year began, Berlin saw no end to a war with multiplying adversaries on a scale undreamed of when Hitler trampled over Poland two years earlier. When Washington promised to ship a reservoir of military and food supplies to Britain and her Allies that winter, the Nazi press responded with fury. In typical style, Joyce smoked out the notion President Roosevelt was spreading the conflict, while Deutschlandsender thundered the action was not dictated by generosity, but purely by American interests. Washington's aid to Britain, known as Lend and Lease, had a profound effect on Americans living and working in Germany. The young CBS journalist Howard K. Smith never forgot sensing the chill as old liberties and 'the futile rose-coloured glasses, disappeared' with the introduction of the Lend and Lease Bill in Congress:

Hotels requested American correspondents to vacate their rooms. All our telephone conversations were obviously tapped, and our houses were watched by not very subtly disguised plainclothes detectives. These little features combined with the growing belligerency of Germans on the streets and in restaurants, made life for us in Berlin more than unpleasant.[1]

On 30 January Hitler, gave a speech before 18,000 people at the Sportpalast declaring any ship carrying aid to Britain within the range of German submarines would be torpedoed. At the same time, he warned the United States if anyone on the American continent tried to interfere in the European conflict, his war aims would rapidly change. According to the Propaganda Ministry, Hitler's speech was broadcast over 667 transmitters in Europe, America and Japan and translated into 26 languages. 'It was,' Deutschlandsender opined, 'a magnificent settling of accounts with England.'

As lines were drawn in the sand, Germany sought to understand the public mood in America, a task which was partly undertaken by the 'Sonderdienst Seehaus', a secret listening post operated under the auspices of the Foreign Office. The facility, Ribbentrop once remarked, 'enriched Germany with information-procurement plucked entirely from the airwaves'. Comparable to the monitoring service of the BBC, Ribbentrop saw the unit as an opportunity to expand his influence on foreign propaganda when it launched in July 1940. To begin with, Seehaus monitored English and French broadcasters, with more 'exotic' programmes from Greece, China, India and the Arab region added later. By 1941, the Foreign Office radio unit had morphed into an entire sub-department, covering all aspects of broadcasting, including the grandly tiled 'Colonial Radio' department tasked with preparing (on paper) the construction of a transmitter network in the African colonies to be acquired by Germany.

Known locally as the 'Schwedische Pavillon', the Seehaus sat on the west shore on Wannsee Lake, close to the villa where the notorious Wannsee conference would be hosted the following year. Hidden behind the walls of this palatial residence – cloaked under the guise of a 'Radio Research Institute' – 500 expert linguists, monitors and transcribers kept the government briefed day and night with what the world was saying – and hearing. The villa's upper floors were crammed with receiving sets, directional gear and equipment for intercepting, identifying and tracing all manner of transmissions. Working on 24-hour shifts, staff monitored and fluently translated news, commercial broadcasts and telegraph services, providing speedy and accurate information from all parts of the globe. Monitors also cooperated with field outposts in Paris, Bucharest, Marseille, Monte Carlo, Shanghai and Rome. Archives show that Seehaus took particular interest in recording the BBC talks of Warren Irvin, an American who spent the early months of the war in Germany:

> Everybody in Germany wonders, how long will these attacks last, how long can it last? Is this just a prelude to the coming invasion, or will England collapse before? I can assure you, this is just Nazi propaganda. I know these German tricks all too well. I do not need to tell you that there is not the slightest sign of a collapse of England.[2]

In true form, Goebbels' territorialism placed Seehaus at the centre of a bitter squabble, leading to his Propaganda Ministry becoming involved.[3] Goebbels was horrified to read Seehaus reports on the 'strikingly unfriendly and positively aggressive' Vatican Radio, which was following the war with painful attention. In an account detailing the 'horror and inexcusable excesses' inflicted on Poles under Nazi rule, a Vatican commentator, newly returned from Poland, spoke about the appalling conditions under German occupation.[4] Another talk, on the measures taken by Nazi authorities in suppressing Catholicism in Alsace-Lorraine and other parts of Occupied France, succeeded in irking the Nazis. Almost daily, Goebbels winced at 'defeatist' bulletins from Seehaus, which filled him with deep suspicion and demolished the credibility of German propaganda. He berated the service as 'nerve-wracking and time-consuming competition [...] with my ministry's existing propaganda machine'.[5]

One department that met with absolute approval in Berlin was the PK propaganda companies, whose embedded reporters continued to churn out action-packed dispatches. From half-a-dozen teams set up before the war, with 150 soldiers per unit, the organisation would grow to 5,000 members in 23 companies spread across the Luftwaffe, Navy and Army.

On 22 January, listeners received an adrenaline rush when Udo Viet, a PK reporter with a reputation for taking extraordinary risks, gave a thrilling commentary from the Mediterranean focusing on Luftwaffe action against the British. Viet threw himself – body and soul – into the broadcast: 'We received reports that enemy naval forces were deployed in the Mediterranean and were pleased that one of them was an aircraft carrier,' he explained, his voice aching with pride. A few minutes later, German fighters swept over Malta:

> The first attack on this war harbour was ordered. The main goal was an aircraft carrier. It was hit so that it will not go into action for a long time. Many strikes were on the arsenal and in the dock area. Probably also a cruiser was hit. The success of these first attacks is a tangible failure for the English.

After describing dive bombers and fighter planes strafing Malta, Viet topped off his report by standing on the airstrip watching 'heroic Luftwaffe pilots' return: 'The whole sky is full of our airplanes. It's a fantastic picture; they merge into a frighteningly dense vision. Our biggest concern now is are they all back?' The following day, Viet was back on air with more exciting reports of Luftwaffe dive-bombing on the British Mediterranean Fleet.

> Our planes were ready on an airstrip when news came in that the enemy warships had been sighted. The Stuka dive-bombers roared off with their protecting fighters. They soon saw an aircraft carrier, two battleships, several cruisers, and destroyers and cargo vessels that were being escorted. The first attack was launched against the aircraft carrier in the face of fierce A.A. fire. The first bombs sent out fountains of water each side of the ship, and then one registered a hit amidships and there was a terrific detonation. A battle ensued between the German and British fighters, while the Stukas went on to engage the warships and cargo vessels. The following day, when they were on their way to attack Malta, the planes passed the enemy warships, which they had attacked

the previous afternoon. A battleship and several cargo ships were missing. The opportunity could not be overlooked, and the German aircraft dived to the attack again before they went on to Malta.

Later, Viet and his colleagues sent equally thrilling dispatches when German troops invaded Greece and Yugoslavia, with both countries falling in late April. In their 1944 book *Goebbels' Experiment: A Study of the Nazi Propaganda Machine*, Derrick Sington and Arthur Weidenfeld perfectly captured how Deutschlandsender established its record for exhilarating, brash announcements:

> On April 5, 1941, the date of the German invasion of Yugoslavia, at 06:00 German Summer Time, Goebbels read the proclamation announcing the invasion, and five minutes later, after a flourish of fanfares, a male-voice choir sang the new 'Balkan Song'. Its first stanza conformed exactly to the propaganda theme of all the news bulletins and talks broadcast later in the day.

Unsurprisingly, prior to the fall of Athens, morale in Greece was sapped further by another Concordia effort. The 'Fatherland' station masqueraded as a free, independent voice for every patriotic Greek purportedly under the auspices of a 'secret political organisation'. Over a scratchy mediumwave signal, it engulfed listeners with calls to loot food warehouses and arrest supporters of the British. There was no restrained behaviour as it accused the British of poisoning water supplies with typhoid bacteria, while Goebbels instructed that the Greek king be verbally attacked on air with the insinuation that he had disposed of the crown jewels abroad, and was planning to hotfoot it to Turkey or Egypt when the Germans arrived.

With the invasion of Greece, British troops beat a hasty retreat from Athens to the island of Crete, which sat 100 miles from Italy's strongholds in the Dodecanese. On 20 May, PK reporter Waldemar Kuckuck was winging his way toward Crete with the Luftwaffe as they prepared to unleash a surprise invasion. Before dawn, the soft stillness of that Tuesday morning was broken when German marines dropped from planes by parachute. Kuckuck described to listeners how 'white silk in these early morning hours glided through the air'⁶ while ammunition boxes attached to parachutes also floated to earth. 'The first chute has landed, the silk rests on the green-brown rock,' he explained. 'German paratroopers are on upper Crete. Here and there is movement down below, the bridge over a river is occupied, a support point is formed.' Several dozen similar reports were broadcast documenting two weeks of vicious fighting, before the battle ended with a German victory, as exhausted Allied soldiers 'with their tails between their legs', evacuated.

Like most PK reporters, Waldemar Kuckuck was probably a grateful recipient of government-supplied stimulants such as Pervitin – a pill sold in small cardboard vials with screw-top lids, as an 'alertness aid' to maintain wakefulness. Over 35 million Pervitin tablets were issued to troops during the French campaign in 1940, and although a prescription drug, due to the danger of addiction, curbing misuse became impossible. In reality, Pervitin was nothing more than neatly packaged, highly addictive crystal meth, known nowadays as 'ice' or 'speed'. After popping a few pills, reporters, soldiers and pilots felt they could defy danger and fight furiously without needing rest or nourishment. Even better, Pervitin activated dopamine, the 'happiness hormone', which made users euphoric and ooze confidence. However, the after-effects of Pervitin could be appalling: sickness, psychotic phases, sweating, dizziness, insomnia, depression, unconstrained fury, hallucinations, and even heart failure. Inevitably, some doctors took a sceptical view of the drug, but it remained in production and use throughout the war.

16

A SINGLE VOICE

At the high point of Hitler's military successes, it was decided to develop a dedicated European radio network to echo a unified voice across the Reich and occupied territories. Using the mediumwave transmitters spread across the Continent, the RRG foreign directorate introduced Die Deutschen Europasender (DES) in April 1941, incorporating mediumwave permanently into international broadcasting plans.[1] At its height, the service operated on 107 long- and mediumwave stations and 23 shortwave transmitters – including Friesland, Calais, Alps, Danube, Vistula, Luxembourg, Vienna and Bremen.

Europasender was divided into six country groups: West, South, North, North-west, South-east and East. Languages included German, English, French, Spanish, Portuguese, Italian, Swedish, Danish, Norwegian, Finnish, Icelandic, Faroese, Flemish, Dutch, Irish, Hungarian, Slovak, Croatian, Romanian, Bulgarian, Serbian, Greek, Russian, Ukrainian, Belarusian, Latvian, Estonian, Lithuanian and Polish. For the most part, Europasender broadcast news and talks in the language of the foreign audience either directly through long- and mediumwave, or by landline from Berlin through a station by the receiving country. DES director Dr Kurt Vaessen described his mission as a fight against foreign propaganda: 'The most important task of the Europasender is to mirror the political, military, cultural and social work of

Germany.'² DES was especially active on the cultural front, arranging special broadcasts marking the 100th anniversary of the Vienna Philharmonic Orchestra with concerts conducted by Clemens Krauss, Wilhelm Furtwangler and Richard Strauss designed to 'brilliantly demonstrate the European reputation of this orchestra'. At the same time, the Danish composer Paul von Klenau performed his three works *Michael Kohlhaas*, *Rembrandt* and *The Queen*, all of which met with audience approval. To improve the audio quality of recordings, RRG taped some shows on to celluloid film, thus eliminating the scratchy sound found on shellac. It was an expensive business, but the audio was so clean even foreign monitors were fooled into thinking some programmes were being broadcast live from Berlin.

The southern Europasender included transmissions geared toward Spaniards, Portuguese and Italians working in Germany. *The Spanish Hour* included lectures, interviews and reports on the life of Spanish workers in the Reich as well as shows for Spanish volunteers on the Eastern Front, who sent greetings and messages back home. An average of 800 letters and telegrams from Spain per week arrived at the RRG, which, the station insisted, provided 'proof of how well the broadcasts were received'. The northern service was limited to a daily news service in all Nordic/Scandinavian languages, which remarkably, included a weekly broadcast for listeners on the Faroe Islands alongside bulletins for Norwegian seafarers.

On top of that, Finnish programmes developed an important link between Finland and her volunteers fighting on the south-eastern front. 'Soldiers convey the greetings of their homeland to these volunteers there and describe their front-line experiences to their relatives.' Programmes for France, Ireland and Holland fell under the Western service, which sent greetings from Dutch and Flemish workers via the Friesland–Calais transmitters. 'The men give their names, their hometowns and shout greetings into the microphone,' the *Rundfunk Archive* journal noted:

Many workers announce their vacation, which they want to spend at home with their relatives; a man is looking forward to his wife coming to Hamburg. So the wishes and interests are different; but the words that go to Amsterdam, Groningen, Rotterdam, to the small towns in Brabant, Friesland and Limburg announce the contentment and wellbeing of the workers. Again and again, those sending requests say 'How wonderful that I can speak to you from Germany!' And there is a little wonder in their voices.[3]

On top of the Europasender contributions, local programming remained robust in Holland, where during his first year as an official mouthpiece, Max Blokzijl – or Moaning Max – was clumsily providing the Allies with a priceless insight into local morale. Blokzijl had become every Dutchman's favourite inadvertent comedian, given his bombastic lexicon and obvious frustration:

> According to general belief you are only a good Netherlander if you wear a button off a soldier's dress in your buttonhole, or a red white, and blue badge; write threatening messages on the doors of political opponents; write anonymous letters to Dutch Nazis; do not speak to anybody who sympathises with the Nazis; believe everything the British and Americans tell you; give a guilder to a street musician to play the same tune for an hour in front of the door of a Nazi just to irritate him; tell everybody 'England always wins the last battle,' say frequently OZO (Oranaje zal overwinner/ Under the House of Orange we will be victorious); scrutinise the Army communiqués from day to day and tell everybody anything there is in them which favour the British.[4]

Besides adding levity to airwaves, Blokzijl unwittingly represented everything that made Germany's invasion seem awkward. That was until the arrival of the Concordia station De Notenkraker. It was designed to discredit all underground pirate radio activities in the Netherlands along with the British-funded Radio Orange, a Dutch programme broadcast daily by the BBC, that had been opened by the exiled Queen Wilhelmina in 1940 to forge 'unshakeable unity'. De Notenkraker interlarded mild criticisms of the Nazis with attacks on the Allies. In an opening statement, the station declared,

> This is the secret Dutch freedom sender De Notenkraker (The Nutcracker). We draw your attention to our daily transmissions on the ultra shortwave ... We do not like Goebbels – that is why we play this dangerous game with a secret sender. We do not like the Dutch Nazis. We like the programmes of 'Radio Orange' in London but we have information they do not possess. This war will probably end in a stalemate, and Holland will have to know where it stands. To make this clear is the purpose of our underground broadcasting station.[5]

The *Netherlands News Digest*, published by the government in exile, noted De Notenkraker, was clearly heard in England, 'but not for one moment were Dutch listeners deceived by it. Not only did the tone of the broadcast stir their suspicions, but when it appeared again and again on succeeding nights at exactly the same time and frequency for a full 20-minute programme, it became certain that the station was a German one.'[6] Almost immediately, the BBC's Radio Orange beamed a message to listeners in Holland warning them against the phony outfit. Unabashed, the station continued to release its nightly stream of distorted arguments against or in favour of Nazi measures, 'always returning to the final conclusion that although it was anti-German it was against the English'. The end came just after four months, when the Germans 'changed' frequency putting it on the same wavelength used by the official Hilversum station. 'That was the last blunder De Notenkraker ever made. It disappeared from the air as unceremoniously as it had sprung into existence,' the *Netherlands News Digest* reported.

Over the border, Deutschlandsender was busy waxing lyrical about the 'bond of friendship' between Moscow and Berlin. Robert Ley, an often-quoted 'authority' on Soviet issues, insisted ties were so warm that his Strength through Joy organisation was launching Russian language lessons for German workers to provide students a 'sufficient understanding' of the language of their ally. Around the same time, Hadamovsky was flooded with complaints flying around about a new Deutschlandsender announcer, who, much to the disgust of many listeners, delivered the news with a 'very irritating' Austrian accent. As a heated debate ensued, the issue was brought before Goebbels, who deemed the radio must speak 'the purest, clearest and most dialect-free German because it speaks to the whole nation'. Furthermore, he told colleagues that 'what Luther's translation of the Bible has done for written German, we on the radio must do for German speech'.

As summer approached, more 'light music' filled the airwaves, provided in the most part by the finely crafted Willi Stech Orchestra, which had been installed as the 'resident radio band' – a position they would hold for the next three years. Although popular, they were banned from using 'muted' horns, and told to avoid numbers with 'distorted rhythms' and 'atonal melodic lines'.

Meanwhile, Anton 'Toni' Winkelnkemper, a former propaganda chief for the Köln district and one of Goebbels' oldest and most faithful disciples, was appointed acting director of the shortwave radio services, thus becoming responsible for foreign broadcasts. Tall, round-jawed and graced with a wicked sense of humour, colleagues remembered Winkelnkemper as an amiable chatterbox but doggedly loyal to his masters and very keen on William Joyce, who, by this point, had plucked up the courage to reveal his identity, proudly informing his audience he had been jailed in England for his political opinions and fled London – because he was 'convinced of German victory'. The disclosure, it seems, was his special 'thank you' to Hitler for letting him help lay the foundations of a thousand-year Reich. Either way, the revelation only confirmed to British listeners his 'fascist thug' pedigree.[7]

That autumn, the shortwave services were producing 154 hours of unique programming daily. 'Technology makes it possible to send shows simultaneously, like an evening programme to Asia, a lunch programme to Africa, a morning programme to South America and a morning programme to North America. More transmitters and directional antennas are used for this,' Horst Clienow, deputy director of the shortwave station, explained.[8]

Following an exotic introductory number, the Brazilian service churned out five hours of Portuguese every day, made up of 43.5 per cent political features and talks. The talk show *Salada mixta*, which peppered politics with Brazilian compositions performed by German artists, became their star attraction. Other South Americans received shows in Spanish, including German language lessons, while North Americans were treated to exclusively English offerings. Broadcasts in English, Dutch and Hindustani were almost exclusively political, while youth programmes and drama, as well as scientific and medical lectures, featured on other services. According to RRG files, during the first year of the war, 200,000 letters arrived from listeners outside Europe – four times the number of letters received in 1937–38.

Around this time, Goebbels was busily devising strategies on beefing up the American shortwave service. 'We must grab America by the horns now. There is no point in treading gently,' he observed, as he drew up plans for a much larger flow of programmes pitched to the average American. His goal, given most Americans supported the Allies, was to push the isolationist agenda. 'Perhaps we shall achieve something with it,' he noted in his diary. He chewed over ideas with Jane Anderson, a 48-year-old journalist described by detractors as his 'female Haw-Haw' who signed on air with the moniker 'Georgia Peach', using the slogan 'Always remember progressive Americans eat Kellogg's Corn Flakes and listen to both sides of the story.' Her trademark diatribes opened with the line, 'Berlin calling the American mothers, wives and sweethearts...'

... And when Berlin calls, it pays to listen in, because there is an American girl sitting at the microphone every Tuesday evening at the same time for a few words of truth to her countrywomen back home.

Anderson had worked as a reporter for the *Daily Mail* in 1915 before travelling the Continent in 1918, ending up in Berlin. British media at the time claimed she had been 'saved from death, after being arrested as a spy by Spanish loyalists' through the intercession of the American State Department.

Before broadcasting, Anderson would light up a cigarette and pace the corridors of Deutschlandhaus, endlessly repeating lines from her script. An FBI monitor tasked with transcribing her efforts noted when Anderson reached the climax of her presentations that 'she gradually works herself into a white heat, her words now tumbling over one another like logs shooting over a waterfall'. She was acquainted with William Joyce socially and he occasionally spoke on her programme, where he was greeted with the familiarity of an old friend. She often quoted the mutterings of Charles Lindbergh, the epoch-making pilot and pro-German isolationist, who prior to the war had been lavishly courted by the Nazis.

After war broke out, the American service of the RRG dropped its classical concerts, 'gentlemanly voices' and polite presentation. Training for work on this revamped service, it seems, was more by threat or bribes than anything else. Output ran along a very basic, very restricted range – mostly monologues, talks, newscasts, record programmes and interviews. Almost 52 per cent of output on the North American shortwave service was of a political nature, with a satirical cabaret show called *Club of Notions* being well received, as was the half-hour show *America asks – Germany answers,* which opened with the catchy melody 'The cables are coming, ooh!'

Similar success was achieved by the *College Hour* presented by Prof. Max Otto Koischwitz, who, before the war, had taught German literature at Hunter College in New York. His topics included 'Good and Evil', 'Surrealism', 'The Problem of Freedom' and 'Morality and Legality'. According to a Propaganda Ministry directive, the following five points had to be subtly weaved into broadcasts aimed at the USA:

1. Bolshevism was the enemy of the entire world,
2. The Jews throughout the world supported Bolshevism,
3. The Germans are the happiest and best-governed people in the world,
4. Germany is invincible,
5. England is economically and politically decadent.

As the biggest bigot on the US Zone, Koischwitz didn't understand subtly, duly earning his stripes spewing outrageous anti-Semitism under the guise of 'Mr OK'. That summer, he tackled the 'Jewish problem' in a lengthy broadcast. 'Confidentially, I want to talk about the Jews,' he told his listeners in a well-meaning tone. 'This is always an awkward subject, especially in America,' he noted. He asserted the average American did not like Jews:

> Political observers who are now wondering at the Soviet–Washington alliance should study the Jewish nation. In Soviet Russia the overwhelming majority of the government officials are Jews, and that Roosevelt is surrounded by Jews at the White House is well known. The preponderance of this Jewish element is the only explanation for the Soviet alliance. The President does not talk about the aid he is giving to the Bolsheviks; he calls it aid to Britain, but Britain is only a stooge.[9]

As with his fellow broadcasters, 'Mr OK' gave all sorts of explanations and excuses for why listeners should be weary of Jewry. While much of this propaganda was unlikely to sway the average American's mind, Kurt G. Sell, the long-time representative of the RRG in New York, estimated in the first months after war broke out, about 500,000 Americans tuned into Berlin daily. That figure then steadily declined, as more listeners felt disgusted by the virulent anti-Semitic, anti-British and anti-Roosevelt abuse.

In an effort to gauge audience figures, listeners in America were offered the one-off opportunity to send free telegraph messages to the RRG, which would be paid for by Ribbentrop's Foreign Office during February 1941. Unsurprisingly, the gimmick was picked up by the entire American press, with some articles giving witty or ironic slant and others just blunt acknowledgement of the idea.

There were also attempts by anti-Nazi organisations to trigger a 'telegram flood' at the expense of the Germans, with some pointing out if they could rack up U$200,000 of telegraph traffic, it would equal the destruction of five Messerschmitt fighter planes. Others expressed concern the telegram offer had been triggered by a German desire to discreetly send and receive espionage reports. The campaign, according to a Foreign Office report, resulted in 10,241 cables consisting of requests, suggestions and 'constructive criticism', with opinions on the war as well as a hefty batch of mockery and insults. The cost of the exercise amounted to little more than 50,000 Reichsmarks, which the RRG considered a bargain.

That year, the US zone expanded their cadre of journalists in Berlin. Altogether, eight Americans, including two women, launched a radio blitzkrieg at the US from Berlin on behalf of the Hitler. Koischwitz, or 'OK', the professor mentioned earlier, served as the programme director. In turn, he hired his lover Mildred Gillars, who became known to her listeners as 'Axis Sally'.

Other US renegades included Frederick Kaltenbach – mentioned earlier broadcasting from Paris – dubbed America's counterpart of Haw-Haw; Robert H. Best, a former Army officer; Edward Leo Delaney, known on radio as 'Ed Ward'; Constance Drexel, a native of Darmstadt; and Douglas Chandler, who broadcast as 'Paul Revere'. Between them, they tried to offset the influence of correspondents like Edward R. Murrow, who was busily churning out pro-British opinions from the heart of London. The previous year, the BBC had also launched *Britain Speaks*, a programme beaming the UK point of view to the States, read by announcers with American accents, who in fact, were mostly Canadians. While CBS's Shirer reckoned Kaltenbach 'would die for Nazism', and Delaney was a 'disappointed actor', Joseph C. Harsch, a staff writer for the *Christian Science Monitor*, opined Kaltenbach was the most formidable weapon in the US department:

> ... he, like Joyce (Haw-Haw), is also sincere in his Nazism. I know because he preached it to me and argued it with me most of the way from Berlin to Paris on a three-day bus trip. He never made any attempt to conceal his position or his relationship with the Germans. He is engaging in personality and has courage even when it comes to differences of opinion with his employers, who show far less cordiality toward those openly on their payroll than toward the independents. Such people have burned their bridges behind them and are at the mercy of German whim.[10]

The following summer, James L. Fly, the chairman of the US Federal Communications Commission, illustrated how Nazi radio efforts aimed at Americans were failing. 'A few weeks ago a German propaganda speaker urged American listeners to go to public libraries to read certain volumes known to contain anti-British material,' he said. To learn how much stock American listeners placed in the propaganda, the FCC asked the American Library Association to check on public requests for these volumes. 'The complete report from the association shows but a solitary request, which occurred at the San Francisco library and that was from a person having an un-related purpose in mind.' By this point, many Americans had already abandoned listening to the US Zone of the RRG, finding it toxic and mentally taxing.

As German advances roared ahead, good times on the home front had started to run their course as shortages inspired little confidence in an increasingly grumpy population. The loudest groans came from the band of radio renegades sulking as the availability of everyday items such as soap and liquor worsened. Smokers noticed well-known brands including Lord Chesterfield and Juno vanished from the Haus Des Rundfunks kiosk, while the cigarettes that were available actually shrank, losing a quarter of their length. Even more perplexing were reports on Radio Paris claiming Marseilles was choked with imports bound for Germany, in spite of the ongoing British blockade. There were other niggles too. The issue of footwear had become a real headache, and accordingly, radio promoted a new office for the exchanging of children's shoes where mothers of children whose shoes were too small, could donate the discarded footwear for other families. For adults, new 'fashionable straw shoes' were promoted heavily on daytime radio. Listeners were advised that straw could be used as a substitute for leather, and could be purchased without coupons.

In May 1941, Rudolf Hess, Hitler's deputy, provided the world with a first-class sensation when he made a dramatic flight in a Messerschmitt-110 and descended in Scotland at the end of a parachute on a self-appointed peace mission. In true form, Goebbels tried to put the best face on the calamity. While mitigating the fallout, he approved an awkward announcement on Deutschlandsender, which floated the false claim Hess had been suffering from a 'mental disorder':

> Party Comrade Rudolf Hess, who had been forbidden by the Führer to undertake active flying because of his illness, which has been getting worse for many years, succeeded in defiance of this ban in taking possession of an aeroplane. Last Saturday at 6pm, Rudolf Hess took off at Augsburg on a flight from which he has so far failed to return. The letter which he left was so confused that shows signs of mental disturbance. This letter leads to the assumption that Hess has fallen victim of madness.

Although rumours abounded that Hess suffered 'various maladies', official acknowledgement that he was in fact mad, unsurprisingly, was met with incredulity and countless cynical jokes:

> In summer 1941, two former friends met in a Berlin prison.
> 'Hello Bert... What are you doing here?'
> 'Well Victor, in 1939, I said: "Rudolf Hess was crazy." And you?'
> 'Well, yesterday I said "Rudolf Hess was not crazy!"'

> Rudolf Hess is introduced to Winston Churchill, who remarks: 'So you are the crazy one?'
> 'No,' replied Hess, 'I am only his deputy!'

To counteract the tremendous effect of the debacle, later variations of the official first 'mad' statement suggested that Hess was, in fact, an idealist and had been snared into an English trap. 'Goebbels and his propaganda department are whirling, themselves into dizziness with their quick reversals in explaining the desertion of Nazi Number 3,' a British commentary gleefully observed. The *Portsmouth Evening News* surmised:

> The fact is that the Goebbels gang have contradicted themselves into a hopeless tangle in a vain endeavour to counteract the tremendous effect of the Hess incident, both in Germany and abroad.

As expected, Joyce, chipped into the Hess dilemma by composing a script for Concordia's New British Broadcasting Station: 'We have no intention of entering into any discussion upon the arrival in peculiar circumstances of Rudolf Hess in Scotland, but since it he has created far more interest than the "Loch Ness Monster" and since we believe this interest to be disproportionate to the event we feel constrained to make some comment on what has become a matter of public opinion.' Furthermore, the commentary continued,

> Hess should be offered a seat in the House of Commons as Independent Conservative Invasion Member. Whether he is sane or insane is of no importance in this connection, for he would be working with the likes of Winston Churchill whose mental condition has long been open to doubt...

While the official line maintained in Berlin was that a one-man defection did not make a crisis, Hess was being fastidiously expunged from history. Mention of him was forbidden on air, in print, and widely circulated souvenir postcards were immediately plucked from kiosk stands. In Dresden, the 'Rudolf Hess Hospital' was quietly renamed for Doctor Gerhard Warner, a well-known surgeon.

***

The 'unbreakable ties' of friendship, with Moscow which had been lauded ad nauseam in the German press since the signing of the Molotov–Ribbentrop Pact, came 'like a bolt out of a clear sky' when Germany invaded Russia on 22 June. Before dawn, Hitler launched Operation Barbarossa aided by Finland, Romania, and Italy. 'Outside the Wilhelmplatz it is quiet and deserted,' Goebbels scrawled in his diary. 'Berlin and the entire Reich are asleep.' The calm was broken just before 05.30 when word arrived at the Propaganda Ministry that the invaders had kicked-off hostilities from northern Finland to the Black Sea.

Script in hand, the minister stubbed out a cigarette, moistened his lips, and took a deep breath. Wochenshau newsreel cameras captured the drama unfolding with a shot of the Chancellery, then the transmitting tower opposite the Haus Des Rundfunks. Narrator Harry Geise marched cinemagoers – shot-by-shot – through those momentous hours:

At the radio station, the broadcasting of the proclamation over all German radio stations is prepared. At the Reich's Ministry for Peoples Enlightenment and Propaganda, Minister Dr Goebbels reads aloud the Führer's proclamation, which exposes for the first time before the whole world, the conspiracy between London and Moscow against Germany. After a month's silence, the Führer expresses at the 11th hour, the only possible consequence with the words: 'I have decided to lay the fate and future of the German Reich again in the hands of our soldiers.'

For the sleepy-eyed public, by this point often dumbfounded by events, the consequences of war with Russia were only too apparent.[11] It wasn't just the contradiction of Nazi policy that was shocking; a two-front conflict represented a nightmare scenario. Like everybody else, the Berlin correspondent of the *Svenska Dagbladet* was left stunned: 'The general public in Germany had been particularly surprised by the announcement of this war with Russia. The durability of the friendship with Bolshevism has never been a good idea.' Indeed, the offensive provided the Nazis with the ideological cohesion which had been absent in propaganda since the signing of the Ribbentrop–Molotov pact. In the first hours of Operation Barbarossa, listeners to Deutschlandsender must have winced at an old-time Nazi sing-song performed by decrepit National Socialist campaigners, from whom no one had heard since 1939. The first bulletin on KWS shortwave service was brief:

On 22 June, special action was begun. The German Army, in collaboration with allied forces, crossed the Soviet border in attack. This battle in the East is the battle of Europe against Bolshevism. The Soviet Russian population has again been placed under terror and horror by the Moscow Government. From reports coming from Radio Moscow, it can be seen that even the least important incident will lead to the death penalty. The population in the Ukraine, in general, has refused to take up arms and support the Soviet system and attempts have been made in this region to liberate the political prisoners.[12]

Over in Russia, vast armoured spearheads, protected by Stuka dive-bombers, blasted gaps in the Red forces as the Luftwaffe destroyed hundreds of Soviet planes on their airfields. PK reporter Karl Holtzhamer took to the skies with the first wave of Luftwaffe pilots. During his broadcast (transmitted the following day), he conceded that having had 'one hour of sleep in two days was of little importance', given the tension and historic significance of the moment. Holtzhamer spoke of being deafened by the 'eternal drone' of aircraft and the 'foreboding clouds of dust all over the east'. Down below, he saw 'smoke roar like a boiler' where Stukas had attacked Russian tanks.[13] Mechanised and marching infantry divisions swept forward, with tank commanders reporting gains of 45 kilometres on that first day.

Foreign Minister Vyacheslav Mikhailovich Molotov took to the airwaves on Radio Moscow to announce, 'This unspeakable attack on our country is a treachery unprecedented in the history of civilized peoples.' He revealed the Luftwaffe had raided Kiev in the Ukraine, the Black Sea port of Sevastopol and Kaunas, the capital of Estonia.

Unable to focus on anything else, Germans hungered for news from the front. Even the endless PK reports and special bulletins could never keep up with the speed of events on the ground. In one day alone, the RRG sent out 14 bulletins from different parts of the Eastern Front to an audience impatient for updates. 'Listeners embraced everything from the Russian front, mainly because so many families had loved ones involved in the campaigns,' says Wolfgang Bauernfeind. 'Every piece of information, however small, was important.' In the newsroom at the Haus Des Rundfunks, an editor had pinned a large map of the Soviet Union to the noticeboard, ready to mark with pins the advance of the Wehrmacht into the USSR. In order to facilitate the undisturbed listening to Wehrmacht reports in restaurants and cafés, waiters were given the right not to serve customers during important Barbarossa transmissions. Franz Liszt's *Les Préludes – Symphonische Dichtung Nr.3* became the standard fanfare used to introduce important radio bulletins. 'When the trumpet announcement sounds three times in the loudspeakers, then during this time in the entire Reich, the radios remain on and everyone runs to the radio receivers,' a mood report noted.

As might be expected, German radio followed a predictable pattern as the USSR came under immediate verbal attack with derogatory language portraying the Russians as uncivilized, primitive barbarians. Another objective was to harden the Wehrmacht, for whom it would be psychologically easier to fight a 'Bolshevik Soviet animal' than a fellow human being. When observing Soviet Prisoners of War, PK reporter Benno Wundshammer noted:

> Anyone who looks into these stubborn crowds as they march past looks in vain for a personality. They are not people, they are goods. Material from the human arsenal of Bolshevism.

Such a description would have warmed the heart of William Joyce, who returned to the airwaves a day after the invasion of Russia. That night, he gave a characteristically bilious, ill-tempered performance, claiming, 'Even in Britain, many people are praying that the Bolsheviks will be beaten, for they realize that a Red victory would mean a communist dictatorship in the British Isles.' From the studio next door, Jane Anderson, speaking to America, compared the action in Russia to a religious crusade backed by 50 million members of the Catholic Church of Germany (which had been persecuted by Hitler since 1933) that she said stood united against Russia. 'The Catholic Church in Germany will support the Führer by word and deed in the crusade against the Communist enemies of the Christian world,' she gushed.[14]

In response to the radio onslaught, the Soviets started jamming German radio, with the thrum and buzz making it completely incomprehensible in Turkey, Greece and the Mediterranean. The Russians, it transpired, had been prepared for a battle of the airwaves and kept 150 jamming stations under wraps specifically for the purpose.

It didn't take long for boasts predicting the German Army would march into Moscow within three weeks to fill the pages of the domestic press. 'We have only to kick in the door and the whole rotten structure will come crashing down,' Hitler once told his military top brass. In fact, records from Goebbels' 'secret conferences' reveal Hitler believed the campaign would take four months, but Goebbels reckoned it would take eight weeks: 'Just as the essence of National Socialism towers head and shoulders above that of communism, so its enormous superiority is bound to prove itself on the battlefield in an exceedingly short period of time.'

In regions occupied by the advancing German Army, initial jubilation at being freed from Communist rule, especially among the populations of the Baltic and Ukraine, quickly soured in the face of the brutal occupational policies. At the same time, the Soviet Army suffered massive losses of men and material in the first months of the war, with about 3.6 million Red Army soldiers ending up in German POW camps, where more than half of them died of hunger, cold or disease.

As mechanised forces continued to thrust east, the German-controlled radio station in Belgrade – known as Soldatensender or the 'Armed Forces Network' – used its mediumwave transmitter to ram home a simple message to workers in the Ukraine by urging them to oppose the destruction of factories by retreating Red Army troops: 'Just think what you and yours will eat if your factories would have been destroyed. The German Army is not fighting you but the Stalin regime.' A separate insurrectionary appeal – transmitted in Ukrainian and Russian – sought to coax Soviet troops to 'turn against' their superiors. Financed by both the Army and Foreign Office, Belgrade was operated by the Propagandaabteilung Südost – alongside stations in Athens and Saloniki. Under the command of Lieutenant Karl-Hein Reintgen, a former producer at Deutschlandsender, the station was entirely staffed by fresh-faced recruits along with combat-experienced officers, with no connection whatsoever with the Ministry of Propaganda. With studios at the former Ministry of Agriculture, it offered music for every conceivable taste, delivered late-night news to homesick soldiers and chronicled every twist and turn in the ongoing conflict. Among the phonograph music programmes, foreign monitors occasionally recorded the odd burst of clumsy propaganda, such as when an announcer declared, 'A German cannot be expected to have the same God as a Negro or a Jew.'[15]

Building the station after the occupation in 1941 had been a challenge given the near-derelict state of the complex. 'Everything was damaged from our Stuka bombs. We had to use umbrellas to protect the microphone and equipment,' a staff member told *Rundfunkarchiv*. 'Right from the start, we tried to fill an entire broadcast day. Today, along with the lieutenant, there are 21 workers at the Belgrade transmitter, including around 300 civilian employees and 150 in the orchestras alone,' which included a Symphony Orchestra, dance and wind musicians, a Serbian folk group and a tambourizza ensemble.

Once the sun set over Europe, increasing the transmission range, the signal stretched from Narvik in Norway down to North Africa covering an audience of 6 million soldiers. The station gained fame as being responsible for the viral spread of Lale Andersen's song 'Lili Marlene', a melancholy tune composed by Norbert Schultze, the man responsible for 'Bombs over England', the unofficial Luftwaffe anthem mentioned earlier. In the late thirties, Schultze had persuaded Anderson, then a little-known entertainer, to perform the song at Berlin's Kabarett der Komiker nightclub where many popular hits had been launched. But even Anderson, armed with seductively husky tones, received no more than polite applause and thus ditched it from her repertoire, but not before cutting a recording of the number for Elecktrola, which remained obscure.

It was not until Corporal Kistenmacher, a 23-year-old army announcer on Belgrade, found a copy in a crate of records and placed it on the turntable that things began to happen. As the sultry tune wafted over Europe, soldiers everywhere began singing:

Underneath the lantern
By the barrack gate
Darling I remember the way you used to wait
Twas there that you whispered tenderly
That you loved me
You'd always be
My Lili of the Lamplight
My own Lili Marlene

Within a week of the first broadcast in August 1941, the song swept on a wave of popularity through the Wehrmacht and the Afrika Korps, leading to over a thousand requests flooding in, as *Rundfunkarchiv* noted:

> The Belgrade broadcaster, which has become very popular due to its daily broadcasts of 'Lili Marlene', was able to donate half a million marks as a gift after accepting donations for requests. The funds will be used at their own discretion for the soldiers on the front and their families.[16]

By the end of 1941, an average of 3,350 letters arrived every day at the Soldatensender Belgrade, most of which were incorporated into request programmes:

> Around 35 letters are used for our 21:45 – 22:00 broadcast in which 40 dedications are sent. Later in the evening from 00:00 to 01:00, 125 letters are dealt with and 200 requests announced. In addition to the news service, all other radio broadcasts are also very popular, especially the light and lively music.[17]

Through Belgrade, 'Lili Marlene' became unique among war songs in that it was a favourite among combatants on both sides. It didn't take long for British troops on the other side of the line to begin humming the tune. Soon after, the American forces joined in; as did comedian Tommy Trinder who first heard it during an ENSA tour in the Western Desert: 'When I got back, I sang it on a talk I gave on the BBC,' he remembered, thus making 'Lili Marlene' a hit on Allied radio.

Daily Herald war correspondent F. G. H. Salusbury, posted with the British High Command in the Middle East, jokingly complained 'something must be done about "Lili Marlene"', which he said lulled the Afrika Korps to sleep and 'nightly tickles the sentimental ears of our own Eighth Army'. Andersen, he wrote, was becoming the 'dope of the British in the Middle East' with her a husky, come-and-kiss-me voice:

She has achieved such reputation that the Prime Minister's last speech was listened to by some British desert audiences with considerable anxiety – lest they should miss their nightly dose of delight. She (Anderson) puts over a song which goes right to the heart of masculine home-sickness and almost produces tears.[18]

The song spread everywhere, even as far away as Ireland where the *Belfast News-Letter* noted the melody 'seems destined to be the "Tipperary" of this war had firmly established itself in Belfast, where it is sung in the streets at night and whistled in the tramcars in the day time'.[19] In later life, Lale Andersen was asked if she could explain the popularity of 'Lili Marlene', replying, 'Can the wind explain why it became a storm?'

17

CALLING AFRICA AND
THE MIDDLE EAST

As 3 million soldiers continued to advance into the wilderness of Soviet Russia, Goebbels kept the home front amused. At the Olympic Stadium the firing gun opened the second German war athletics championships, attracting more than 60,000 spectators. Escapist drama and comedies filled cinemas, with the romantic comedy *Drei Zeiten Hochzeit* becoming the summer hit. Gustaf Gründgens played the title role in *Friedemann Bach*, an exciting tale about the son of Johann Sebastian Bach, which premiered in Dresden. The war flick *Stukas* – showing the daring exploits of the Luftwaffe – captivated audiences across the Reich.

Not long after the start of the Russian campaign, as harder battles were fought, life in Germany was increasingly showing signs of strain as the RAF unloaded bombs on Hamburg, Kiel, Bremen, Köln, Hanover and Mannheim. To make matters worse, confidence among tradesmen, farmers and factory bosses ebbed as more men were called up, prompting another soft push to recruit women into the labour market for work of 'supreme national importance'.

In a country warped by war and lulled by lies, the public grew tired at the slow progress in Russia. Several Deutschlandsender commentaries urged listeners to 'neither be surprised, nor puzzled if the promised sensational announcement on the Russian front is not made for some time'.

But it wasn't all doom and gloom, as good news dripped in from North Africa where Hitler had dispatched his newly formed Afrika Korps under the command of Erwin Rommel to chase the Allies. The initial onslaught stunned the British, forcing them back toward Egypt. Soon after, Rommel cut the British off in the coastal city of Tobruk, sending German propaganda into overdrive. On one occasion, a Luftwaffe pilot gave a thrilling performance describing an attack on Tobruk when the sky was full of British fighters, which he escaped by taking cover in the clouds. 'During the flight,' he explained to Deutschlandsender listeners, 'we passed, among others, a formation of 20 Blenheim bombers, protected by 30 Curtis fighters, and here again we were lucky enough to find some clouds!' Then there was the battlefield trauma of a German soldier praying for salvation. The recording was allegedly made while a German unit was being strafed by the RAF in the Western Desert:

> Time has come to a standstill. Seconds are eternity. A mouse can scuttle into a hole. If I could only shrink! Mother Earth, do not forsake me; swallow me up.

The RRG's English shortwave service penetrated well into the Middle East, especially in comparison to the BBC. With war's outbreak up-to-date newspapers and reliable information became scarce for the huge British colony in Egypt, making Cairo a breeding ground for gossip. 'There was a rumour last week that London had been bombed,' a NAAFI (Navy, Army and Air Force Institutes) canteen worker noted in her diary at the start of the war. She talked of being lent a radio, which, despite her best efforts, could only receive 'German propaganda' while reception of the BBC was near-impossible to decipher among the crackles and hisses.

The Middle East presented a golden opportunity to bombard the air with Nazi slogans and incite sympathetic Arabs to cause disturbances with talks of British arrogance, hypocrisy and oppression – and, most importantly, the assurance of independence. The beauty of such propaganda, Goebbels mulled, was the ease of making promises which may or may not be fulfilled.

The Arabic radio service aimed at Arabs, Turks and Persians fell largely under Ribbentrop's control. That year it was busy spreading anti-Semitic diatribes and calls for resistance to the British, with the aim of 'galvanising cowed Arabs' and elevating the aims of Germany. To achieve its goals, The Voice of the Free Arabs targeted sparsely settled populations across North Africa and western Asia stretching from Casablanca to Baghdad, by offering a dazzling variety of transmissions aimed at bringing Arab countries and their Diaspora together. The section aimed at the Arab world was titled the 'Near Eastern Department', which debuted in April 1939, with shows produced by Arabs from Palestine, Syria, Jordan, Morocco, Algeria, Iraq, and Tunisia.

Iraqi journalist Younis Bahri, with Muhammad Taqi-al-Din al-Hilali, an academic best known for translating Sahih al-Bukhari into English, oversaw the day-to-day operations. Bahri trained 'an elite group of announcers' and Islamist commentators and, in his own words, the service became a miniature Arab League, with a 'tumultuous army of editors, writers, interpreters, and male and female typists'. His staff also translated secret daily reports – 'for our personal information', which arrived from various armed forces commands and ministries.

Articulate and assertive, Bahri at just 30 years old, thrived within his role and pioneered new ideas including broadcasting verses from the Koran at the opening of each transmission, a technique given special permission by Hitler himself. 'He is today the principle and most important Arab Quisling in German hands,' a British intelligence report asserted.[1]

According to his autobiography *This is Berlin! Long Live the Arabs*, Bahri first encountered Goebbels in 1931 when seeking support for his anti-British newspaper *al-'Uqâb*. But now, as a fully subsidised Nazi propagandist, he was enrolled into the SS and charged with recruiting like-minded collaborators. Bahri's fame even spread to the pages of British newspapers, including *The Scotsman*, which observed in March 1941,

Everywhere in the Near East, Arabs tune in their sets to listen to Younis Bahri broadcasting from Berlin. This is not because they sympathise with Hitler, but because Bahri is bawdy, funny and exciting, while the London broadcasts, Arabs say, are refined, sensible and dull.

Other notables working at the Near Eastern Department included Rashid Ali el Gailani, the Iraqi rebel leader who had been behind anti-British riots in Mosul. He became an honorary 'Chief of Staff', but was most often to be found sipping gritty coffee in the Kürfurstendamm, hidden behind the pages of Arabic newspapers. Haj Amin Effendi el-Husseini, the former Grand Mufti of Jerusalem, was another 'employee' enjoying comfortable refuge and a huge salary, thanks to his tireless instigation of just about every anti-British movement in the Middle East. In return for their services, the Nazis promised Rashid Ali would triumphantly lead Iraq to victory, as the ex-Grand Mufti unified the Arab world.

From the very start, like the broadcasts to South Africa in 1939, the Arabic programmes left the British dumbfounded as they indulged in outrageous fantasies, which would have even made William Joyce blush. For example, in one 'news bulletin' it was stated a poor, destitute Egyptian woman was begging in Cairo for a piece of bread and was immediately shot by a British sentry. Wholesale atrocities were invented, with no basis in fact, while Nazi military successes were exaggerated even more than they were for other audiences.

Just how effective this infiltration was became clear when the Iraqi government condemned Rashid Ali to death as a traitor. In response, Berlin Radio screamed, 'The judgment was delivered while the leader was far away in the capital of a friendly country,' where, it said, he was respected and esteemed:

The Arab world knows that the British dare not judge Rashid Ali, so they found a dirty gang of slaves who were willing to do their filthy work. These are the real traitors who will one day be judged in their turn. They have sold their consciences in the Jewish fashion; they are cursed by God, now and forever. Arabs, listen carefully; the British are always talking of justice and liberty, but when they speak these words they have no intention of fulfilling them. This British judgment, against the leader and his collaborators is another dark spot in the annals of British crimes and atrocities.

Meanwhile, back on the boiling sands, a seesaw tussle between Rommel's Afrika Korps and the British was fought out in the flat wilderness of the Western Desert. Through constantly changing offensives, the campaign developed into a mobile war stretched out over hundreds of miles, draining the strength of the Wehrmacht, who were inexperienced in desert warfare. The scorching daytime heat and bitter temperatures at night left many troops in ill health. By the time the Germans retreated a few years later, enthusiasm for a free Arab world at 'Near Eastern Department' had long vanished.

By late summer, the German advance into Russia was becoming bogged down as the mighty Wehrmacht battled with terrain, supply backlogs and resistance from the Red Army, which had recovered from the shock of the lightening invasion. Despite the changing situation, Deutschlandsender insisted 'the Bolshevik Air Force had been annihilated', and claimed the 'beginning of the end has come. Russia, and with her the entire British Empire, is on the eve of disaster'. Even Hitler predicted, 'This enemy (the Russians) is beaten and will never rise again,' a statement, repeated by Reich Press Chief Dietrich and endlessly re-echoed by all home and overseas radio services. A perfect example of this hubris was beamed to the USA in German during October:

> The Soviet Union is finished militarily. In spite of every exertion they will never succeed again in establishing any sort of defence. How long they will be in a position to offer resistance is a question that we are not even prepared to answer today. But just as the Polish campaign was already decided on the 18 September 1939, and the breakthrough at the Seine resulted in the decision over France, likewise the history of the Soviet Army is sealed with the new destructive battles.[2]

Even when presented with such positive messages, the untroubled confidence of the German people was giving way to nervousness.

The most trustworthy barometer of morale on the home front was the anti-Jewish campaigns, which fell somewhat in fine weather, 'but rose immediately when the people sensed danger or anxiety'. Some questioned how long the Wehrmacht intended to thrust into the bottomless depths of Russia, as an endless succession of hospital trains from the East, as well as a new calling up of fresh blood, made people tetchy. Obituary notices of fallen soldiers began flooding German newspapers but were soon restricted to the advertisement columns at the back of each edition.

From the beginning of hostilities on the Eastern Front, Russian radio gave a remarkable lead in the matter of effective propaganda by introducing the actual names of prisoners into the news as a way of making every civilian listen, no matter how harsh the penalties. Night after night, Radio Moscow called 'wives, mothers and sweethearts to come to the wireless to hear some distressing news' about captured lovers, sons and husbands. At the heart of their effort, Russian propagandists prioritised scooping up letters found on German prisoners or on the corpses of the dead. From this, they pieced together a picture of their interests, fears, family, hopes and worries. Curt Weiss, a notable journalist and author on the Nazi period, heard the material being used and noted that correspondence concerning family suffering – especially parents' – received special prominence:

> I don't know what to write you. I do not wish to lie, yet if I told you the truth, it would only be depressing.
>
> Mother is weak. She spends most of the day in lines for food. Yet for months past we have not seen butter, we have forgotten how it tastes or what eggs look like... We once wanted a child, do you remember? How happy I am that we have none...

Another letter to an infantryman named Rolf, also painted a desperate picture of food shortages on the German home front:

> I have received your princely gift of 31 eggs. You cannot imagine how happy I was. I have eaten not less than five at once and gave Monica one, too. And then we even had salad — just think of it! So for once we had a square meal.

On top of this, Russian technicians had developed an unconventional method of disrupting Deutschlandsender transmissions by deploying a 'ghost voice' into the ether, a phenomenon witnessed by a *New York Herald Tribune* reporter:

A voice cut in on the news broadcast of the Deutschlandsender — the biggest station of the Third Reich. The German announcer had just reported that a certain number of Russian planes had been shot down on that particular day. And, as he paused for breath, the strange voice broke in with: 'All shot down on the desk of the Propaganda Ministry in Berlin.' The voice proceeded to ridicule every statement the German announcer made. It told the German radio audience that it was listening to lies and that no one in his right mind would believe them. But as soon as the announcer tried to sneak in news again, speaking at top speed, there was that voice again, cutting in when the Nazi paused for breath, speaking as clearly as ever.

Despite their best efforts, RRG technicians failed to silence the mystery voice, which always signed off at the end of the news with the line, 'The lying will continue tomorrow.' This obstructionist tactic against Deutschlandsender was described in a *Liverpool Evening Express* editorial as 'another example of Soviet radio engineering skill. Its accomplishment has astounded technicians all over the world.'

It certainly impressed Goebbels, who briefly tried generating his own 'ghost voices' by saturating the BBC Forces programme with a barrage of abuse against Churchill, Eden and the British government. 'If you are hearing interruptions, particularly during short intervals,' the BBC calmly informed, 'you may take it that these are due to direct interruptions from the enemy.' However, the agitation sparked a BBC warning to Berlin threatening retaliation by using the Nazi wavelengths during air raids if the interruptions continued. 'What the Germans do, we can also do, and much more effectively because their stations go off the air when the RAF makes its frequent attacks, and we would then have the air to ourselves,' engineer A. E. Moore told the BBC's European service. 'Under this development it is the German people who would at last hear what their leaders have been doing, and without fear punishment from the dreaded Gestapo.' Moore added that even to the most casual listener Goebbels's hand is only too obvious. 'It betrays that lack of finesse which has provided cartoonists the world over with a profitable subject. What the Germans completely forget is that listening to foreign broadcasts in Britain is not forbidden. The cumbrous German mind cannot help thinking that conditions in Britain are similar to those in Germany.'[3]

Examples of the 'ghost voice' repartee were recorded by Radio Royal, the listening station of the *Aberdeen Press and Journal*:

> **Announcer:** In last night's raid over this country two raiders were destroyed.
> **Voice:** Rot.
> **Announcer:** Casualties were small.
> **Voice:** You wait till next time.
> **Announcer:** We lost four fighters in North Africa.
> **Voice:** Why don't you say nineteen?
> **Announcer:** Newfoundland contingent in Britain.
> **Voice:** Poor fellows.

The Voice then grew indistinct and there was a background of laughter. When the announcer said, 'That is the end of the news,' the Voice said, 'Thank God!'

The 'ghost voice' agitation came as Britain prepared to take the offensive in the war of words with the formation of a new directorate of political warfare composed of representatives of the Foreign Office, Ministry of Information, Ministry of Economic Warfare, BBC and other bodies with the aim of coordinating all foreign propaganda. Until this point, there had been doubt regarding the aptness of British foreign propaganda, with some considering it too heavy and too dull.

Japan entered the war by assaulting Pearl Harbour on 7 December, when hundreds of Japanese fighter planes swooped from the sky in a surprise attack on a US Hawaiian naval base, leaving more than 2,300 Americans dead. The action not only stunned and outraged the United States, it would have dire long-term consequences for Germany. But in the excitement of the moment, the attack presented a whole new theatre of triumphs for William Joyce to distract listeners from the sluggish Russian campaign:

> It would be the height of hypocrisy for either Roosevelt or Churchill to profess surprise at the extension of the war for which they have been working. They know perfectly well that the conflict with Japan could easily have been avoided, and yet, when Japan struck, the British and American Forces seemed at a loss to act. The Japanese plan of campaign was one of the most remarkable in the history of war.

Four days later, Hitler – apparently offhand and without consultation – stood before the Reichstag and declared war on the United States:

> Despite the years of intolerable provocations by President Roosevelt, Germany and Italy sincerely and very patiently tried to prevent the expansion of this war and to maintain relations with the United States. But as a result of his campaign, these efforts have failed.
>
> Faithful to the provisions of the Tripartite Pact of September 27, 1940, Germany and Italy accordingly now regard themselves as finally forced to join together on the side of Japan in the struggle for the defence and preservation of the freedom and independence of our nations and realms against the United States of America and Britain.

Even the most optimistic Nazis could see Berlin had boxed herself into an un-winnable situation in a conflict. 'In such circumstances the halo around Hitler's head must have paled little, despite his efforts to find a scapegoat for failures,' a British newspaper columnist opined.

As Hitler was speaking, PK journalist Hans Beyer on the Eastern Front was busily documenting his painful experiences of suffering hypothermia: 'First signs of freezing on nose and ears even with protective headgear,' he noted. 'Finally, a big van took us off to the next village. We first thawed our noses and ears with snow. Then we crept into an air force house for shelter. It was teeming with rats, bugs and lice. The window was boarded up. We froze the whole night.' From June to the end of 1941, more German soldiers died than in the entire previous course of the war, many having fallen victim to the ill-conceived plans of the military command, which had been convinced of a quick victory and provided no winter equipment. In such freezing temperatures, thousands of soldiers died agonising deaths from the cold or starvation.

In an effort to address the problem, without exposing its real horror, Goebbels was forced behind the microphone on 20 December to reveal all was not well in Russia: 'We are up against an enemy superior in numbers and materials,' he glumly admitted, before acknowledging German soldiers had not been properly supplied. He pushed the blame onto an early winter, which, he said, had been more severe than usual. Then, listeners were left stunned as he rattled off a shopping list of what the troops needed: socks, insulated boots, stockings, vests, jumpers, underpants, blankets, ground sheets, thick gloves, scarves and windproof jackets. 'Those at home will not deserve a single peaceful hour if even one soldier is exposed to the rigours of winter without adequate clothing,' Goebbels barked, lacing his plea with a threat demanding collections 'be more generous than any previous one'. That night, if British newspapers are to be believed, Deutschlandsender reportedly dropped the sign off 'Heil Hitler' and replaced it with 'Bidding a cordial good night to all listeners who now want to enjoy a well-deserved night's rest.'

Meanwhile, over in Holland, Max Blokzijl, who, if one did not know his antecedents, might easily be taken for a secret opponent of Nazis, made another remarkable admission on Hilversum: 'While the bombs were whistling down during the recent RAF raid, men and women came down the streets singing "That's Going Well".'

That Christmas, the writer Friedrich Hussong took to the airwaves, when festivities, in contrast to 1940, were markedly low-key. 'We must celebrate this Christmas with a clear conscience, remembering the hundreds of thousands of our men who will pass it in the Russian winter,' he observed. 'Therefore, we must joyfully follow the precept, "Do not give me a present, I shall not give you one".' He said kids would understand that 'we are celebrating the third war Christmas', that 15 million parcels sent to the Front were 'more important than any passenger traffic'.

> The energy of German workmen and women is infinitely more necessary in armament factories than in the production of dolls, toys, and other useless articles. [4]

Hussong called for a no-nonsense approach for a nation that, in the wake of the fight in Russia, wanted desperately to seal victory and get back to a semblance of normalcy; he also provided a few tips on how to celebrate:

> Let us imagine that we have Christmas sausage and marzipan and Christmas cakes, that the shopping centres are changed into fairyland and that the pleasure of making gifts has been restored to us ... Only those who neither give nor receive presents during this Christmas will have the right to exclaim: 'War Christmas 1941!' And this Christmas will have been the supreme Christmas Festival of all German generations.

The year ended with the German people having seen their supposedly invincible armies driven back, as they faced another winter under the shadow of terrible casualty lists.

Above left: 1. Hans Bredow, the visionary once known as 'Germany's Marconi', became chairman of RRG having served at Telefunken and as director of the Department for Wireless Telegraphy.

Above right: 2. Standing less than five feet tall, Joseph Goebbels proved to be a skilled bureaucrat with an insatiable appetite for work and boasted the most impressive academic résumé of all the Nazi hierarchy. (Bundesarchiv Bild)

Below: 3. Designed by Hans Poelzig, the *Haus Des Rundfunks* knit together fine acoustic qualities with faceted ceilings, non-parallel studio walls and absorbant vanes. (Photo: Nathan Morley)

Above: 4. The Königs Wusterhausen transmitter site, where a 900-foot mast made it the highest in the world, with the exception of the Eiffel Tower.

Left: 5. The Königs Wusterhausen transmitter site today. Back in the 1920s, 14 kilometres of copper wire and buried metal tubes formed the earth system, extending the reach of *Deutschlandsender*. (Photo: Nathan Morley)

Below left: 6. The *Volksempfänger*, a budget Bakelite radio launched at the tenth radio exhibition in Berlin in 1933. The device retailed at the remarkably low price of 76 marks – the equivalent of two weeks' wages for the average working man. (Photo: Nathan Morley)

7. The surviving annex from Goebbels' Ministry of Propaganda in Berlin, which was attached to an old stucco-and-granite palace on Wilhelmstrasse. (Photo: Nathan Morley)

8. The letter Hadamovsky shot off to Herbert Antoine advising that the continuing payout of the salary would work according to the legal requirement of three months – 'therefore you are no longer entitled to additional benefits'.

9. The Nazis maintained that 'true sport is a carrier of culture, which is politically determined according to our National Socialist view'. This 1937 cartoon from *Volksfunk* highlights a feature about motor-racing which was transmitted on Saturdays.

Above left: 10. Eugen Hadamovsky. As an ardent Nazi disciple and faithful protégé of Goebbels, Hadamovsky was perfectly suited to the role of RRG's 'Reich Programme Director'.

Left: 11. An advertisement for a loudspeaker from 1935. Radio sets were installed in restaurants and shops, while authorities announced a scheme to place 6,000 loudspeaker pillars at bus stops, town squares and railway platforms.

Below left: 12. A *Reichssender Berlin* reporter 'interviews a horse' at the Ruhleben trotting track. Station manager Otto Stoffregen said that through the news the 'life of the imperial capital with its great political, military, artistic and sporting events must be captured and conveyed to the listener'. (Author's collection)

Below: 13. Staff from *Reichssender Berlin* setting up for an outside broadcast, presumably from a municipal hall. (Author's collection)

Right: 14. Expectant mothers dance to tunes on the radio at a 'Mutterheim' in Berlin. During the day, silly, melancholy, propagandistic and sentimental gramophone records transported housewives far from domestic chores. (Author's collection)

Below: 15. The Summer Games catapulted Germany into the focus of the world as hundreds of thousands of tourists descended on Berlin's Olympic Stadium, built to hold 106,000 spectators. The German athletes received a rapturous reception from the crowds, as did squads representing Finland, the United Kingdom, Norway and the USA. (Author's collection)

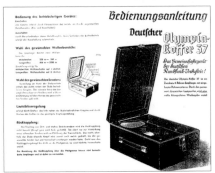

16. An *Olympiakoffer* – the first battery-powered portable radio. Priced at 156 RM with tubes and batteries, the green mock-leather device was advertised as a 'receiver for travel, weekends and sport'.

17. Some reporters at the Olympics required direct relays, whilst others were eager to make recordings for later transmission.

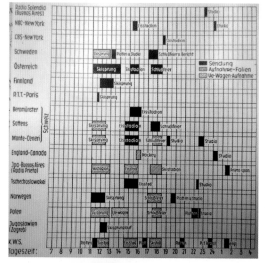

18. An original RRG broadcast chart from the Winter Olympics 1936. The enormous scale of broadcasting the event required pioneering spirit, with the laying of cables alone taking over half a year.

19. The first TV studios in Berlin today. Before RRG began transmissions from Berlin-Witzelben, an ultra-short-wave antenna was hoisted atop of these studios on Rognitzstrasse, not far from the *Haus Des Rundfunks*. (Photo: Nathan Morley).

Right: 20. TV announcers Anne-Marie Back and Ursula Putzschke at the Nipkow TV station, *circa* 1935.

Below right: 21. Watching television in Berlin, 1936. Although the first tests were described by viewers as 'satisfactory', the low-definition picture was so poor at first that some visitors depended on the audio commentary to understand what they were 'watching'.

Bottom right: 22. The Brocken TV transmitting station. Plans were also underway in 1935 to build two mountaintop TV transmitters – one on the Brocken (where a five-story building had been constructed on the summit) and the other on the Feldberg, near Frankfurt – enabling TV to reach a quarter of the population. (Author's collection)

Below: 23. The television service moved to the *Deutschlandhaus* (pictured in 2020) on Adolf Hitler Platz in late 1937, given the building was more 'optically and acoustically suitable for television broadcasting'. (Photo: Nathan Morley)

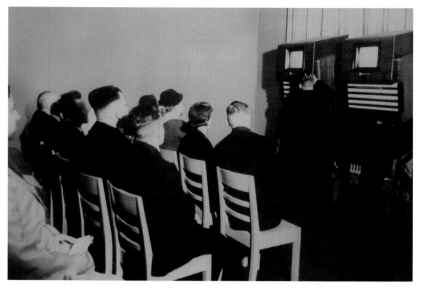

Above: 24. Special 'television theatres' invited crowds to gather in front of tiny screens to watch free of charge.

Left: 25. A ticket allowing entrance to a special TV room in Berlin. The first of these rooms opened at the Postal Museum using two television sets and seating for forty people.

Below left: 26. Television cartoons from the *Volksfunk* magazine. For the Nazis, television presented a world of possibilities when it emerged from the experimental stage to become a practical reality on its debut in 1935.

Top: 27. William Joyce (left) clocked-in for duty at the German broadcasting station two weeks prior to the outbreak of war. Having felt uneasy in London, he stuffed his world in a suitcase and fled along with his wife Margaret (right) to Berlin to avoid internment.

Above: 28. William Joyce lived in a beautifully decorated apartment in this building at Kastanienallee on a leafy street near the studios. (Photo: Nathan Morley)

Above right: 29. At 05.48 a.m. on 1 September 1939, the duty editor at the *Haus Des Rundfunks* took a sharp intake of breath when this crucial telex from Hitler's office – Ref 8004-ddd bln – arrived. 'We kindly ask you to make the following announcements at 06:00, 08:00 and 10:00.'

Right: 30. Joyce worked in an office along this corridor in the *Haus Des Rundfunks* during 1939. He later moved to the *Deutschlandhaus* on Adolf Hitler Platz. (Photo Nathan Morley)

31. A PK Company attached to the Wehrmacht enjoys the snow in Poland, 1939. From the beginning of the war, Wehrmacht Propaganda Companies (PK) began providing a vast amount of material for radio, newspapers and magazines. (Authors private collection)

32. A PK Company attached to the Luftwaffe relaxes at Christmas 1939. Thankfully, for both reporters and listeners overwhelmed by the pace of developments, Christmas brought a semblance of normality back to the airwaves. (Author's collection)

33. The 'U Wagen', used by PK Companies, in which wax discs span on a cutting machine, capturing the action. (Volksfunk)

34. The 'black propaganda' effort was led by Goebbels' little-known aide Adolf Raskin.

Above right: 35. PK correspondents armed with recording equipment and microphones on a raid over London to witness the thrilling spectacle of 'bombs of the heaviest calibre' raining down on the British capital. (Volksfunk)

Right: 36. Performing for the troops in 1940. The KdF radio crew always received a tremendous reception during tours, and by early 1940 they had clocked up 247 transmissions since the beginning of hostilities. (Author's collection)

Below right: 37. Soldiers and airmen often performed songs and humorous sallies used in KdF radio shows. (Author's collection)

Below: 38. Choosing a trusted news source could be a difficult task, as this cartoon shows.

RADIO LONDON—NEW-YORK

"...Stockholm reports that London overheard from Madrid radio that a Swiss announcer said Ankara heard Berlin deny the Rome report that Tokyo did not, as Reuters had previously announced, have anything to report on this..."

Above left: 39. Dutch Nazi Max Blokzijl, who had earned his stripes contributing fervently fascist articles to pro-Hitler papers under an assumed name, was installed as a senior announcer and commentator. (Dutch National Archives)

Above right: 40. Heinz Goedecke, a master of nimble comic timing, hosted the popular *Wunschkonzert für die Wehrmacht*. (Volksfunk)

Below: 41. The shady *Büro Concordia* broadcast from these offices at the Olympic Stadium. The unit was set up to produce subversive radio propaganda and stir up defeatism, strife and dissent. (Photo: Nathan Morley)

42a. In a letter to Goedecke marking the fiftieth edition of the *Wunschkonzert*, Wilhelm Keitel, Chief of the Armed Forces High Command, noted, 'These concerts have become an increasingly important link between the German people and their soldiers.'

42b. The show was performed live in the concert hall at *Haus Des Rundfunks* and featured a high-wattage cast. Pictured is the concert hall in 2020. (Photo: Nathan Morley)

43. Known locally as the 'Schwedische Pavillon', the Seehaus sat on the west shore on Wannsee Lake. Hidden behind the walls of this palatial residence – cloaked under the guise of a 'Radio Research Institute' – 500 expert linguists, monitors and transcribers kept the government briefed day and night with what the world was saying – and hearing.

44. Anton 'Toni' Winkelnkemper, a former propaganda chief for the Köln district and one of Goebbels' oldest and most faithful disciples, was appointed acting director of the shortwave radio services, thus becoming responsible for foreign broadcasts.

GOEBBELS-ENTEN

45. A Russian propaganda leaflet dropped over German territory in August 1941. The message was that Goebbels was not telling the truth and it was better to trust the Soviet government.

46. Hans Fritzsche established himself as something of a national radio institution. Known for his unflappable delivery and well-structured arguments, he would guide listeners through triumphs and tragedies alike, always opening his talks with the words, 'Hier spricht Hans Fritzsche!'

47. Helmuth Hubner, a seventeen-year-old from Hamburg, was executed in Berlin-Plotzensee after being charged and convicted of listening to the BBC and spreading the information he'd heard.

48. Fritz Kuhn and his German-American League, a New York-based Fascist organisation run on Nazi lines, warmly welcomed the RRG's growing influence and enthusiastically distributed programme materials, such as this schedule, far and wide.

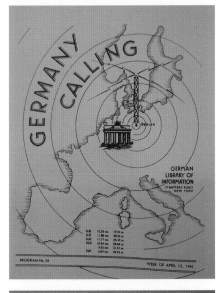

49. The German short-wave schedule spawned a host of talks, commentaries and features aimed at all parts of the world.

50. Since the occupation, the Nazis used the *Radio Luxembourg* headquarters in the *Villa Louvigny*, a building spread throughout an old fort with a moat and rows of flowerbeds dotted around it. (Photo: Nathan Morley)

51. In 1943, Richard Baier was employed as an announcer at the RRG. 'Imagine that! I was 17 years old, and working on the radio in the heart of Berlin.'

52. The *Haus Des Rundfunks* today. The bunker, which was demolished in the 1990s, was located where the two white office blocks now stand. (Photo: Nathan Morley)

53. The Soviet military administration ordered all transmitters and antennas in Zeesen to be dismantled and sent to Russia as reparations.

18

THE TURNING TIDE

As Germany grappled with supply problems, bartering gained traction at the margins of the economy during winter 1942, presenting a worrisome new sign for the Nazis. With the public seeking creative new ways to cope with the radically changing economic landscape, a decree threatened death for using forged coupons and stiff jail terms for black marketeering. As pressure began to mount, a nationwide scavenge was launched for clothes to supply German and foreign workers in the East, while the Hitler Youth canvassed house-to-house seeking surplus shoes and boots. Deutschlandsender abandoned caution to request the public rummage around for old swimming trunks, which could be remodelled into balaclavas, while Goebbels extended his appeal for warm clothing to citizens in Bohemia and Moravia.

Anyone who lived in Germany in 1942 and kept their eyes and ears open could have picked up on the ominous signals arriving from the East. On 3 January, a Deutschlandsender talk, *The Invisible Menace*, described how Soviet ski troops – clad in white capes with hoods – swooped down on the German units in surprise attacks:

> The enemy soldiers do not know fear or death. Hand-to-hand fighting decides the issue. In one battle on the Central Sector, the Bolsheviks attacked for four days and five nights. Our troops

had no rest for this period – and this was in severe frost and snowstorms.[1]

Considering frequent claims that the Soviets had been 'officially destroyed and crushed', such reports baffled many listeners. 'They make a mockery of anyone with a tidy mind,' a diarist in Dresden scowled. As usual, regular radio briefings from Army Generals Rolf Bathe, Erich Murawski and Lieutenant-General Kurt Dittmar added saccharine to bitter situations. 'It was not a closed presentation of the military operations, but explanations for the layman,' Murawski recalled. 'They created a spirit of sharing the situation and enjoyed all-round popularity.' That said, the briefings frequently turned the attention of listeners away from Russia by playing on the alleged U-boat successes in the Atlantic, or the progress of the Japanese in the Far East, which had rendered a fundamental challenge to the British with the fall of Singapore, the loss of Java and their successful invasion of Burma.

In the immediate wake of these humiliations, German shortwave propaganda spawned a host of talks and features aimed at the British and their Allies in Asia. The English actor Jack Trevor produced the weekly *Anzac Tattoo*, a 'typical English variety entertainment show', similar to an ENSA concert.[2] Douglas Reed, a *Daily Herald* reporter, had met Trevor in 1928. 'He was an exceptionally good-looking, well dressed, well-mannered man, and yet none of the British colony (in Berlin) seemed to know him.'[3] For his efforts, Trevor was paid 280 Marks per week for writing and appearing alongside a cast of English-speaking Germans in *Anzac Tattoo*. During a brief encounter at the Haus Des Rundfunks, CBS reporter William Shirer remembered Trevor as being a ranting Englishman with a 'burring hatred of the Jews'.

For once, the Büro Concordia found a receptive audience when it launched a hail of radio agitation directed against the British occupation of India with the help of exiled Indian leftist leader Subhas Chandra Bose, a man dubbed by the British as 'the Indian Quisling'. Filled with anti-English animosities which bubbled to the surface on Free India Radio (Azad Hind/Voice of Free India), Bose doled out half-baked claims, crass generalisations and appeals for national liberation, delivered in accent-free English, Hindustani, Bengali and Tamil:

> Against our brutal foe, no amount of civil disobedience, sabotage or revolution can be of any avail. If therefore we want to expel the British from India, we shall have to fight the enemy with their own weapons. But it is not possible for our countrymen at home to organise an armed revolution and to fight the British army of occupation with modern arms. This task must, therefore, devolve on Indians living abroad and particularly on Indians living in East Asia.[4]

His second-in-command, Arathil Chandeth Narayanan Nambiar, recounted how Bose selected the main lines of propaganda, commentaries and talks. The following instructions were distributed to all members:

> Britain would lose the war for military, economic and moral reasons: Militarily because Britain's enemies were better prepared. The air weapon had reduced the value of the Navy – of which the British were proud – and Germany had the best Air Force.
>
> In the last war, Italy and Japan were against Germany: in the present war, they were on Germany's side. France, which played an important part in the last war, had ceased to exist as a major power. Economically, there was no question of Germany being starved, since the resources of the whole of Europe were at her disposal.
>
> Morally, England had not the same vigour that she had in 1914. The British forces were scattered all over the globe, distances and time were against Britain. Britain had no monopoly on propaganda as in the last war. National consciousness had become much stronger in countries such as India, Arabia and the Colonies. British imperialism in its present form and Indian freedom could not exist side by side.[5]

Bose cobbled together his scripts at Lichtensteinallee-2, a granite villa cosseted in the leafy diplomatic enclave of the Tiergarten, opposite the Italian Embassy. He revelled in his celebrity status and lucrative offers to compose anti-British pamphlets for Ribbentrop's Foreign Office and 'advise the German press' on India-related matters. 'Bose was obsessed with the idea that the

Azad Hind transmission was proving very effective in stirring up the masses in India,' Nambiar recalled during his testimony to British interrogators after the war:

> The Azad Hind radio had been established as an independent shortwave station. The duration of the transmissions was fifteen minutes and in the beginning, they were made in two languages Hindustani and English. Bose was of the opinion that a secret station would attract more listeners than official transmissions. Secondly, a secret station could transmit things which the official station could not.[6]

Ribbentrop not only believed implicitly in Bose's ability to stir up the masses in India, he continued to invest eye-watering amounts into the project: 'In this war, like no other war before, the struggle for public opinion in the countries of all continents plays a decisive role,' the opening preamble of a Foreign Office finance report stated. 'Here, the experiences of the war have shown broadcasting, as the most modern, global instrument of propaganda, has made the possibility of influencing the peoples almost unlimited.'[7] Nambiar testified that Bose was anxious to launch two other secret stations: 'Congress Radio' to win over supporters of Gandhi, and 'Azad Muslim Radio' to counteract the activities of the Muslim League. 'He wanted to keep these stations secret in order to give the impression that transmissions were coming either from India itself or from a neighbouring country.' Eventually, the stations spluttered onto the airwaves, but in traditionally slapdash Concordia fashion it was an utterly transparent ruse. 'It was obvious,' Nambiar said, 'that the same wavelengths and frequency was used for all three stations, but there was a hiatus of fifteen minutes between different programmes.' Transcribing the content of the Bose soapbox – night after night – could be an excruciatingly tedious task for the British monitors:

> The time has come when India should play a dynamic role in the struggle against British imperialism, so that our freedom may come – not a gift from any foreign power – but through our own strength.

Another important collaborator – Radio Himalaya – also pretended to operate from India but was bankrolled by the Italians and run by anti-British firebrand Fakir of Ipi, who had fomented trouble in North West Waziristan, before reappearing in Rome. The station purported to represent Indian peasants and reported the raising of a 'Free Indian army' alongside promises that the Axis offered India freedom from the British yoke. At one point, fifth columnists in Tibet reportedly ran a chain of shortwave transmitters rebroadcasting Radio Himalaya, with the most powerful of these situated somewhere near the sacred city of Lhasa. 'From its transmitters pours a steady stream of lies and distortion aimed at creating suspicion and disquiet between India and Britain,' the *Daily Herald* observed.

For all its audacity, the effectiveness of these broadcasts confounded Nazi analysts. The German embassy in Bangkok – referencing an Indian informant – stated listener interest in news from Berlin was minimal, given it was devoted primarily to the war and events in Europe. On the other hand, the informant assured Bose's talks on Indian topics were well received.

The British – overwhelmed by the sheer volume of outrageous material on Radio Himalaya and Free India Radio – reached a similar conclusion. In response, Colonial authorities opened a campaign of jamming alongside the BBC's new production *Through Eastern Eyes* featuring commentaries read by Indians and occasionally scripted by George Orwell, then an employee at Broadcasting House.

Back in Germany, Goebbels displayed true Nazi elasticity by lauding the 'enthusiastic response' to his Russian clothing appeal, boasting 67.2million items had been donated, 'evidence that the public wanted to carry the war through to victory'.

From the other side, Radio Moscow broadcasting in German reported how medics embarked on a war against lice after an outbreak of 'spotted typhus' in Germany and the occupied areas, with the scourge blamed on troops returning from the Eastern Front. The disease is born amid filth and is prevalent in the winter when more clothes are worn and cleanliness is difficult to achieve. As a preventive measure, grimy and unkempt troops were forced to shave their heads and incinerate filthy uniforms at the frontier.

The onset of spring provided a comeback opportunity for William Joyce, who predicted the day was 'not far off' when the Wehrmacht would wipe the remains of the Russian Army from the face of the earth. 'Hitler's Germany is now preparing one of the greatest offensives – perhaps the greatest offensive in history – an offensive which will condition the history of the world for a thousand years to come.'[8] Talk of this threatened action featured heavily on Radio Metropol, a new 'black propaganda' station targeting Russia under the auspices of Ribbentrop's Foreign Ministry. At a time when misinformation was in ready supply, Metropol piped up from studios in Wannsee (probably at the Seehaus) to target the Eastern Front using transmitters at Zemun in the suburbs of the Serbian capital. Beaming 11,925 kHz and 9,480 kHz, Metropol displayed skilfully feigned impartiality, with a format of news, music, and cheerful patter in Georgian, Uzbek, Tatar, Russian and Ukrainian. Unlike Concordia efforts, the operation was so slick, that few listeners suspected they were listening to programmes of German origin. News editors on Radio Metropol made wide use of 'International Information Bureau', a non-existent neutral news agency, which German radio referred to when cooking up outrageous statements and false stories. Metropol and other services, including Radio Paris and Hilversum, quoted it in the same way as the BBC quoted Reuters or the United Press, or other well-known agencies, except that as it was fake, it enabled them to start rumours and drop hints in the hope somebody somewhere would believe them. It also allowed them to broadcast extreme claims and escape the consequences. 'When they (the Germans) want to say something which they would like to say, and which they yet feel to be so extreme or absurd that they don't want to have it quoted back at them later, they can now do this by saying that this neutral news agency has reported it,' W. A. Sinclair, the scholar of Philosophy at Edinburgh University, who had previously monitored William Joyce, explained. After months of listening to German radio to hear how often this 'fairy tale' agency cropped up, Sinclair submitted his conclusions to the *Listener*:

If you listen to one of the Nazi news readers broadcasting and hear him quoting this news agency, it all sounds quite normal.

For instance, the German radio on 3 November said: 'The special correspondent of the International Information Bureau in North Africa reports that the large-scale British attack which was started by the heavy artillery preparation yesterday morning on the El Alamein (Egyptian) front ... has collapsed,' and so forth. You may think that a news agency which says things like this is not particularly reliable, but it certainly sounds as if some such agency did really exist, whatever its reliability or unreliability. But, as a matter of fact, no such agency exists.

According to Sinclair, German newscasters kept up the pretence it was a real agency with ingenuity. 'They always speak about it with an air of not very interested detachment, as if it really had nothing to do with them.' Other 'favoured sources' included the German-controlled Scandinavian Telegraph Bureau and the pro-German Swedish daily *Aftonbladet*.

Whether it was pensioners moved to tears in the front row, or legions of music fans singing along from the gallery, Germany had become besotted with the Berliner Rundfunkspielschar children's choir. There had probably never been a time when music and the public were so close together emotionally: 'We broadcast over the Deutschlandsender every Sunday afternoon at one o'clock. People tuned in to listen to our young, innocent, fresh and enthusiastic voices,' recalls Peter Meyer, a former member of the ensemble. Even over scratchy mediumwave radio, its members displayed remarkable purity of tone, accompanied by a piano and mandolin. In early spring, the choir was packed off on a 14-day concert tour to Alsace and south-west Germany to perform a whole gamut of works, including songs by Brahms and Schubert, Handel's opera *Xerxes* and a selection of German and Finnish folk tunes. Although exciting, Meyer joined the Rundfunkspielschar to avoid conscription in the Jungvolk where 'they did nothing but war preparations. I went once to my assigned unit and ran away':

The next week, I followed my friend Hartwig Berlin to the Funkhaus (Haus Des Rundfunks) were the group met and practiced and transmitted. My mother, as was Hartwig's, was a singer and had given me the training that allowed me to become a member after my audition. I joined in 1940; I was eleven years old.[9]

The weekly broadcasts were a combination of 'aggressive and romantic renditions' of German folk music which, Meyer said, gave Berliners a lot of false hope:

> Our conductor was called Lodze, he wore a Nazi uniform and was handicapped, walked with a strong limp. During the week we often met in smaller and local groups, mine was in Schoeneberg, where we practiced new songs and worked on our overall repertoire. We competed against the Koenigsberger Sängerknaben and the Wiener Sängerknaben with three songs each. After two songs we were dead last, the famous group from Vienna was number one. Our last number was an old German freedom song adapted by the Nazis for their cause: It was an electrifying number that brought the audience to their feet and gave us second place which we really did not deserve. We only sang three verses, one, seven and eight:

> *Heraus, heraus die Klingen,*
> *lasst Ross und Klepper springen,*
> *der Morgen graut heran,*
> *das Tagewerk bricht an.*

> I never forgot the text which helped our German audience to forget momentarily the fact that their house might be burning upon their return home that night.[10]

In addition to performing at angelic concerts, Meyer participated in Concordia broadcasts: 'I remember signing a paper that swore me to silence about this ruse,' he recalls. On one occasion he imitated a Polish teenager: 'The recordings took place in Berlin, never in Poland or Czechoslovakia. This was perpetrated in the Berlin Funkhaus without a single foreigner in sight.' The fake story being 'played out' was that young foreigners were delighted the Germans had come and that they got along so very well with their new-found German friends:

I also went to Babelsberg, which was like the American Hollywood for that time and there I participated in films and the newsreels called Die Wochenschau. Again, we made films of the same kind of propaganda as mentioned above; I played foreign or German youth members and had to learn a few words of foreign languages for my roles.[11]

Wherever there was the slightest possibility of cheering up the public, the Nazis left no stone unturned. A popular distraction came from the German Broadcasting Association's special sports performances at the Funkturm radio tower, opposite the Haus Des Rundfunks. It was hoped spectators – mostly Berliners, wounded soldiers and armaments workers – would find relaxation and enjoyment in the KdF, Police, Luftwaffe, Nazi Flying Corps and Hitler Youth performances. Various tournaments, including basketball, hockey, fencing, handball and boxing were transmitted on both radio and TV, along with a special 'Day of the Air Force' organised by the Luftwaffe Sports Association with 400 participants.

As hard as they may try, such events provided only a brief respite. 'Berlin was not a jolly town,' a Swedish journalist noted, as he heard more grumbling, saw more anguish and noted a decline in self-confidence.

Hans Fritzsche – the man who had impressed Goebbels with his oily eloquence – made the same observation. On returning from a brief stint on the Eastern Front, he took control of the radio division at the Propaganda Ministry with a mission to bridge the void between reality and propaganda. 'Radio must reach all or it will reach none,' he insisted, arguing more candour about everyday worries such as the black market, strained relations between soldiers and civilians, air raids and food shortages, was needed. 'Instead of maintaining the previously adopted sanguine attitude, the aim of which had been to minimise first the British and then the Russian strength, the Propaganda Ministry began to paint everything in sombre colours,' Swedish writer Arvid Fredborg recalled in his memoirs *Behind the Steel Wall*:

Stories began to circulate about what would happen to Germany if the British and the Russians were victorious. The transition was a little too fast for many Germans, but the propaganda was carried on so cleverly that the only conclusion to be drawn from Goebbels' presentation by the man-in-the-street was that he had to do his utmost. Obviously, the Propaganda Ministry had spent quite a little time on phrasing his explanation so as to make the situation look as black as possible without causing people to despair of victory.[12]

On a tour of Berlin, fellow Swede George Alexsson, a former correspondent of the *New York Times,* saw public apathy everywhere, but 'the reverses in Russia', he thought, had 'caused little reaction ... the home front did what it is told, accepts restrictions and considers it has done its duty'. Understandably, unlike in previous years, Hitler's birthday was a subdued affair. As a token gesture, Goebbels arranged for 5,000 Kleine Empfanger (small radio receivers) to be handed to the relatives of those killed in the conflict, while coverage was given to a Tokyo radio broadcast to Germany, in which the General Secretary of the Japanese State Youth delivered a speech:

> There is a will in the hearts of Japanese youth to fight this war to the end with the aim of breaking up the old order defending England and America and building a new world of justice. To achieve this great goal, Germany and Japan have formed an inseparable alliance with Italy. The youth of Japan offer their warmest congratulations to the great leader of Germany.[13]

As the war situation grew increasingly tense, Red Army and partisan attacks slowly splintered Hitler's hold on the Ukraine, a territory vital for grain supplies. Those tasked with exploiting occupied land faced critical seed shortages and a lack of tractors for the spring sowing. The situation was made more remarkable, as less than a year earlier, Germany had planned to raise sheep in the Ukraine to make it not only the granary of the Continent, but also the source of its entire stock of wool, lambs' meat and vegetables. The government had even set in motion a plan for teenagers to take a two-year farming course, with the gift of a farmstead in the Ukraine.

But from early 1942, the agricultural situation only degenerated. Deutschlandsender urged German farmers to 'make all efforts in the coming season for the next harvest', a tall order given the scant support for home farming crippled by the manpower shortage and the dearth of phosphates essential to maintain healthy crop and livestock production. At every turn, the public was deluged with advice about preparing for intensive summer sowings, with speeches reheated from previous campaigns calling for calm when the meat, butter and bread allowance was slashed further.

When 19-year-old Irma Weinknecht graduated from high school, she was required to complete six months of national service with the Reichsarbeitsdienst or Labour Corps. 'All the great dreams one had as a young girl – I wanted to study drama – had to wait,' she lamented. Like every other girl of her age, Irma was packed off to do manual work with spade and hoe in the countryside, while, at the same time, receiving regular instruction in the pervasive dullness of National Socialist politics:

> It started with me being examined at the health department, which, in my mind, was all about whether or not I was pregnant. But, since I was fit in every way, I was told I could start shortly thereafter. It was not at all a question of whether I really wanted to go there – it was a clear command.

After four weeks, Irma was sent to plant potato seeds 'after sorting out the stinking remnants of the previous harvest'. The farmer hitched her onto a horse-drawn cart to lug jute sacks filled with seeds. 'It was a terribly heavy burden for a city girl! I could not keep up the pace, which earned me some rude remarks, so I was glad when the work was over.'

19

NEW IDEAS

On 20 May 1942, the Wehrmacht High Command ordered a long-defunct TV station in Paris to come back to life. The motivation for this strange move, if reports are to be believed, was to derail plans to tear down the Eiffel Tower which could provide the Nazi war machine with 7,000 tons of scrap iron. News of the scheme filtered through to British media, which unsurprisingly lamented that the effect on Parisians would be 'similar to that which Londoners or New Yorkers would feel if a Hun committee were considering the razing of Nelson's Column or the Statue of Liberty'.[1]

Those in favour of demolition insisted the tower was in poor shape and rusting badly. Soon after, a committee tasked to looking into dismantling the structure – including engineers from Telefunken – found the idea so repulsive that they argued in favour of resurrecting the old 30kW PTT Vision transmitter, which was stored under the base of the tower. Before the war, experimental TV broadcasts from the Rue de Grenelle had become ambitious in scope, transmitting weekdays from 15.30 to 16.30 and on Sundays from 15.30 to 17.30.

Although the Paris television station had been abandoned in 1939,[2] the new idea was to revive it to entertain battle-scarred soldiers cooped up in Parisian hospitals, with the added bonus of using the tower as a jammer for enemy aircraft. Alfred Bofinger, the head of the Broadcasting Group in the German Military

Administration, thought the moment right for a German TV channel and enlisted Kurt Hinzmann, a member of the so-called Staffel K – a group charged with taking over the BBC in the event of an invasion of the UK – to run the operation. At the same time, the Reichspost oversaw all the technology issues.

Hinzmann, a veteran of the Nipkow station in Berlin, christened the station Fernsehsender Paris and ordered the transmitter be converted from the French 455-line to the German 441-line standard. Then the search for a suitable location for the studios also got underway with the Chaillot Theatre on the Place du Trocadéro being considered, but in the end Magic City, a former dance hall on the Rue de l'Université, was chosen.

Until the refurbishment of Magic City, the Fernsehsender Paris set up a makeshift studio at the former Czechoslovakian Embassy opposite the Eiffel Tower, where experimental transmissions – flickering faintly in hazy grey – featured live pictures of the Paris landscape, *Die Deutsche Wochenschau* newsreel and France-*Actualités du Gouvernement* from Vichy along with relays of Deutschlandsender over a test card. Over the coming months, Léon Smet – the father of Johnny Hallyday – found employment as a director, while the youthful singer Mouloudji, choreographers Serge Lifar and Serge Reggiani, and the actor Jacques Dufilho also worked on early programmes.

In all, Fernsehsender Paris reached about 300 television sets in the capital area, most in German military establishments and hospitals, but it's thought more than a thousand pre-war sets in private homes could also tune in. There were also a few uninvited spectators. An English radar surveillance station near Beachy Head in Sussex succeeded in receiving Fernsehsender Paris over a distance of 240 kilometres using a spiderweb antenna construction strung between two wooden towers at a height of about 30 meters to amplify the signals. 'The whole thing was unreal, fantastic. We were actually looking in at the Germans in Paris,' gushed technician RAF Wing Commander George Kelsey. 'Our job was merely to provide the picture, but in satisfying ourselves that reception conditions were stable, we stayed long enough to appreciate at least one valuable service that the enemy was unwittingly rendering. His newsreels depicting our bomb damage in France, with a commentary to whip up hatred of the British, provided a wonderful record at close quarters of the success of our efforts!'³

By and large, Goebbels was uninterested in small-time TV experiments in Paris as he concentrated on pepping-up morale on the home front and to the armed forces. After 'much preparatory work', two new shows were launched on Deutschlandsender for serious and classical music, and another on the old Reichssender transmitters for light entertainment. 'It is important to secure good humour at home and at the front,' he explained in an article for the *Völkischer Beobachter*. Remarkably, slithers of jazz music were readmitted to the airwaves so 'soldiers at the front, after a hard battle, could appreciate what they call decent music, which means light music, in their cold and inhospitable quarters'. Listeners were, he said, in general, too strained to absorb more than two hours of an exacting programme: 'If a man who has worked hard for 12 or 14 hours wants to hear music at all, it must be music which makes no demands on him.'

The real reason for the format tweaks came amid reports of German soldiers seeking light relief by listening to jazz and swing music on foreign stations. To propel themselves through this listener downturn, Hans Fritzsche claimed Germans were suffering from a 'radio disease' syndrome: 'You are bound to feel ill,' he explained during a broadcast, 'you listen to Anglo-Saxon radio, and are swung between extravagant hopes and the deepest despair.'

Tuning in to such programmes on the home front remained a dangerous pastime. That year, eight people were jailed for 33 years for listening in to the BBC. The death sentence was reserved for those who met to listen as a group or passed on what they had heard. Helmuth Hübener, a 17-year-old from Hamburg, was executed in Berlin's Plötzensee after being charged and convicted of listening to the BBC and spreading the information he'd heard. In many cities, similar cases against 'traitors' came before the courts. Sentences were announced in the press, with the *Volkischer Beobachter* leading the campaign against 'the voice of the enemy':

The fact has been established that listening in to the BBC causes considerable weakening of the power of resistance of those

Germans who listen and generally paralyses them mentally. The effect of listening in to the BBC is only comparable with soldiers who inflict self-wounds in order to escape army duties.

But it wasn't just the public barred from listening to foreign radio. Earlier in the year, Hitler had ordered that Goebbels, as well as the head of the Reich Chancellery Hans Lammers, Foreign Minister Ribbentrop, Marshall Goring, Field Marshal Keitel, Post Office Minister Wilhelm Ohnesorge and Interior Minister Wilhelm Frick, were the only ones allowed to listen to foreign radio broadcasts. All other senior officials – including military commanders – required direct permission from the Führer. Remarking on the order, Goebbels noted it was

> disgusting how many big shots are now trying to prove to me that they can't continue their work unless they receive permission to listen to foreign radio broadcasts. In almost all cases I deny their requests. I agree to place at the disposal of every individual only such material that is essential for his special work. The task and duty of listening to foreign broadcasts must devolve on the political offices created for this purpose.[4]

On some days, it seemed to Hans Fritzsche that he was riding on the crest of a wave, on others that he had crashed into the shore. When asked by Goebbels to spearhead the thankless task of a 'politeness campaign', he must have sighed. As war prospects worsened, concern over abrasiveness, rudeness and the infrequent use of such words as 'please' and 'thank you' became widespread and it was decided polite people should be applauded for their civility. A radio talk was followed by a poster campaign. The slogan, 'In this room, it is the duty of everyone to act and speak with politeness,' was plastered throughout the Reich. The campaign worked when members of the public wrote to the Ministry of Propaganda to nominate people who were especially polite. Then Goebbels would distribute prizes, including money, radios and tickets to the theatre for politest ones. 'Politeness was filmed and shown in the movies,' Swedish journalist Gunnar Pihl recounted. 'Polite people received a pin as a sign of their civility, a pin with the Berlin bear on it. When distributing the pins, Goebbels declared the people of Berlin were fundamentally tremendously polite. Humorous and polite.' Never to be left out of matters of the national conversation, Goebbels opined,

> ... if sometimes there is no coal and no potatoes, if one can no longer travel by rail when one wants to, if the means of transport in towns are overcrowded, if one has to wait hours in a queue to get a seat in a cinema or a theatre, if the shop assistant says there is nothing left – good heavens! If they were the only things our soldiers had to put up with at the front they would think the life they were leading was a veritable paradise!

Politeness had never been abundant at Berlin pubs, known locally as Kneipen. Tired and thirsty, a newly arrived Swedish correspondent in Germany spat out his glass of local beer, which was little more than 'gassy coloured water'. A decree forbidding deliveries of hops, ersatz hops and malt to breweries had a devastating effect on its quality, as the last genuine ingredient was removed. According to reporter Howard K. Smith, by mid-1941 the bar at the Adlon – the best hotel in Berlin – was also squeezed for refreshment: 'It caused visible pain to the old bartender to answer an order for a cocktail saying he was dreadfully sorry, but today, precisely today, he had run out of ingredients.'

A stiff drink would have probably helped the staff at the Olympic Stadium, where the Concordia station, Radio Caledonia, was clinging on for dear life. BBC monitors noted programmes were becoming the stuff of legend, as German announcer Phyllis Markgrah demonstrated an uncanny ability to deliver convincing Highland vocal impersonations. During her 15-minute rambles, many written by Baillie-Stewart, she asserted pre-war Scotland had suffered higher child mortality than any other part of the United Kingdom, and furthermore Britain was spending £13 million a day on war materials when three out of 10 Scottish children were undernourished.

In its weekly chat to members of the 'Scottish Peace Front' (a fictional organisation), Donald Grant, a Scottish fascist recruited in 1940, urged listeners that Scotland would 'continue to be a pawn in international capitalism' after the war. The station often called for a 'Scottish Socialist State, governed by patriotic Scots, solely in the interests and for the welfare of the Scottish nation'. A selection of scratched 78 rpm Scottish folk records – many featuring Jimmy Shand – provided the musical backup for Caledonia's musings. By late July, both the Propaganda Ministry and Ribbentrop's men realised they were flogging a dead horse and interest in Radio Caledonia evaporated with astonishing speed – it faded from the airwaves soon after.

Around this time, the spurious New British Broadcasting Corporation stumbled across a rumour 'going round London to the effect that a serious attempt will be made to invade the Continent and relieve pressure on the Russians before the winter'. The report suggested US troops would play a prominent part in the attack: 'Commandos are known to be standing in several parts of the country, while large numbers of American troops have recently been moved to the East Coast.' What's even more striking, though, was for the first time ever, the station had hit on a genuinely truthful rumour, as planning for the 'second front' was, in fact, well underway in London. Finally, the rumour mill deserved much more credit than it typically got.

William Joyce must have laughed out loud at the demise of Radio Caledonia given it was largely a Baillie-Stewart effort. That spring, he was elevated to the position of 'Head Commentator' at the princely salary of 1,200 Reichsmarks a month in return for placing the 'whole of his work at the disposal of the RRG'. Toni Winkelnkemper confirmed the appointment in writing:

I hereby appoint you, with effect as from the 1 July of this year, as chief commentator for the group of countries 'England'. This is an instruction to you to prepare the political comments in the English language for our news service in accordance with the directions of the superior authorities and suggestions by the director of the group of countries. I also ask you to examine the news services from the language point of view and to allocate the announcers in concert with the editorial chief who is on duty. In order that you may obtain the necessary time for your further extended duties you are released from the news announcement service. Having regard to

your extended responsibility and your many years of efficiency as
an announcer and commentator, I am considering a readjustment
of your remuneration. You will hear further on this matter shortly,

(Signed) Winkelnkemper

The thrill of the promotion for Joyce was sweetened when Eduard
Dietze was elevated to Editor-in-Chief of the English services,
which by this point was transmitting round the clock. Edwin
Schneider, a 23-year-old newsreader, remembered the hectic
English programme schedule:

From January 1942 until the middle of 1943, I broadcast in
English from Berlin at 14:30, 15:30, 16:30, 17:30 and 18:30 daily,
with the exception of two days off in a fortnight, when others
deputised for broadcasts, which all lasted for 15 minutes. At
15:30 was the German High Command Communiqué, which was
repeated at 16:30. At 17:30, I introduced a feature programme of
commentaries and music.[5]

The English-language service joined in the spectacle of enforced
mourning for Reinhard Heydrich, the Deputy Protector of
Bohemia and Moravia, who had died from gunshot wounds
inflicted by an attacker in Prague. Deutschlandsender declared
Heydrich would 'live in history as one of the most striking
personalities of the German revolution'. Once his funeral was
over, the news agenda shifted to the anniversary of the invasion
of Russia: 'The first year of the Eastern campaign closes with the
battle of Kharkov, a happy omen for the coming destruction of
the Russian armies.' But, as one commentator decided on a policy
of caution, hinting not everything was rosy on the Eastern Front:

The hot summer sun blazes down on the dry and dusty, hilly and
rugged landscape. This is a most peculiar country. In the winter
the cold is unbearable; in May there is stifling heat, which is just
as unbearable as the cold of the winter. The ground is tough.
Long stretches of this hilly country are covered with grey smoke
clouds; over there on the enemy side of the elevations German
grenades are bursting. Here on the German side, where our troops

are concentrated, Soviet shells are exploding. Great stretches of scorched, blackened, gnarled brushwood are in flames. Amid the dense smoke clouds which are rising over the valleys, one can occasionally see tufts of green in the distance. Innumerable filthy brown dust clouds are drifting along the heights and hollows of the countryside.[6]

Throughout autumn, Wehrmacht troops rolled along the banks of the Volga prompting Deutschlandsender to announce the fall of Stalingrad was a foregone conclusion:

Upon reaching the banks of the Volga north and south of Stalingrad the basic part of the strategic objective of the battle of Stalingrad was achieved. Even though the fighting is going on along the banks of the Volga for the purpose of annihilating the Soviet opponent, it seems to have lost some of its former character. Stalingrad is no longer of the same strategic importance. The game at Stalingrad can be said to be virtually over.[7]

The reality, though, was somewhat different as the Soviets had launched an attack in the Caucasus, then struck southwards across the bend of the Don and cut off a large portion of the German 6th Army in front of Stalingrad. From then onwards, Russia had Goebbels stumped most of the time, and his explanations became more and more difficult to swallow – they came thick and fast, losing all trace of consistency. While one commentator explained just why the Wehrmacht weren't getting anywhere, another assured victory had already been won. Sometimes, a commentator covered both angles in one commentary, as Dittmar did on 13 September. 'The decision has already been reached,' he announced, then, a few minutes later, explained Germans were handicapped by poor rear communications, while the Russians had raised the fortress of Stalingrad to a 'symbol of victorious resistance'.

On the threshold of the fourth winter of the war, as Stalingrad faded from view, Goebbels received a belated birthday present in the form of John Amery, the son of Leo Amery, the Secretary for India in the Churchill government. Greatly to the surprise of many within the ProMi, Amery had been picked up in France and became a willing recruit to the Nazi cause after spending a few days in a private conclave with Foreign Ministry officials. From there, he was whisked off to the Haus Des Rundfunks to begin broadcasting on the English service. He told Ribbentrop he was much more 'in tune' with the mood of the British public, while his opinion of Joyce was unenthusiastic.

His first broadcast introduction stated Amery was 'speaking of his own free will and at his own request. The German Government takes no responsibility for what he says.' But, as an émigré anti-Semite with fascist leanings, his presentation sounded perfectly placed, despite the fact he sounded like a bundle of nerves:

> Listeners will wonder what an Englishman is doing on the German radio tonight. You can imagine that, before taking this step, I had hoped that someone better qualified than I would come forward. I dared to believe that some way of common sense, some appreciation of our priceless civilisation, would guide the councils of Mr Churchill's Government. Unfortunately, this has not been the case. Not only the priceless heritage of our fathers, of our Empire builders, is being thrown away in war which serves no British interests, but our alliance with the Soviets – what is that, really? Is it not an alliance with a people whose leader, Stalin, dreams of nothing but the destruction of that heritage?
>
> Morally, this is a stain on our honour. Practically, it can only lead, sooner or later, to disaster and Communism in Britain, to the disintegration of all the values we cherish most. I appeal to you tonight to use your common sense, to see through the propaganda with which such a small group of people try to blind you.

Amery added 'between you and peace stand only the Jew, the Bolshevik and the American Government. There can no longer be British victory.' In one respect, Joyce's life was made a little easier, as the focus was diverted to the toxic utterances of the wayward aristocrat who seemed to relish flirting dangerously with treachery, but his sense of satisfaction, though, would not last long.

20

1943

William Joyce loved to quote – from memory – long verses of Yeats, his favourite poet, or certain lines from the Greek classics. Although he had no particular expertise, his grasp of the military situation shaping the war was just as impressive. As 1943 got underway, Joyce sketched out the four fundamental factors in play, all of which led to anxiety. The first: a humiliating German retreat in North Africa had left Italy exposed to the Allies. Secondly, the ferocious RAF bombing campaign was reducing cities across the Reich to rubble. Third, a critical manpower shortage eroded arms production, and fourth, the perilous situation facing the Wehrmacht in Russia which was being stunned by the ferocity of resistance.

On New Year's Eve 1942, as Allied bombers rumbled above, Deutschlandsender fell silent just as Goebbels' annual address had begun. The roar of explosions and the staccato of flak fire sent radio staff racing to the basement. Targets in Lubeck, Köln and Rostock also felt the weight of the RAF's arm, while Turin, Milan, and Naples shared similar experiences. When his oration resumed, Goebbels asked listeners to display tough endurance and 'stake all' for the Fatherland: 'Whether we like it or not, we are forced to hold out till the victorious conclusion of the war.' His speech opened the tireless repetition of three new key themes spearheading propaganda that winter. Firstly, the war was forced upon the German people. Secondly, the war was a matter of life and death and, thirdly, the country needed to adopt a 'total war' effort. [1]

> What was a few years ago merely a question of courage and national enthusiasm has now become a matter of toughness and moral endurance, and on this, the enemy has pinned his hopes. He thinks we may be equal to a long war as regards material things, but not spiritually. He will be disappointed in this supposition.

Morale assessments originating from the nib of Goebbels' pen hardly constituted an accurate barometer of the national mood. Publicly, he batted away assurances that 'not one symptom of grave internal weakness on the home front had been recorded', while in private, he expressed concern that Rhinelanders were getting weak-kneed: 'This is understandable,' he conceded to his diary, 'for months the working population has had to go into air-raid shelters night after night, and when they leave they see a part of their city going up in flames and smoke.'

An immediate measure was to exercise greater restraint when reporting air raids on radio newscasts, fearful that bombing reports encouraged the RAF. The reality though was that 'shelter life' had assumed a regular form as the public spent more time barricaded in basements. More worryingly, the number of civilians killed and maimed by bombs had assumed significant proportions.

In a half-hearted attempt to play down the situation, William Joyce claimed 'there was not even any excitement', when taking a tour of Berlin after a raid. 'There was just a grim and purposeful recognition of the fact that these attacks on civilians will be avenged.' Corporal Francis Paul Maton, a POW working at the Concordia outfit, was surprised by the amount of courage Joyce showed during some of the worst raids: 'While most of us were shivering down in air raid shelters he stood alone on the top of the Reichssportfeld making a recording of the raid.'[2]

Behind the brave theatrics, seesaw fortunes and increased nostalgia for home were leading Joyce into alcohol problems, which would stymie his once-popular nightly dramas. Occasionally, when circumstances allowed, he snuck out of the capital and pitched up in a village or town on the outskirts and lived for a few days undisturbed. Occasional relief came during recordings at POW camps, which were proving a rich source of material, as well as an inducement for British listeners. Eduard Dietz fostered the policy of trying to persuade Allied troops in prison camps to broadcast or send messages – his work paid off, resulting in a whole gamut of content ranging from simple dedications to full-blown POW variety concerts staged in Stalag barrack huts.

After hearing one such offering over the Hamburg transmitter, a British journalist remarked, 'the show might well have been taken for a BBC production'. The songs – humorous and sentimental and all in English – were interspersed with dance numbers by a jazz band and applause. The organiser was described as Henry Mollison, 'the well-known film actor'. Another reporter tipped his hat to a cabaret staged by British officers:[3]

> He paid glowing tribute to the men of the cast, not only for the excellence of the presentation, but also for the ingenuity they had displayed, and the time and patience they had devoted to the play. He referred to the members of the cast by name, some of them being the sons of distinguished personages.[4]

Using an outside broadcast van containing a disc-recorder, two-channel mixer and ribbon microphone, roving reporters from the show *On the Spot* visited POW camps in Italy to meet British soldiers. One of them, Frank Burton, was thrilled to be handed the microphone: 'Hello, mum!' he shouted, 'hope you are listening to this broadcast! I am OK and safe, and being treated all right.'[5] On the other side of Europe, personal greetings (all of which were similar in tone and content) were taped for broadcast and weaved between a selection of tango, rumba and jazz records. Royal Navy officer Reginald Ivor Oakes was clearly moved when invited to send a message to his young wife: 'Hullo, darling. I am really in Germany. I am quite well and not injured at all. I hope you are all right. Hope you get on all right and that the new baby is well. Keep heart until I come home. It won't be very long.'[6] A memorable contribution came from Pilot Officer Colin Shaw Hodgkinson, who, having lost both legs, was inspired by the deeds of Wing Commander Douglas Bader and succeeded in becoming a Spitfire pilot. The first announcement that he had been captured came with a message over the Hamburg transmitter: 'Dear Mum, – Sorry to give you so much anxiety. This is to say I am OK and well looked after. – Love, Colin.'

As British POWs shrugged off their predicament with a smile, Germans were beginning to feel the strain. That winter, Hitler mobilised all men aged 16 to 65, and women aged 17 to 45 years old for defence purposes. Long-held beliefs that a woman's role was as a 'mother and housewife' – which had long been the raison d'être of daytime radio – were abandoned. To hammer home Hitler's call, the Labour Front leader Robert Ley was wheeled into the Haus Des Rundfunks to enlighten the nation. Given his supply of traditional Nazi cohorts – white, male, Caucasian 16 to 35-year-olds – were no longer available, Ley demanded 'every man capable must carry a weapon and every healthy woman must help forge the weapons needed by her soldiers'.[7] For a country which had spent a decade striving for Aryan purity, its ethnic make-up was in flux, as foreigners poured in to plug manpower gaps. In a bout of self-reassurance Douglas Chandler, speaking on the US Zone, claimed the Allies had started a whispering campaign that Germany was prepared to discuss terms:

> This is no café rumour, but was started by good old Reuter. A five-day tour through bombed areas of the Reich convinced me of the people's continued solidarity. The Winter Help Collection was nearly 100 per cent up on last year's total. The rumourmongers must have failed to take into account the Special Communiqués with their combined total of over 200,000 tons of shipping sunk. To Roosevelt's war cry of 'Unconditional Surrender' Germany's answer is 'Total War'.[8]

In the wake of the mobilisation, radio began reducing sports bulletins, while football matches and inter-city tournaments were cancelled. Concurrently, tennis, swimming and golf and most other sports were ignored by the press. Furthermore, a solution was needed to revamp the daily 13.00 *Sonderanmeldung* which usually trumpeted news of U-boat successes against Allied shipping[9] but given the circumstances, Goebbels felt they had become irrelevant. Then, with no realistic prospect of securing raw materials (and little demand), Goebbels read with outraged surprise that production of his famous cut-priced Volksempfänger was to be discontinued.

In any case, Goebbels seldom neglected an opportunity to demonstrate his ability to adapt. He ordered news and commentaries replace entertainment on the Kurzwellensender and, for the first time, Chinese news bulletins (which had been proposed by the Foreign Office in 1941) were cobbled together by two announcers, a producer and a clerical assistant, with a similar effort aimed at Japan following soon after.

There were changes afoot at the South American service too, where half-hourly newscasts replaced propaganda, anti-Jewish talks and lectures on non-war-related topics.[10] Concerned about their effectiveness, Goebbels toyed with the idea of eliminating commentaries from the European and American service in favour of straight news. He was dubious of the need for 'tedious' talks, reckoning he could 'compel the collaborators in our foreign radio services to increase our stock of news'.

Surprisingly, despite the obstacles and upheavals, the Kurzwellensender expanded during 1943 with productions in 31 languages to Europe, the Americas, Africa and Orient as well as to overseas Germans, totalling 228 daily transmission hours.[11] In an added sign of productivity, there were few relays of domestic services and only a handful of repeats (see Appendix F).

Meanwhile, from across the Channel, the BBC mounted an intense counter-broadcasting campaign at Germany, unleashing 20 daily transmissions along with relays of *America Calling Europe* and news in slow Morse, which, according to an editor, 'was harder to jam and excellent for the editors of underground newspapers and news letters on the Continent'. The year began with German prisoners of war in Britain being allowed to broadcast direct personal messages to their relatives on Christmas Eve and Christmas Day. On top of that, features for the Luftwaffe, Navy and Army played alongside general interest talks and expert commentaries. Moreover, 12 daily transmissions beamed at Italy, as well as a relay of *America Calling Italy*. The differences between the output of the BBC and RRG were stark. Whereas, the organisation of National Socialist broadcasting revolved around working on the 'leader principle', the democratic structures of the British propaganda gave BBC employees greater individual freedom and left more room for creativity.

But there were some similarities. The BBC, like the services from Hamburg, mentioned the names of prisoners of war and, to gain a hold on hearts and minds, arranged a weekly Lutheran service, which, given the suppression of religion in Germany, gained a vast audience. For many listeners, such offerings were perceived not just as a radio programme but as a gesture of moral support.

Erika Mann, the eldest daughter of Thomas Mann, occasionally appeared in front of the BBC microphone, as did Austrian actor Martin Miller, famed for his hilarious Hitler parodies. English language courses presented by Sefton Delmer, who at the outbreak of the war was a professor of English literature in Berlin, won a following, given his edgy humour and wit:

You probably know that we Englishmen are known for not being able to learn foreign languages. That's why it will be best if you learn some useful English expressions before you visit us.
As the topic of our first lesson, we choose: The channel crossing ... the channel crossing. Now please repeat after me:

The boat is sinking ... the boat is sinking.
The water is cold ... the water is cold.
Very cold ... very cold.
And now you should learn a verb that will be very useful to you. So please repeat:
I'm burning ... I burn.
You're burning ... you burn.
He's burning ... he burns.
We burn ... we burn.
You are burning ... you are burning.
They burn ... they burn.
And now I would like to suggest another sentence for you to memorise: The SS-Sturmbannführer burns pretty well ...The SS-Captain is burning quite nicely!

21

STALINGRAD

In Russia, the campaign at Stalingrad continued to unravel as dwindling resources, artillery bombardments and the brutal winter took its toll. The 6th Army had been surrounded, starving and dying since the previous November, as the city became a vast graveyard for Wehrmacht troops left rotting in the very earth they had wanted to enslave.

In many ways, the public back home – although knowing the situation was fragile – were kept in the dark as to the extent of the unfolding catastrophe. But when phrases like 'heroic commitment', 'unyielding perseverance', and 'heroic defence' began filling the airwaves in mid-January, a clearer picture emerged. 'Goebbels is breaking it to them a little less gently day by day,' a British journalist observed. A military communiqué broadcast over Deutschlandsender on 24 January made the critical admission 'that the situation at Stalingrad had become more serious because of major enemy forces breaking in from the west'. 'Nevertheless,' it added, 'the defenders of Stalingrad in the best German military tradition, still hold a circle around the city which is continuously being narrowed. By their heroism, they have pinned down strong enemy forces for several months.'

On 30 January, Friedrich Paulus, the commander of the 6th Army in Stalingrad, was promoted by Hitler to the rank of Field Marshal. The point being that no German of that rank had ever surrendered; Hitler banked on Paulus either fighting to the bitter end or committing suicide, but as it turned out, he chose to surrender.

On that same day, Herman Goring tallied the cost using Deutschlandsender to usher in the final act: 'From generals to the last man, everyone is playing a unique part. With unflagging courage, and yet exhausted, they fight against a mighty superiority for every block, every stone, every hole, every ditch.' The longer his bleak assessment went on, the clearer it became Stalingrad was lost. It was against this background that on 3 February, the calamity ended as 90,000 Wehrmacht troops, including Paulus, his generals and thousands of officers, trudged off into captivity.

Back in Berlin, the duty announcer at the Haus Des Rundfunks was poring over a mercifully short communiqué, weighing every word. Eventually, taking his place behind the microphone – he announced:

From the Führer's Headquarters.
3 February 1943.
The High Command of the Wehrmacht announces the battle for Stalingrad has ended. The Sixth Army, under the exemplary leadership of Marshal Paulus, true to its oath to fight to the last breath, has succumbed to the enemy's superiority and unfavourable circumstances.

The message was repeated three times, before 'Ich hatt' einen Kameraden', a march customarily heard at military funerals was played. The nation was stunned.

That evening, as the sun was beginning to set, Deutschlandsender went off the air – from 19.25 to 20.00 and from 20.45 for the rest of the night – not as a mark of respect for the fallen, but due to RAF action over Berlin.

Once the British fliers had gone, William Joyce emerged from the shelter on the Adolf Hitler-Platz and attempted to disguise the hollowness of his mission by tackling the debacle in Russia. On *Germany Calling*, he insisted it would be a profound, 'cardinal error to suppose the German nation does not know how to take one defeat after so many victories'. Furthermore, fortified by schnapps, he triumphantly declared his battle against the 'Russian menace' would rage on from behind the microphone. A talk on the same grand theme was in full swing in the adjoining studio from where Francis Stuart, speaking on the Irland-Redaktion, poignantly declared Stalingrad had moved Germany more than any other event, 'for while such victories as the fall of Paris might be attributed to the perfection of the German war machine, this is a triumph of flesh and blood'.[1]

Goebbels sent an order to editors that 'henceforward the heroic struggle of Stalingrad will become the greatest epic of German history'. With that in mind, Deutschlandsender stopped transmission for 60 seconds the following morning as the nation joined in 'silent contemplation to enable the soul of the living warriors in Christianity's fight to stand in symbolic contact' with those who had paid the supreme price at Stalingrad.

Two days later, radio's foremost military commentator, Kurt Dittmar, gave an unusually frank assessment: 'For the first time an entire German army has ceased to exist,' he said sombrely on Deutschlandsender:

> What we used to inflict on others has happened to us. We have been encircled; attacked from all directions, compressed into a narrow space and split up into pockets. It is still difficult to realise. We feel it like a sharp physical pain. Three years of unparalleled victories lie behind us.
>
> We must form a new estimate of our Soviet enemy. Perhaps we have judged him too much by Western standards and have not realised how sudden can be the transition from disorderly flight to furious counterattack.[2]

Stalingrad marked the turning point of the Second World War as the struggle for national survival began. From then on, hopes of German victory on the Eastern Front or, indeed, in the wider conflict, faded. With declining fortunes in Russia, Ribbentrop's Radio Metropol abandoned shows in Uzbek, Tatar, Russian and Ukrainian and began focusing more on English, French, Polish and Persian programming directed towards Africa, the Middle East and Iran. RAF Warrant Officer Raymond David Hughes, a POW, was despatched to Radio Metropol where Margaret Joyce and Eduard Dietze lectured him for two or three hours on how to speak into the microphone. 'They all insisted on me making a record, and I eventually made one.' Hughes did nothing at Radio Metropol for a month and then started announcing musical records, 'speaking a few words in some small plays, one of which was *The case of Mr Ramsbottom*, which I had written, having heard it two or three times on the radio'. Hughes broadcast under the name Raymond Sharpies, 'Raymond being my proper Christian name and Sharpies is a family name':

> After I had been there for a time, I told them I spoke Welsh, and as there were Welsh regiments in Italy and Africa I suggested that I should do broadcasts in Welsh. I wrote a script with the Welsh National Anthem, 'Land of Our Fathers', then I gave an address which included the Lord's Prayer. At Radio Metropol my salary was 600 marks a month, but I only drew 400, the remainder going in taxes. I was paid extra for broadcasts I made and also for scripts I wrote, according to the value placed on them.[3]

Henry William Wicks, another Radio Metropol veteran – described in court files as an insurance manager with no fixed address – told prosecutors after the war how he wrote commentaries, produced plays, and on one occasion, took part in a fake interview with Winston Churchill.

Like Metropol, the US Zone of the RRG also began turning its attention toward Africa. That winter, Otto Koischwitz was on top form, dispensing advice to Allied soldiers: 'When you get back home,' he told Allied troops, 'you'll have a tough time finding a job. And if you get home without a leg or an arm you will have an even tougher time. Your heroism and patriotism won't count for a thing. As a matter of fact, it doesn't count for much even now... so think before you risk the loss of a leg or an arm. Better be a coward for a few minutes than a cripple the rest of your life.'[4]

Ironically, just when genuine news was needed most, it became more elusive. That combined with a rise in air-raid warnings and proliferation of information designed to deceive, led to a general exhaustion with radio itself. Unsurprisingly, enraged by the Nazis' failure to report accurate news, security services noted an up-tick in 'black-listening'. Teenager Alfred Müller from Könnern

Beesedau, a small village north of Leipzig, recalled his father had stopped paying attention to RRG news about a year earlier:

> He did not doubt banned foreign broadcasters provided truthful coverage. Most of the time we heard BBC London at 20:00, it began with the four droning beats on shortwave. Likewise, we could hear the Voice of America just as well. I still have the theme tune of that time in my ears. We also received Radio Moscow and we knew the transmission times in German. From Moscow, we learned about the founding of the National Committee 'Free Germany'. I remember hearing a speech by the captured German General Walter von Seydlitz.[5]

In a wildly understated personal admission, Goebbels accepted the obscure Nazi news policy had given the public scant insight into the war: 'Our reticence regarding Stalingrad and the fate of our missing soldiers there naturally leads the families to listen to Bolshevik radio stations, as these always broadcast the names of German soldiers reported as prisoners,' he confided to his diary.

He was right. Given the paucity of news on German channels, Radio Moscow had been accurately predicting a messy outcome at Stalingrad since the previous autumn. 'From dawn to dusk the air is filled with the drone of engines,' the Moscow evening news reported on Thursday 17 September 1942. 'Air combat goes on practically unceasingly. Fighters in dozens swoop over the battlefield, while Messerschmitts and bombers crash in flames.' Soon after, bulletins focused on Soviet troops driving a wedge into German positions north-west of Stalingrad. Then on 8 October, Radio Moscow described how Soviets were 'persistently and methodically' breaking up the enemy's defences. By 19 January, the Russian Army was 'steadily narrowing its ring of death around the remnants' of General Paulus's trapped army.

In addition to news coverage, Radio Moscow spearheaded the fears of the German public at any given opportunity and became very adept at it. The station saw its main task as 'exposing the criminal character of the Hitler regime and its aggressive actions', as well as disseminating instructions for resistance fighters in Germany and calls for an internal uprising. Exiled communist politician Walter Ulbricht – who, in later times served as leader of the German Democratic Republic – delivered talks with thunderous fervour. He specialised in urging German women to hide their sons and for soldiers to 'turn arms against their tormentors'. His popularity, however, was not only achieved by zapping public morale; he gave credible and timely news reports, especially, as seen, during the Stalingrad debacle. Occasionally, Ulbricht was joined on air by former Reichstag members Wilhelm Pieck and Wilhelm Florin, where, between them, they faced off in dissecting the Nazis and their allies. Between 1933 and 1945, almost all the important communist emigrants to the Soviet Union wrote scripts at Radio Moscow's German-language editorial office in the 'All-Union Radio' building in central Moscow.[6] Important meetings at the level of the national communist parties usually took place in the 'Hotel Lux', where hundreds of exiles were housed including Ulbricht. For the most part, senior Radio Moscow editors were partially exempt from censorship, while official news and background material arrived from the TASS news agency and Sovinform. A few editors received radio interception reports and intelligence from the secret services in addition to growing quantities of captured German documents and field post letters. Furthermore, Radio Moscow had access to German and international press from Soviet embassies abroad. The station – relayed from Kiev, Odessa, Sverdlovsk, Leningrad, Minsk, Kuibyshev and Ufa – opened each evening with the call, 'Proletarians of all countries unite! Here is Radio Moscow in German!' After 1942, the sign on was modified to 'Death to the German occupiers! Here is Radio Moscow in German!' At the beginning of transmissions, the German version of the 'Internationale' was played in its entirety along with the chimes of the Kremlin Church.

Despite the formidable opposition, Goebbels' faith in his own anti-Bolshevik propaganda – which stoked public fear of 'barbaric Bolsheviks' and Mongol hordes of Reds – was, he reckoned, 'the best horse we have in the stable'. Shortly after Stalingrad, Lieutenant-General Andrey Andreyevitch Vlasov, a prisoner captured during the siege of Leningrad, lent colour to the roster of willing radio recruits, making his debut with a call for Russian soldiers to desert their posts. It is not clear how many broadcasts Vlasov made, but he was actively involved in covering the German discovery of 11,000 corpses' in Polish uniforms at Katyn, near

Smolensk, that had been captured during the Soviet advance into Eastern Poland in September 1939 and massacred by the Russians. With Poland back in the news, US Zone commentator Douglas Chandler was dispatched to Krakow to look at conditions. In true form, he couldn't resist yammering on about the 'progress every town experiences as soon as it is rid of the contaminating influence of the International Jews'.

> Krakow's ghetto is today free of Jews, its former inhabitants being removed to the Polish Jewish Settlement of Lublin. I found plenty of good food in the restaurants at prices which were just about the same as in the German Reich. Eggs were the special treat. After the very strict egg rationing in Berlin, I smacked my lips over the portion of six scrambled eggs at my first breakfast.[7]

The so-called 'Jewish threat' was also wheeled out at the Sportpalast on 18 February when Goebbels delivered a battle call for 'total war' with the message that Germany faced a 'new realism'. As the Party faithful trooped into the arena, the doors were bolted at 16:30 to stop overcrowding. The building was stuffed to the last seat with soldiers on leave, 'popular intellectuals' and actors including Heinrich George, whose compliant reactions were caught on film. Albert Speer sat in the front row, while Goebbels' wife Magda and two eldest daughters, Helga and Hilde, were seated to his left. The speaker's platform was decorated with two swastika flags and dangling from the balustrade a banner read, 'Total War – Shortest War'.

That afternoon, Goebbels took no chances of being disturbed by a mischievous RAF raid, so the event was recorded at teatime and broadcast at 20.15. In a simple piece of bluffery, the radio announcer described the scene that night as if reporting live, before playing Goebbels bravura performance:

> The great heroic sacrifice that our soldiers have made at Stalingrad has become of outstanding historic importance for the whole of the Eastern front. It has not been in vain. Why? The future will show. There is no time for fruitless discussions. We have got to act, and without delay, quickly and thoroughly, as has always been the National Socialist way.

Playing to a Nazi tribe desperate to hear fantasies in defiance of all the evidence, he gave creative reasoning to justify Stalingrad as 'the great alarm call of fate to the German nation', claiming 'behind the advancing Soviet divisions, we can already see the Jewish liquidation commandos':

> Two thousand years of Western civilisation are in danger. European countries, Great Britain included, claim to be strong enough to oppose the Bolshevisation of the European continent in good time and with good effect. Such a claim is childish. Should the strongest military power in the world not be able to break the Bolshevik danger, who else would have the strength to do it?

Then, in a final, desperate plea – with perspiration running down his brow – he made a pronouncement that became infamous, when he asked the audience a set of questions:

> Do you believe with the Führer and us in the final total victory of the German people?
> Are you and the German people willing to work, if the Führer orders, 10, 12 and if necessary 14 hours a day and to give everything for victory?
> Do you want total war?
> If necessary, do you want a war more total and radical than anything that we can even imagine today?

In what looked like a collective meltdown, 15,000 audience members jumped up from their seats screaming, 'Yes!' Deutschlandsender extended coverage to let listeners share in the 'euphoric mood'. Josepha von Koskull, who, with her roommate Frau Schramm, 'heard the crowd roar from the small radio, but we were not thrilled, but horrified! We wondered what the enthusiastic crowd might think when Goebbels spoke of working 'ten, twelve and, if necessary, fourteen to 16 hours a day'. Frau Schramm then chipped in: '... and the other 8 hours we sit in the cellar'.[8] The following morning, police intelligence reports noted some listeners had 'just now become aware of the terrible seriousness of the situation. They are extremely shaken but they have not abandoned hope.'

22

THE SHOW GOES ON

Despite the setbacks, radio propaganda continued to insist victory was assured as leading Nazis, including Hitler's Press Secretary Otto Dietrich, were instructed to dramatise the dangers of Bolshevism. Incessant talk of the 'Russian threat' also acted as a distraction from military problems in Tunisia and the crumbling submarine warfare effort.

In another elaborately publicised ploy to divert attention, commentaries began assuring an Allied invasion of the Continent was doomed to failure. Not a day passed without listeners being told the Atlantic Wall – 6,000 km of coastal fortifications stretching from France to Scandinavia – was impregnable.

The campaign followed a prescribed format that grew during April as the net tightened around the last Axis forces in North Africa, which surrendered with the fall of Tunis in May.[1] Accordingly, Deutschlandsender spun the line that British victory came due to 'arms superiority', while Hans Fritzsche argued 'our main success was that owing to the German resistance in North Africa we were able to pass through the danger in the East last winter'. In the days to come, other commentators maintained the war 'would never be decided in Africa'. The humiliation was completed when a regular Sunday wireless feature, *Rommel is Rumbling On* – tailored for the German forces in the desert – was axed without warning. While the combat fighting ended, the radio war continued. Mildred Gillars from the US Zone was awarded a new show, *Home Sweet Home*, to drain the morale of US troops in North Africa: 'While you are over in French North Africa fighting for Franklin D. Roosevelt and all his Jewish cohorts, I do hope that way back in your home town nobody will be making eyes at honey.'[2] These efforts, with other relentless clumsy propaganda, continued for the rest of the year:

Well, boys, I guess all of you have felt the same about some girl. Well, you've parted now, and you may dislike my repeating this to you, but it's the truth, especially if you boys get all mutilated and do not return in one piece. I think then you'll have a pretty tough time with your girl. Any girl likes to have her man in one piece, so I think, in any case, you've got a pretty hard future ahead of you.[3]

In these broadcasts, Gillars was referred to either as 'Midge' or as 'Axis Sally'. Her selections of songs were aptly woven into her remarks by way of emphasising the loneliness and discomfort of the soldier's life and the recollection of all the good things that they were missing back home. 'In such comments,' US monitors noted, 'the subject cleverly exercised all of her powers of bitter-sweet sentiment, nostalgia, and insidious intimacy':

It was her special pleasure to hammer away at the theme that the war was bound to be a long one; that the fate in store for most of the soldiers was to be killed, wounded or taken prisoner; that there was little likelihood that the soldiers' sweethearts would be content to wait out a long war.[4]

Gillars, like Eduard Dietz, made frequent visits to prisoner of war camps accompanied by technicians, and portable recording equipment to solicit prisoners to speak brief messages to their families in America.

Over at the Haus Des Rundfunks, amid the roar of sea shanties on *Ankerspill* there was no mention of German submarines fleeing the Atlantic to avoid new Allied anti-sub tactics which had sent 43 U-boats to the ocean floor, leaving countless heartbroken families back in the Reich. By this point, German sailors were

receiving a dose of misery via the Deutscher Kurzwellensender
Atlantik, a new subversive effort dreamed up by the British
Political Warfare Executive, with the Admiralty and Sefton
Delmar. It aimed to 'undermine the morale of the German forces
in Western Europe and U-boat crews in the Atlantic by unsettling
their faith in their arms and equipment and in their leaders, by
rationalising bad discipline and performance of military duty, and
wherever possible by encouraging actual desertion'.

Broadcast over massive shortwave transmitters in
Crowborough on the 30-, 38- and 49-metre bands, it always
opened with the words, 'This is the German shortwave
broadcaster Atlantic. In all of our programmes, we bring you
news from the front, news from home and from all over the
world. And, in between, we always have the latest popular music
for you.' A British Political Warfare Executive (PWE) report
disclosed prisoners of war had paid tribute to the quality and
popularity of Atlantik:

> Several have expressed admiration for the cleverness of its use
> of cover; some saying that if an officer entered the room during
> an Atlantik news bulletin, listeners were able to prove that they
> sincerely believed it to be an ordinary German station.
>
> Reception is good in the Mediterranean, with no jamming,
> and in the Atlantic, the station can usually be heard well, though
> jamming is strong in certain areas. There is also evidence that the
> station can be heard fairly well as far away as Salvador, 5,000
> miles from Europe, while its popularity in Sweden and Switzerland
> suggests that it can easily be listened to on ordinary sets both in
> Northern and in Central Europe.
>
> News bulletins consist of reports from the front, from inside
> Germany and from Germany's allies, together with items of special
> interest to servicemen, and they include information taken straight
> from the official German news agencies as well as material slightly
> 'doctored' for subversive purposes and items which are out-and-
> out, but nevertheless plausible, inventions.[5]

The Deutscher Kurzwellensender Atlantik devoted extensive
airtime when the Italian island of Lampedusa – between Tunisia

and Sicily – surrendered to the Allies. Then, its news focused on 'total war' in the Ruhr, which arrived in the shape of massive attacks from British bombers.

Soon after, on a beautiful sharp moonlit night in May, RAF crews launched devastating raids on German dams, triggering massive floods, wrecking munitions factories and rendering thousands of people homeless. Using the 'Bouncing Bomb' technique devised by Barnes Wallis, the RAF's 617 Squadron (latterly known as the Dambusters) attempted to blast infrastructure that was impossible to destroy with conventional weapons. By the following morning, the situation was so serious that all radio stations broadcast hastily thrown together flood warnings for areas along the Rhine, Weser and Ruhr. RAF Bomber Command, listening in to Deutschlandsender on 191 kHz back at RAF High Wycombe, whooped with joy given the flood alerts confirmed their achievement.

By day's end, Goebbels – who had been watching the drama unfold – was handed a Reuters report written by a former Berlin correspondent. In it, Guy Bettany suggested the dam raids were the brainchild of a Jewish émigré in London.[6] In a fit of rage, Goebbels personally composed a news bulletin screaming the 'attempt against the dams was a crime inspired by the Jews. Like all other Jewish crimes, this one too, will find just punishment.'[7] In propaganda terms, the success of the Dambuster raid was invaluable to the British war effort when a boost was needed.

Right across Germany air defences were proving tepid as the RAF onslaught escalated over Dortmund, Essen, Bochum, Duisburg and Düsseldorf. A newspaperman in Essen observed the people of Western Germany looked 'eye-to-eye with death and the fight is made more difficult by their realising that they are condemned to passivity'. At the same time, a remarkably candid radio commentary painted a picture of the upheaval in North-Western Germany: 'Even our soldiers from the Eastern Front go silent when they see the devastation from the windows of their leave trains.' The announcer described a nightmarish chaos with civilians on the front line. 'If any region could exemplify total war, this region would,' he said, adding that during 1,365 days of war, every second or third day had seen an air-raid alarm:

Often the heaviest raids have been preceded by several smaller advance warnings interrupting the daily lives of the population. It is a population which has given soldiers for all fronts. It has had its men killed and missing in the fighting. It has had also to sacrifice the health and happiness of its children, to sacrifice cherished belongings, homes, the lives of their nearest and dearest. To these people, the war has been brought nearer than to many a soldier in the front line. Those who have not experienced the war directly will never understand the circumstances in which these dwellers of the threatened areas are living. Even soldiers from the Eastern Front bow before their spirit. One wishes that one could bring other German families here for half a day, or even for only an hour.[8]

The raids were taking a very familiar form. First, there was a pre-alert, then, about five minutes later, the main air-raid sirens went off. After that, it was a matter of minutes before bombs began falling. 'During night attacks, the bombers always came at a time when you are usually in the first deep sleep. That gnawed,' a Berliner remembered. After the all-clear, the public groped their way out of basements, muttering thanks for salvation. Witnesses recall how emerging into the street was like re-encountering another world. The dust and acrid smoke brought on asthma, bronchitis, chest weakness, and other respiratory troubles.

An RRG reporter, speaking after a raid on Düsseldorf, remarked 'a lot of courage and strength was needed to live through that night. This can be seen from the look of things and from the expression on the faces of the people gathering after overcoming the first shock of the hours of horror.'[9]

As June ebbed away, Goebbels was quoted as predicting Berlin would be the target of more enemy attacks, prompting an evacuation of children, young mothers and pensioners. To make matters worse, the housing crisis was spiralling out of control in Hamburg where 20,000 people were homeless, while in Bremen, 30 per cent of its population sought shelter in 'unfit buildings'.

As a special precaution, essential spares, transmitter tubes and archives – including recordings of Hitler's speeches – were moved from the bowels of the Haus Des Rundfunks to a potash mine, safely hidden from the RAF. Works saved included exquisite wartime performances of *Strauss conducts Strauss* with the Vienna Philharmonic, and the Dresden Opera's *Don Giovanni* conducted by Karl Elmendorff.

The beginning of the end for German radio came when Deutschlandsender transferred operations to a deep bunker opposite the Haus Des Rundfunks during raids. The structure – at the corner of Masurenallee and Soorstrasse – had been approved by Ernst Himmler, and enabled programmes to be switched from the main studios to the bunker at the flick of a switch. Built with reinforced concrete, it became known as the 'Hochbunker' and contained a control room, studio equipped with a single condenser 'Neumann bottle' microphone and a teletype machine. 'The bunker also had a special concrete ceiling of 4.5 metres and sidewalls of 2.5 metres in diameter,' announcer Richard Baier told the author in 2019. 'It was bombproof and could withstand any attack with the weapons of that time.' He remembered there being a power station, emergency generator, water treatment room, boiler room, and medical bay at a lower level. In 1943, Baier's father secured him a job as an announcer. 'Imagine that! I was 17 years old, and working on the radio in the heart of Berlin':

> Life in the bunker was largely normal for us. The various floors of the bunker had workspaces for announcers, a small orchestra and we worked without any restriction. There were also bedrooms, toilets and bathrooms, very comfortable lounges, a kitchen with a grocery store and rooms at the entrance and exit for the SS guard.[10]

Baier still has particular memories of the heavy raids, when the earth shook so violently the control panel instruments were unreadable. The blasts often shattered his sense of balance, causing giddiness. Astonishingly, even now, at the age of 93, he can still visualise his former life deep underground, where he rattled off army reports and news bulletins in a damp world 'devoid of natural light – a bleak environment'. Within minutes of a raid ending, he would be back on the air, 'as if nothing had happened':

> The bunker was only used when an air raid or other warlike events threatened our lives. It was connected to the transmission towers in the Berlin suburb of Tegel using an underground shaft system. This connection existed until the end of the war and remained intact.

Around this time, Baier recalled newscasts began detailing judgments of those caught stealing from bombed-out homes. In one such case, the death sentence was handed down to Hans Dobroszczyk, a 36-year-old factory worker arrested for having picked up a handbag from the ruins of a building, which was construed as looting. He was charged and sentenced to death that same day by a Special Court.

The Paris television station burst onto the airwaves that summer. The impressive new studios at Magic City had been soundproofed and built across a surface of 70 by 35 meters, with a raised stage, air conditioning, 3,000 Lux strong spotlights, technical areas, dressing rooms, a telephone exchange, as well as editing rooms, fast film photocopiers, offices, wardrobe, telecine area, a scenery block, a restaurant building and seats for a 300-strong audience. Initially, the station broadcast three and a half hours a day, which later went up to about five hours. As the Reich was crumbling, Kurt Hinzmann was busily shaping the look and tone of the channel, which, given the circumstances, was remarkably perky. It included light entertainment, coverage of topics specific to Paris, rudimentary education spots, sports events – including amateur boxing bouts – and features. From the outset, two announcers introduced the programmes, first in German and then in French. The station gave pride of place to its meticulously structured live musical variety shows. In one of the most infamous moments, a thoroughbred racehorse was brought into the studio for a demonstration of vaulting. After a successful routine in front of the cameras on the first floor, things went pear-shaped when the horse refused to descend the stairs – and had to be hoisted out through a window by the fire department. The amount of time, money and effort producing shows for a virtually non-existent audience was staggering.

With the war in the desert over, all eyes turned to Italy, where a combined Allied invasion of Sicily began on 10 July, with both amphibious and airborne landings. As if that wasn't bad enough, an Allied raid on Hamburg, known as Operation Gomorrah, wiped much of the city off the face of the map on 25 July. On the ground, fire and destruction left 1,500 people dead. Three nights later, the RAF returned to carry out another saturation raid, surpassing anything imaginable. Goebbels was left stunned by the raid, noting in his diary that a city of a million inhabitants had been destroyed in a manner unparalleled in history: 'We are faced with problems that are almost impossible of solution,' he observed. 'Food must be found for this population of a million. Shelter must be secured. The people must be evacuated as far as possible. They must be given clothing. In short, we are facing problems thereof which we had no conception even a few weeks ago.'

In the days after, shock about the devastation spread across the broadcasting apparatus – from the domestic home services to the overseas propaganda channels. Hetzler at Büro Concordia began seeking temporary accommodation outside the capital, while the Joyces and Eduard Dietze, by then Controller of the North-West European Service, shuttled off to the safety of Luxembourg.

The task of dealing with the connection between Berlin and the Grand Duchy fell to Edwin Schneider. 'My duties merely consisted of feeding material to Luxembourg, by landline, where it was recorded and broadcast as required,' Schneider recounted. 'This material consisted of news items and commentaries written by various people, including Baillie-Stewart and Professor Haferkorn,' he recalled. 'In the latter days, before Luxembourg finished, much of the news was broadcast from Berlin through Luxembourg, to Bremen, Friesland and Calais as hitherto, and I did some of this too.'

Since occupation, the Nazis used the Radio Luxembourg headquarters in the Villa Louvigny, a building spread throughout an old fort, with a moat and with rows of flower beds dotted about round it. An SS-unit guarded the drive that curled to the station entrance, where high double doors were ornamented with the station coat of arms. Over the coming years, vast sums of money would be spent on the villa and early visitors remember an enormous glass chandelier hanging from the ceiling and walls covered with silken panels. Mahogany furniture was upholstered in red leather and heavy draped windows gave visitors the impression they had walked into a palace. An assessment of achievements titled the 'Luxembourg broadcaster under German administration' gave glowing praise:

> The Luxembourg broadcaster, which was previously financed by English capital, was one of the largest hate broadcasters in the West before the war. When the war broke out in September 1939, it temporarily stopped broadcasting. After the invasion of German troops, the Luxembourg transmitter, which is one of the strongest in Europe with five transmission towers, was initially used as a Wehrmacht transmitter. On November 15, 1940, it was taken over by the RRG. In the period from 21 November 1940 to 31 January 1942, Luxembourg has produced 1,400 broadcasts. In the cultural-political work and the home service, particular importance has been attached to raising awareness among the Luxemburg population that they are part of the German war effort.[11]

Back in Germany, the Hamburg bombing, combined with increased raids on Berlin, turned out to be a trigger-point for the RRG, which was creaking under the strain. Amid the destruction, a British newspaper monitor asserted that German domestic news bulletins were 'degenerating into anaemic bilge', and cited a newscast on Deutschlandsender:

> It lasted exactly five minutes instead of the normal fifteen minutes. After saying that news from the Eastern front was not yet to hand, the announcer read a quotation from an obscure Bulgarian paper, obviously in Goebbels pay, on the criminality of the democracies in daring to bomb innocent German war industries. The second item was an alleged message from Teheran stating that the whole of southern Iran was in the throes of revolt against the British regime.[12]

As time went on, the material beamed to the United States became more acidic. In a broadcast to North America, the US service attacked the actor Leslie Howard, who had been killed in a plane shot down over the Bay of Biscay. Referring to him as 'Leslie Howard alias Steiner', the commentator (presumably Mr OK) said,

I do not myself like Howard, though I will admit he was better than the common run of Hollywood actors. But passing him off as an Englishman was a sheer fraud. After Howard, who are the best-known of English actors in the United States? Robert Donat and Charles Laughton both of them Jews. Probably their real names are Finkelstein and Cohen.[13]

Funnily enough, when Joyce had mentioned Howard during a broadcast in 1940, the actor wore the acknowledgement like a prized medal. 'Lord Haw-Haw paid me the honour last week of blasting me out as a perverter of the emotions,' he beamed to reporters while making *Pimpernel Smith*. 'Another Nazi said "of course, you can't rely on people like actors".'

As his empire disintegrated, Hitler took to the airwaves on 8 November for a 'grand review' of the war. A listener – dissecting the nuts and bolts of the broadcast – noted the Führer's irritation was 'concealed by defiance and forceful delivery'. He spoke about his steady nerves, his religion and his excellent relations with Party and army leaders, as well as military events. 'Also, he talked about twice as much about himself as he had a year ago,' the listener observed.

What Hitler failed to mention was the horrific air raids, which were ramped up on 22 November, when a hurricane bore down on Berlin. That evening, 764 bombers laid waste to large areas of the city centre, obliterating the Kurzwellensender headquarters at Deutschlandhaus as well as the State Opera House, National Theatre, National Gallery, Romanische Café, Charlottenburg Palace, Technical University, Hotel Bristol, Charité Hospital and the embassies of Sweden, France, Turkey and Iran. Tens of thousands of incendiary bombs ravaged whole districts. Diarist Marie Vassiltchikov was taking shelter with her father that night:

We had hardly got there when we heard the first approaching planes. They flew very low and the barking of the flak was suddenly drowned by a very different sound – that of exploding bombs, first far away and then closer and closer, until it seemed as if they were falling literally on top of us. At every crash, the house shook. The air pressure was dreadful and the noise deafening.

By this point, according to a Swedish correspondent, quarrels were continually breaking out 'among the nerve-frayed population', and plundering and petty theft became rife. The devastation prompted the Kurzwellensender to move to Königs Wusterhausen, where studios were knocked together at the Bahnhofs hotel and in the post office basement. Other radio evacuees included Charlie and His Orchestra, a propaganda band playing bastardised versions of western hits, which upped sticks and continued to play from the studios of Reichssender Stuttgart.

Although a large part of Berlin lay in ruins, RRG soldiered on as best it could. By this point, Peter Meyer, the young Rundfunkspielschar performer, was also on the move. 'I participated in the choir till 1943 when too many bombs caused us to flee Berlin to a place in the Harz Mountains of Germany.' He vividly remembered his last broadcast concert after the first bombs had fallen in Berlin. 'I doubt that any survived the war. My friend Hartwig Berlin was blown to bits by an American bomb.'

At the end of November, the 10th anniversary of the Strength through Joy organisation was commemorated with a special show that noted the purpose of the movement had adapted to the 'cultural caretaking of the bomb-battered population and our soldiers'. Ironically, just a few weeks later, an RAF raid destroyed the KdF headquarters, along with the artist index, contracts and tour plans – setting off the rapid disintegration of the organisation.

As autumn turned to winter, British monitors heard Margaret Joyce on air, waxing lyrical about the 'benevolent manner' in which Germans were governing occupied Russia and Poland. Her talk – recorded in the safety of the Radio Luxembourg studios – also touched on Germany's contributions to music and how William Caxton, the father of English printing, learnt his trade in Gutenberg and how the Victorian author Charles Dickens admired the German people, as did Carlyle.

By Christmas, Margaret and William, and Dietze, were back in Berlin announcing more anti-Communist horror tales. Brooding on his lot, William Joyce gave a memorable Christmas night performance, devoid of the humorous or sarcastic touches which had made him famous. 'I've never heard him rave so much since he started his broadcasts for the Nazis,' the correspondent of the *Wireless Whispers* column declared. During his 15-minute slot, Joyce denounced the British Conservative cabinet minister Brendan Bracken and then launched a bitter attack on General Eisenhower. In a calmer moment, he spoke soberly about the 'battle-scarred' capital of the Reich saying he was proud 'Berlin is the city of my adoption'. In response, the *Wireless Whispers* composed Joyce a sly open letter:

> William, you evidently know which way the wind is blowing, and are anxious to keep on the right side of those to whom you have played up to for four-and-a-half years. But I wouldn't be in your shoes for the whole world. The time is rapidly approaching when there'll be no further use for you by the Führer and what then? Somebody else will be waiting for you. And I repeat with greater emphasis—WHAT THEN?[14]

As the scenes grew more desperate, Brita Bager, a star announcer on the RRG Swedish service, called time. With her co-host Dagmar Cronstedt, she had gained popularity for a weekly talk show in which they chatted about topical issues in the style of 'girlfriends gossiping'.[15] Bager had also achieved notoriety after seductively inviting Spanish recruits for Russia to visit Berlin where she 'would convince them southern women have no monopoly in sex appeal'. But by late 1943 the jokes were exhausted and gossiping had turned to griping as constant upheavals prompted both women to return to Stockholm.

Once across the swirling waters of the Baltic, Bager became a busy and distracted woman. For cash, she sold her tale of woe to the North American Newspaper Alliance, complaining the German radio system had been 'scattered to all parts of the Reich by Allied air raids'. She cooked up a grim picture of conditions at the wireless network, which, she said, was 'becoming too much of a strain to follow this radio circus on its many moves back and forth across the Reich'. For added spice, Bager sarcastically noted – in a jibe at her old master – that the Allies did not respect Goebbels' broadcast schedule. 'First, we were in Berlin, then Königsberg,' she squawked. 'When danger seemed imminent that the capital could share Hamburg's fate, it was back to Berlin, or rather the suburbs when the Russians and Americans made Königsberg too uncomfortable.'[16]

A brace of well-known journalists in Sweden weren't impressed with her outpouring, which some found ethically indefensible. The *Göteborgs Handels- och Sjöfartstidning* opined the 'things this Ms Bager has to tell contain nothing of value'.[17] The public was equally cool, branding her a 'rower' (roddare), a popular expression after the debacle at Stalingrad. 'That was a reference to people who earlier had been proud Nazis,' says author Niclas Sennerteg. 'After the turning-point of the war, they started rowing across the water to the proper coast and pretended they had not cheered on Hitler.' Sennerteg discovered Bager and Cronstedt were not the only 'rowers' fleeing the sinking Swedish radio ship.

The translator Bertil Kronvall, who had married a Berlin woman, did not follow the rest of the staff to Königsberg, neither did Edvard Gernandt and Hillevi Lagergren, whose contract with the radio ceased. Also, Alexander von Strussenfeldt quit when the staff moved. To the Swedish Security police, Strussenfeldt later claimed that he certainly earned a lot of money in Germany but that there was nothing to buy with it. Then he had concluded that he, in spite of everything, would be better off in Sweden.

As 1943 drew to a close, the names of Tunis, Stalingrad, Italy, and Eastern Ukraine conjured up bitter memories for the Reich. While many people thanked God 1943 was nearly over, 1944, it seemed, was shaping up to be much worse.

23

1944

It was scarcely an auspicious beginning to 1944 when the announcer on the KWS opened its first transmission by welcoming listeners to 'January 1, 1943'. The blunder led a British paper to quip, 'Don't They Wish It Was!'

With New Year's Day falling on a Saturday, Deutschlandsender beamed cheerfulness by playing '60 colourful minutes of film, opera and entertainment', followed by Carl Millöcker's operetta *Das verwunschene Schloss*. Then, the brilliant talent of Austrian actress Auguste 'Gusti' Huber was deployed for a special hour-long edition of *Erzählt Märchen*, featuring celebrities reading children's stories. That winter, Mihail Sebastian, the Romanian novelist, was thrilled to hear the airwaves awash with music all the time. 'Yesterday, on Deutschlandsender, there was a Mozart piano concerto that I did not already know, and Haydn's Symphony No. 13, which I think I heard for the first time.'[1]

But no amount of beautiful music could disguise the lack of cheer, as the war returned to its country of origin. 'Almost anything may happen these days. The very air is pregnant with expectation,' Kurt F. Wagner, an overseas radio commentator, said in a talk on the spirit of the German Army. Wagner insisted far from being defeatist or even dispirited, German soldiers on the Eastern Front breathed 'an air of confidence and smile at the idea that the Red Army might ever get to Germany'.[2]

Wagner could hardly have failed to notice smiles were in short supply on the home front, where Allied air raids over industrial areas had laid waste to 60 per cent of the 1.6 million homes. To make matters worse, the decreasing value of money had elevated tobacco to becoming the de facto second currency. But, even in the face of such hardships, the population remained resilient as people continued to go to work and support the war effort. Radio newscasts afforded greater prominence to the work of the special 'people's court' for the sake those thinking of stepping out of line, such as Vaclev Hotovee and Werner Rossette, two 23-year-old Berliners, executed as 'enemies of the people' after being caught breaking into cellars and stealing goods stored as a precaution against bombing raids. In another incident, a mineral water manufacturer was beheaded after having been sentenced for 'disruptive talks to German soldiers'. According to a radio bulletin, the man frequented army leave canteens. At one, he 'insulted two much-decorated sergeants by minimising their deeds on the front'. Such defeatism prompted the regime to clamp down on rumour mongering among the population. A 'Whoever whispers lies!' poster campaign was rolled out, along with the slogan the 'enemy is listening', featuring a shadowy figure representing a spy eavesdropping on 'reckless babblers' in everyday situations.

Over the next months, much of Hitler's legacy in southern Europe was undone. Down in Italy, puffing on his last cigarette, PK radio reporter Lutz Koch told listeners how the British and Americans roared forward with strong infantry and armoured forces against German lines at the Anzio beachhead: 'The battle for Cassino has reached its full strength now,' he explained on 14 February. 'Three times we have recaptured a lost position and thrown the enemy out of Cassino after he had already gained a foothold. Three times, too, the enemy troops in the bridgehead had entered Aprilia and were thrown out again.' As the battles deepened, American troops reached the town centre, sparking a hurried German retreat.[3]

That same week, a PK radio reporter embedded with troops in the freezing wilderness of Russia gave a harrowing account of how 'our soldiers know that they must hang onto the last man and the last bullet until the command to retreat comes and they are put on another sector to renew their attacks'. A cold wave from the north had swept the entire Eastern Front, with the temperature falling to minus 10 degrees. Ice covered swamps, lakes and rivers:

> They dig themselves holes in the snow and frozen ground to shelter from the cold and wind. We can hear the howling of Siberian wolves.[4]

By now, this kind of dispatch had become well-trodden ground for the PK units in Russia whose correspondents – skilled in preparing victory features – now shone at composing haunting nightmarish reports.

The war Goebbels was waging in 1944 had become very different from the one he had expected to fight. Even as Deutschlandsender slipped in hints of the existence of large Luftwaffe reserves in Western Europe and quoted an Air Force spokesman as a making the dubious assertion that production of planes in Germany had never been higher, Goebbels seethed that the entire radio network was, in essence, controlled by the RAF. Compounding matters, constant power cuts across the Reich often prevented the public from tuning in when the stations were broadcasting. That winter there was an air of desperation in Berlin, which was experiencing a rise in diseases, electricity cuts, gas shutdowns, lack of fuel and the frequent failure of local transport. It was unsurprising then that Goebbels' weekly conferences, held with Fritzsche and other Propaganda Ministry officials, mostly focused on damage limitation because forward programming planning and commissioning was hardly possible anymore.

At the same time, tensions grew between Goebbels and Hadamovsky, the man who had been so crucial in moulding the RRG. In foul temper and suffering from a terrible kidney illness, Goebbels fumed his apparatchik had 'hardly been seen in the Ministry in recent months' due to travelling and writing books. 'In a lengthy interview, I sharply criticise Hadamovsky,' the minister noted to his diary. 'I unequivocally make it clear that he will either have to worry more about his job or make his office available again.' For his part, Hadamovsky had lost interest, opting to leave RRG soon after to join an SS tank unit.

Living on cheap cigarettes and wine, the grisly horrors of wartime Berlin continued to impact William Joyce, who was already reeling at news that he and other traitors who had assisted the enemy would be charged with offences against British law and brought to trial in a British court, a fact confirmed by Deputy Prime Minister Clement Attlee on 22 March. From then on, much of the attention showered upon Joyce from the British press focused on predicting his ultimate fate. Still, for all his worries, Joyce continued to grapple with the news, while being personally swallowed by events in the rapidly changing war. A hastily arranged return to Luxembourg increased his foreboding as he tried to reverse a growing impression of German weakness.

24

D-DAY

Talk of the oncoming Allied invasion became increasingly common during the early part of 1944. After months of guesswork, wishful thinking and misguided speculation, German radio reported on 25 April that Erwin Rommel, the one-time desert hero, had inspected Western defences and found the coast to be impenetrable – any attempted Allied invasion would fail.

Hans Fritzsche, who by this point was getting dog-tired of 'absolutely reliable invasion reports', spoke of streets criss-crossed with barbed-wire defences and light artillery peering dangerously from lofty barricades. Listeners were told the strongest sectors were on the Channel coast, from Holland, via Ostend and Boulogne, running towards St Valerie. Fritzsche seldom ventured away from his office, as he pecked away on his typewriter peddling the line that south-eastern and southern Europe had been transformed into an 'ever-growing state of preparedness'. He waxed lyrical that fortifications of 'monstrous proportions' had been built 'against whatever the enemy may be planning'.

At the same time, Deutschlandsender started re-popularising First World War favourites including 'The Watch on the Rhine' and 'Germany's Army Guards Against Invasion'. As a further deterrent, the US renegade Mildred Gillars directed her attention at American troops waiting for D-Day in England. On 11 May, she starred in a horror drama entitled *Vision of Invasion* intended to frighten Americans with forecasts of staggering casualties.

Operation Overlord – or D-Day – was finally launched on 6 June 1944, when 156,000 troops under the command of General Bernard Montgomery, supported by 8,000 ships and 13,000 planes, headed for France. On the eve of battle, General Eisenhower told Allied forces, 'You are about to embark upon a great crusade, toward which we have striven these many months. The eyes of the world are upon you.' As Allied troops waded into the waters off France, Deutschlandsender was quick off the mark, reporting the 'long-expected invasion had begun', before the crack of dawn. An early morning mathematics lesson was pulled for live accounts of air, sea and land engagements. As this was going on, the German station at Calais kept up a remarkable running commentary throughout the day and night with the announcer, at one point, reportedly having said, 'And now we bring music for the invasion troops.' In the skies above, the busy drone of RAF planes could be heard to 'soften up' the Germans – salvo after salvo, as the planes swooped overhead, dropping bombs and firing at machine-gun nests in the famed Atlantic Wall. At the end of the first day, more than 150,000 men, as well as 22,000 jeeps, cars and tanks, had been landed.

In Berlin, Fritzsche was jolted into the real world after being told the armada of Allied forces swamping Normandy was so enormous as to be difficult to comprehend. His reputation as a straight shooter ebbed with his assertion, 'We are calm in Germany and we know how to impose restraint on ourselves, because from now on arms must speak.' Joyce's only armaments came in the form of a bottle of brandy and handwritten script when he yammered identical platitudes in an attempt to make D-Day look like a mere setback:

On the whole, I can assure you that Germany's military position is much better than it has been for some time. The enemy in the West has been so obliging as to select the very ground upon which the German Command desired the decisive battle to be fought. Not all at once, not in every skirmish, will the accumulated strength of the German reserves manifest itself. When in due course the campaign can be assessed on the basis of established fact, the optimism which Churchill nurtured amongst his people will sink into ashes and dust. Before us lies a period in which many riddles will be solved and in which much that has been obscure will become clear.[1]

This was like a red rag to a bull as far as a journalist at the *Evening Dispatch* in London was concerned. An editorial on 7 June stated,

Joyce, alias Lord Haw-Haw, spoke last night as if the invasion is already a fiasco. He reached his zenith as a master of contemptible sarcasm. There is stupidity rather than mystery behind this German propaganda. It can only be based on an ineradicable conviction that British people don't believe their own news.

A few weeks after D-Day, during a broadcast of *Views on the News*, Eduard Dietze recited a specially composed poem, which given its style and tone, almost certainly came from the pen of William Joyce:

The Great Day

Oh, D-Day was a great day in the history of the world,
When the Allied flags of freedom were so bloodily unfurled.
The boys who did the fighting were engulfed in Hell on earth,
While the Jews at home delighting watched their stocks increase in worth.

Oh, D-Day was a grand day on the good old Stock Exchange,
For the paratroops of pockets, well outside the German range.
Like the vultures, they descended on the battlefield of gain;
By the time the day had ended, they'd made sure 'twas not in vain.

Oh, D-Day was a great day, when they gathered up the loot,
These money-grubbing Hebrews who'd never launched a 'chute,
While England's lads were dying amidst the hellish roar.
And their heroes' blood was drying on the fatal Norman shore.[2]

Despite diminishing resources and audience interest, the day after D-Day Fernsehsender Paris remained unaffected, starting programmes at 10.00 with the film *Flea in the Ear*, and in the evening running the feature *Venetian Wedding* followed by a documentary called *Baroque City Dresden*.

The atmosphere was less relaxed at Deutschlandsender where Kurt Dittmar admitted both Britons and Americans were fighting with tenacity and fierceness. 'It will, therefore, be no easy and above all, no rapidly concluded struggle with which we are faced in the west.' Huge Allied losses were recorded, with over 10,000 men killed in those first days. The ensuing Battle of Normandy resulted in Allied casualties of more than 190,000 and reduced nearly 610 towns and villages to rubble.

In response to the new situation, Radio Paris cobbled together *Siegfried Line Calling*, a propaganda effort aimed at the invading armies to give the 'latest information and news flashes about the new fighting front in France'. To lure listeners, 'the names of those boys who have been taken prisoner' were included on the broadcasts.

Not long after, Mildred Gillars was on the road visiting POW transit camps and war hospitals near Paris to record prisoners' messages, which were later incorporated into a series of programmes called *Survivors of the Invasion Front*. Her visits were evidently made very soon after the invasion, probably in June or early July 1944. When Gillars first ventured to obtain messages by roaming around POW camps she met with considerable hostility from prisoners, and was forced to change her tactics and approach. There is evidence that on later visits she described herself as a representative of the Swiss government and even made herself out to be a member of the International Red Cross so that by thus misleading the prisoners was able to secure their confidence and cooperation. She utilised the Radio Paris studios from where her audio was forwarded to Berlin for ultimate transmission, with the first programme in the series transmitted by shortwave to the USA on 1 August 1944:

Hello, America! This is Midge speaking and presenting now some of the survivors of the Invasion Front. I'm very happy to be able to present these boys to you tonight. I can just imagine how very much ... especially at this time ... you are missing them ... wondering with all your hearts what has happened to them. And they are particularly happy to be able to have this opportunity to relieve your minds as much as it is possible. First of all tonight (name obscured by US censor) of Cleveland, Ohio, is going to speak to you. Then (name obscured by US censor) calling his wife in Providence, who hopes his little boy won't beat him up too much when he gets home, (name obscured by US censor) with a message for (name obscured by US censor) as well as one for his grandmother in Ontario, California. All right, now, folks stand by for these voices ... *Survivors of the Invasion Front* speaking to America.[3]

Subsequent instalments came on Tuesday and Friday nights until sometime in October when the series was concluded.

After the initial shock of D-Day, a note of sober calm took over the domestic airwaves, but 'in the Ministries, as well as among the masses, an atmosphere of serene confidence prevails. There is no nervous expectancy here,' an announcer said in an attempt to assure listeners that life in Berlin was unmoved.

Such reports must have bemused the growing number of voices outside – and, significantly, inside – the regime who believed the war was lost, with the upshot being a daring assassination attempt on Hitler at his field headquarters near Rastenburg. On 20 July, the aristocratic Colonel Graf Claus Schenk von Stauffenberg placed a briefcase bomb in the conference room where Hitler was due to meet military brass, and then, when the conference got underway, he slipped outside just prior to the explosion.

To ensure success, Stauffenberg and other members of the internal German resistance had tampered with Operation Valkyrie – a plan designed to suppress domestic uprisings. Thus, after the assassination attempt, most army units obeying Valkyrie were unwittingly working for the conspirators.

So, at 12.42, when Hitler's headquarters was blown apart, Operation Valkyrie swung into action. Back in the capital, an unsuspecting army unit – Wehrkreiskommandos III, based at Spandau – were duped into thinking they were obeying legitimate orders when instructed to occupy the Haus Des Rundfunks. Company commander Major Friedrich Jakob was given four objectives, but only the first was part of the genuine Valkyrie operation, the three others having been added by the conspirators:

1. Occupy the radio station
2. Phone a specified telephone number when accomplished
3. End transmissions from the building
4. Establish contact with Army High Command

With the telephone call to the Army High Command, Jakob would have been further duped by being connected to 'the future head of state' General Ludwig Beck, another conspirator, who was awaiting news eagerly at the Bendlerblock, the main army headquarters in Berlin from where he planned to address the nation.

At 17.00, Jakob, accompanied by 400 men, set off from Spandau in a convoy along Heer Strasse toward Charlottenburg and the Haus Des Rundfunks. Twenty minutes later, his men replaced an SS guard unit without incident and placed machine guns and other infantry weapons on ground-floor window sills. Jakob's mission preceded apace, as troops occupied every floor, the studios and the main concert hall. 'The Company made its way into the courtyards, removed machine gun nests and seemed to be absolutely in control of the situation,' recalled RRG employee Rudolf-Günter Wagner.

Major Jakob's first order – the genuine one – was completed at 17.15 with the building secured. But lacking technical knowledge, he was forced to summon Reichsintendant Dr Heinrich Glasmeier at 17.30 to pull the plug on all output, as per his third order. So, as instructed, Glasmeier and Jakob, along with two technicians, proceeded to the main control room, where arrayed before them was a huge panel of dials, knobs and speakers. In a grand gesture, Glasmeier flicked off a few switches, dusted his hands and announced, 'Sendung ist beendet.' Jakob glanced at his watch, lit up a cigarette, thanked Glasmeier, and then marched off, relishing the near-perfect execution of his orders. But unbeknown to Jakob – and probably on the orders of Ernst Himmler – programmes continued to cough out from the concrete bunker across the street. Thus, the conspirators' plan had, in fact, already failed. At 18.45, a telex message from Hitler's headquarters piped to the bunker studio confirming the assassination attempt but noting, 'Apart from minor burns and bruises, the Führer himself suffered no injuries.'

So, just hours after 'Valkyrie' kicked into action, news of Hitler's survival spread like wildfire across the world. By 19.30, Major Jakob spoke to Goebbels himself, who gave him clear instructions: 'Accept no orders from the Bendlerblock.' Thus, the Haus Des Rundfunks remained in Nazi hands.

Later in the evening, normality returned to the radio building. 'Robert Krajewski, the canteen owner had fixed a warm soup for the crew. After midnight, with the help of a bottle of red wine that Krajewski had conjured up, we sat together with the officers of the battalion,' employee Oskar Haaf remembered. An hour later at 01.00, Hitler – clearly in an agitated state of excitement – was connected by landline from Rastenburg to the Haus Des Rundfunks for a dramatic broadcast:

> The bomb was placed by Col. Graf von Stauffenberg. It exploded two metres to my right. One of those with me has died. A number of my collaborators, very dear to me, have been very severely injured. I myself sustained only some very minor scratches. I regard this as a confirmation of the task imposed on me by Providence to continue on the road of my life as I have done hitherto.

He claimed the circle of conspirators was small and had nothing in common with the spirit of the German Wehrmacht, and above all with the German people. 'It is a miniature group of criminal elements who will be now ruthlessly exterminated.' The first news bulletin on that morning declared, 'The conspiracy against the Führer has completely collapsed.' Soon afterwards, Hans Fritzsche described the assassins and conspirators as 'sand in our war machine', which was 'being thoroughly washed away'. That evening, Joyce had some special words for his leader:

> In Germany, however, today the universal feeling is that God has protected the supreme leader of the nation, and that this protection has been given to him because he has a historic mission to fulfil. Twenty-five years ago Adolf Hitler was unknown to the world, although those about him were beginning to realise the power of his personality. (...) Remember it was Hitler that raised Germany from her agony and suffering to a new nationhood.[4]

It was around this time Richard Baier first saw William Joyce.

> He was in the atrium of the broadcasting station talking to the highest SS leader for propaganda, Gunter d'Alquen. He was the SS standard leader and, after the assassination attempt on Hitler on June 20, 1944, directed the entire war broadcast reports in the Haus Des Rundfunks.
>
> I remember Gunter d'Alquen was also the editor-in-chief of the SS newspaper *Das Schwarze Korps* and leader of the SS unit 'Kurt Eggers'. The programmes directed against England were made by Haw-Haw in the Deutschlandhaus near the broadcasting centre and therefore he was only very occasionally in the main building.

In response to the assassination attempt, a Gestapo 'Special Commission' arrested more than 600 people in connection with the plot, with the notorious 'People's Court' sentencing most of them to death. An early victim of this post-coup purge was the Seehaus listening post at Wannsee, which it transpired, much to Goebbels' satisfaction, had been a hotbed of anti-Hitler activity after all.

As a veracious armchair warrior, Goebbels thought himself by far the best tactician – and military strategist – in Germany. His final diary entries, as usual devoid of compassion, read like a campaign journal. After D-Day, he exerted his powers of 'Reich Plenipotentiary for Total Warfare' with added gusto placing the entire machinery of the State into war services. Theatres, orchestras, art academies, colleges, cabarets and cultural institutions were closed, with only cinemas exempt. Actors, singers and other artists were obliged to serve at the front or in the armaments industry, while many newspapers were merged, to free up journalists and editors for front-line duties. At the same time, the famed PK propaganda troop units were gradually being disbanded, given the rapidly shrinking size of German territory. PK reporters had suffered heavy losses in the battles that followed D-Day and Goebbels now felt the organisation had outlived its usefulness, as he pointed out in a speech to his officials:[5]

> An example: the Army propaganda. Its boss was a little Major who oversaw a battalion of correspondents and propagandists. That was at a time when our fronts spanned almost all of Europe and

there were still some joyful things to report about. Then Wedel became a Lieutenant-Colonel, a Colonel and finally a General. The organisation he directed had to grow, of course, along with his rank. This happened not because it was practically needed (to the contrary — his tasks have been shrinking along with the fronts), but because a Colonel commands a regiment and a General commands a division. So today we have a division of war correspondents — and no paper for printing their reports.[6]

Any hopes things might get better were dashed when Karl Scharping, one of Goebbels' leading political spokesmen, announced Germany was 'on the defensive and there is no getting away from the fact'. In a national broadcast, he told disbelieving listeners 'this time, however, we do not intend to let the war go to the dogs at the last moment as we did in 1918'. Adding to the gloom, propagandist Heinz Liebscher worried aloud on Deutschlandsender about how it would be useless to bury 'our heads in the sand and pretending that we are not concerned – that things are not half so bad'.

In typical style, Joyce found himself trying to salvage something from the wreckage of D-Day. Within a week of the landings, he forecast the war would be waged on new and more dangerous ground and began dropping sinister hints about a new 'secret weapon'. As it happened, the first of these mystery missiles, known as the V-1 – or Kirschkern – burst upon the world a few days later, hitting a target near London. 'The very term V-1 implies, of course, that Germany has other new weapons which have not as yet been employed against the enemy,' Joyce explained to his English listeners. '"V" is the capital letter of the German word "Vergeltung", which means "retaliation" and its use to denote the concept of victory must be familiar to nearly all of my listeners.'

In a move calculated to stir the feelings of the home front, the public in Germany were treated to films about the V-1, which took pride of place in *Wochenschau* newsreels throughout July. Over in London, Vivienne Hall noted in her diary, the new weapons came as an appalling shock to the civilian population:

God what a week! And how many more of them are we to have? After a lull, when we had hours at a stretch without flying bombs and we began to feel we had got the measure of them and that they were dying down, on Tuesday night we lay and listened to an almost continuous stream being poured over us – all night long the sky was filled with the drone of the approaching, passing, stopping engine of a flying bomb; and so it has more or less gone on through the week.[7]

In the event, however, the vengeance rockets or 'doodlebugs' were no engineering marvel and soon faded. 'The flying bombs gave him (Haw-Haw) a chance for a short come back,' a listener in Britain noted, adding there was no longer a specific line to Haw-Haw's talks: 'He could no longer use the old mixture of lies with half-truths. Wider and ever wider were his threats of defeating the Allies by destroying England, ever more grossly exaggerated became his claims as to the effects of V-I, V-2, V-3, etc.'

The V-1s disappeared from the news agenda when the press was directed to prepare the public for the possibility of the military abandoning France. On 16 August at 21.42, the Fernsehsender Paris television station politely bade goodbye to viewers and shut down, while the following morning, the Eiffel Tower transmitter was destroyed and the Magic City studios stripped of equipment. The German adventure in Paris ended 10 days later when the Second French Armoured Division liberated the city, immediately pulling the plug on Radio Paris.

Meanwhile, as Allied troops made a triumphal entry into Brussels in September, the entire Concordia effort at the Olympic Stadium hurriedly relocated into the thick stone corridors beneath the spectators' terraces as a protection from the bombing. That same month, Joyce received the Cross of War Merit for his services to Germany, while at the same time, had been pilloried for bad mouthing an air-raid warden during a testy exchange in a bomb shelter. Soon after, he was enlisted into the Volkssturm, a last-ditch self-preservation unit. Those drafted were aged between 18 and 60, prompting a foreign correspondent to remark, 'To press gang untrained, ill-equipped and in many cases crippled men like this to face the overwhelming might of the Allies is like giving an order for national suicide.' After five years of war talk, Joyce's sole measure of military notoriety came with a lesson in firing makeshift rocket launchers and marching along the Unter den Linden. As of October, all news bulletins transmitted abroad were preceded by a newly composed song, 'Volkssturm take up your rifles'.

Lieutenant Günter Heysing, a broadcaster on German forces radio, was rebuked by the Wehrmacht for inadvertently giving a rare insight into public attitudes about this pensioner army. 'Lots of people have adopted a peculiarly jocular attitude towards it,' he revealed with merciless candour.

> One hears such remarks as: 'A fine bunch of duds we are going to get now,' or 'Now boys, let's all play at Robin Hood in the forest and shout boo at the enemy'. But the men who make these swinish, drivelling remarks are mere inoffensive clowns compared to the others, the more dangerous type, who just dismiss the Volkssturm with contemptuous shrugs of the shoulder and declare that they are going off to draw up their will before it is too late.

Meanwhile the only copy of 'Lili Marlene' was thrown into a packing crate as staff at Soldatensender Belgrade took to their heels in a mad scramble back to Germany as Tito's partisans and the Soviet Army closed on the Serbian capital late in 1944. To the north, Allied forces captured the Radio Luxembourg transmitter in working order. Back in Germany, the public began muttering about the wisdom of so many German soldiers remaining in Norway, the Balkans and Italy, while at the RRG, thoughts turned to where they should base themselves, as the borders of the Third Reich continued to shrink. Compounding matters, the Allied invasion was causing a multitude of problems for industry. Steel production suffered a huge blow when a transport crisis, caused by the pre-D-Day offensive against rail centres, effectively put a stop to the movement of iron ores to the steel mills of the Saarland. The near collapse of the railway network – and the economy – also triggered a huge decline in the dispatch of coal from the Ruhr region, meaning less fuel for cooking and heating.

Allied troops reached the German frontier on 12 September, before battling their way into Aachen where most of its civilian population had already been evacuated. Over in Holland, Max Blokzijl, the Dutch quisling commentator was claiming that 'Dutch terrorists, backed by the British, are active everywhere' during a panicky broadcast on Hilversum.

After the daring Operation Market Garden – in which Allied troops dropped into the Netherlands on parachutes – a fresh propaganda station named Radio Arnhem appeared to serve these new arrivals using the talents of Helene Sensburg, a 31-year-old Canadian brunette broadcasting from Hilversum. Sensburg had been born in Germany and returned there in 1939 after a 10-year stay in England, as a result of which she had mastered the English language. Her husband, a German war captain, had been captured by the Russians, so she found a job at the RRG and was transferred to a Wehrmacht propaganda section, which gave her the task of seducing the Allies. British journalists dubbed her 'Mary of Arnhem', and during her brief career she gained notoriety as the first 'woman radio poacher', as she filled in a transmission break in the daily BBC European service. No sooner had the BBC faded out at 15.30, than the notes of Beethoven's *Fifth Symphony* and Mary's voice popped up on the same wavelength with a news bulletin in English and a hotchpotch of excerpts from the German High Command and SHAEF bulletins. A British correspondent noted,

> Mary of Arnhem tried very hard indeed to pass herself off as a BBC announcer, giving genuine British news, but as a confidence trick it is a poor piece of work. Her tone is thin and school-girlish. She is exceedingly nervous, and her greatest difficulty is beginning a sentence. To judge by her accent, she really is English, and that is why Goebbels must have thought she was good enough to take in the troops on the Western Front. The manner of presentation is typical of Haw-Haw himself.

Meanwhile, Radio Luxembourg returned to life in Allied hands as a wholly new propaganda service aimed at Germany named Radio Free Luxembourg. It commenced on 23 September with *The Frontpost* – a news programme – and *Letters That Didn't Reach Them* (*Briefe Die Sie Nicht Erreichten*); the latter production was stolen from Radio Moscow and adapted using a female announcer reading excerpts from German post captured by the Americans. Sacks of private mail were sent to producers who cultivated the emotional intensity of the programme – the powerful and deeply moving letters recorded an astonishing impact on those who heard them.

Some soldiers wrote home telling their parents of the loneliness they endured, while others cursed Hitler and the 'hopeless war', but most wrote about their desire to be reunited with loved ones. Another show, *One Minute Which Can Save Your Life*, gave a basic lesson on how to surrender. A surviving script gives more insight:

> Single soldiers or small groups should surrender by laying down their arms, helmet, and belt raising their arms and waving either a handkerchief or a leaflet. If Allied soldiers are in the immediate vicinity, they are to be hailed.

Radio Free Luxembourg paraded captured Germans in front of microphones to send emotional greetings home, assuring their families they were safe, while encouraging those still fighting to surrender. The station is also noted for a broadcasting watershed, when a recording of the execution of two German soldiers convicted for spying was transmitted, much to the horror of some listeners, who heard the click of the trigger – followed by the shot. 'When surrendering, please mention our programme,' the announcer quipped. But Radio Free Luxembourg also became a trusted news source delivering the latest headlines from Europe, with its reports often picked up by major news agencies.

A note must also be made of a lesser-known station operating secretly alongside Radio Free Luxembourg in the dead of night. The future head of CBS William S. Paley, then a colonel working for General Eisenhower, controlled Operation Annie, the code name for radio station Nachtsender 1212. When Radio Free Luxembourg signed off at night, the transmitters would be turned off, set to a different wavelength and flicked back on under the guise of Nachtsender 1212, which duped listeners by claiming to be broadcasting from within Nazi Germany and span a series of hoaxes, misleading and false information. 'Annie's objective: to win the enemy's confidence by giving him aid and comfort, the better to dupe him later,' recalled Hans H. Burger, who worked on the project.

Subtly, Annie became bolder as more and more Nazis accepted her authenticity. Soon, she appealed for help from other sectors to rescue surrounded party leaders. More men and equipment were thus lured into capture. On other occasions, Annie would innocently report 'facts' that troubled civilians. Example: the Reich's cartographical institute, said Annie, was short of maps numbered 315 to 318; they were badly needed for national defence. Why, the Germans asked themselves, did the high command need maps of Westphalia, still 300 miles inside the Reich?[8]

By December, Nazis in Vienna were in total confusion as the Russians moved up more tanks and cavalry to prepare for a mobile spearhead against Hitler's homeland. RRG staff made desperate efforts to open backup connections to Berlin in case of landlines being torn out of action. By this point, Reichssender Vienna was actively relaying Deutschlandsender alerts about enemy bombers over Reich territory. At the same time, postal communications with foreign Germans became more difficult and, in some cases, completely impossible, prompting KWS being given a new task of transmitting of personal information and messages to all continents.

As Christmas approached, the US Zone's 'Paul Revere' was experiencing good, solid, sound health, albeit sounding like a unhinged desperate man: 'With the landing of the American troops on the European Continent, I realised that the purposes for which I had made my broadcasts were in vain,' American renegade Douglas Chandler told listeners. 'I realised that perhaps my continued adherence to my course of action had been the result of coloured thinking.' What was on display was American Chandler's anger, animated by panicked fear.

By the end of 1944, over 2.7 million German soldiers had lost their lives on the Eastern Front, while in the space of a little less than a year, the Allies had driven the German Army back from the beaches of Normandy, across France, through the Low Countries and into the brick and slate wastelands of Germany.

25

SHOUTING INTO THE ABYSS

The year 1945 was the beginning of the end of the Hitler government. The mistakes and blunders had been made and the tragedy would now play out on the streets of Germany. Capturing Berlin held a strong appeal for vigorous young Russian soldiers, keen to avenge their country's humiliation at the hands of the Nazis. By the beginning of the year, Red Army units had established makeshift camps 90 kilometres from the German capital in preparation for the coming onslaught, which, when it happened, would involve more than 2.5 million soldiers and 6,000 tanks.

The vast majority of Germans, including Lieutenant Heinrich Schwich, a soldier of the old school, knew nothing of the Russian movements, or the scale of attack being planned. In any case, Schwich had no intention of letting anything undesirable happen to the Haus Des Rundfunks. Aided by 30 SS guards, 12 anti-aircraft gunners, and 450 Volkssturm conscripts, Schwich spent January cobbling together barbed-wire entanglements around the building, as well as defence posts in the studios and on the roof. Outside, opposite the Fair Grounds, his men cleared a mass of rubble and tangled telephone lines as refugees hurried toward Kantstrasse and the city centre.

'The atmosphere inside the Haus Des Rundfunks was fragile,' recalled Richard Baier. 'Morale had reached its lowest ebb.'

Deutschlandsender began sounding more like a numbing presence as it mixed gramophone records with incessant air-raid alerts warning of 'bomber formations approaching', leading the foreign press to nickname it 'achtung radio'. As all hell had been let loose in the sky, repeated alarms – sometimes at the rate of one every few minutes – indicated the course of Allied aircraft over Reich territory. It was often Richard Baier's voice that emerged from the wireless during these chilling broadcasts:

> Bomber formation is approaching North-west Germany. Other formations coming from the south are now over the Upper and Lower Danube.

> Bomber formations from the west are heading for the Berlin province of Brandenburg and other bombers from the south making towards Saxony.

> Other bombers were reported over Kassel area and flying east from Quackenbrueck and Gutersloh.[1]

The enforced passivity of being unable to strike back at the RAF spawned a popular joke: 'If you see a silver plane, it's American. A black plane is English. If you can't see anything, it's the Luftwaffe.' The joke was lost on shallow-witted Douglas Chandler, who found himself in a dismal predicament that winter. After surviving an air raid, he feigned glee to regale his listeners in America with details about a visit to the crash site of an RAF Lancaster bomber. 'On the desk beside my microphone, lies a handful of machine-gun cartridges found beside the shattered tail,' he explained in an awkward tone, adding the wreck had been plastered with blood and human hair:

> ... and a scrap of uniform with the name and address of a London army tailor, a few strands of copper wire from the timing mechanism of the bomber's motor, and three fragments of aluminium alloy from the aircraft's framework. I collected these ghastly souvenirs, not for any morbid interest, but because I felt that some of my listeners in America might care to know what

happens when an air bomber has dropped its eggs of death on a sleeping city and then has received its own death blow from the city's air defences. I have many relatives at home in the U.S.A., including three nephews of military age. One I know gained his commission before 1941 as reserve flying officer. Perhaps it had been his fate to end his joyous life as a crumpled mass.

Over in East Prussia, countless joyous lives were destroyed as citizens fled the onslaught from the Red Army. 'No one had any idea that the Soviet Army was in the neighbourhood apart from Nazi Party officials, who had all fled to safety with their families,' a distraught Swedish refugee explained, describing how six Russian tanks rolled into her town. For most Germans, Hitler's promise of a happy new life in the occupied territories ended in blind panic as the enemy came steadily closer. For men, fears of swinging on the end of a rope, or being marched into slavery, dominated every thought.

As this ghastly ordeal was going on, another struggle was playing out in central Berlin where senior Nazis praying for a retreat to the safety of Berchtesgaden watched in dismay as Hitler took up residence in a bunker underneath the ruins of his Chancellery. Only a few days before, on 14 January, Albert Speer noticed Hitler sporting a limp, violent tremble and broken voice. Although suffering from jaundice and having undergone the knife to remove a vocal cord polyp, his distress was more than physical. Sleep deprivation, stress and a cocktail of quack drugs administered by a clueless doctor exacerbated his malaise.

As Hitler's leadership quietly faded, RRG technicians opened the landline linking his subterranean command post to the Haus Des Rundfunks to carry what turned out to be his final address to the nation. Exactly 4,381 days after his radio debut, the Führer limped to the microphone at 23.00 on 30 January, the anniversary of his accession to power. It had been a day crowned with bad news, including a new Russian surge toward the Oder and battles in Pomerania, Brandenburg and East Prussia.

From the outset, he gave a dismal performance: 'Any sufferings our enemies may inflict,' Hitler said that evening, 'are nothing beside the irretrievable suffering and misery which would follow a victory by the Plutocratic Bolshevist conspiracy.' Despite exasperation, Hitler went on to blame the usual scapegoats, insisting he had no intention of abandoning his leadership: 'Only God,' he scathed, 'could absolve me from this duty.'

> In this hour, I appeal to the whole people, and above all to my old comrades and all soldiers to arm themselves with even greater and tougher spirit of resistance. I expect every German to do his duty to the last. Every fit man must stake his life and body. The sick and infirm must work to the last ounce of their strength.[2]

With defeat inevitable, few paid any notice to the plea, given the love affair – known as 'Führer liebe' – between the nation and its leader had long soured. Reuters described the 15-minute oration as one of the shortest speeches of his career, and 'certainly the gloomiest',[3] while Radio Moscow was quick to laugh off the broadcast, insisting Hitler only spoke as silence would represent a confession of complete bankruptcy: 'The times when a Hitler speech was an event are gone forever.' BUP correspondent Jack Flesicher predicted the Nazis were determined to go on with the war 'in a sort of frenzied desperation regardless of the hopelessness of their position'. According to an Associated Press radio monitor, the famous heckling ghost voice – similar to that heard a few years before – broke into the speech at intervals.

Inside the narrowing limits of the Reich, the damage and dislocation put the home front increasingly out of government control, but the fantasy world of domestic administration rolled on, divorced from reality. In one case, as a basis for future food distribution calculations, Deutschlandsender announced every pig and chicken in Germany would be counted on 3 March 'no matter to whom they belong, or where they happen to be'. Beyond that, nothing else was ever heard of the ridiculous scheme. At the same time, another commentary insisted government ministers hadn't the 'faintest intention of deserting the capital', while chapter-and-verse updates on Goebbels' workload as 'Reich Defence Commissioner' – a role in which he found adventure inspecting bomb damage and delivering pep talks to his pensioner home guard – became a daily news highlight. 'I saw Dr Goebbels this morning,' one Berlin radio commentator said in full voice. 'As always, he was wearing his grey overcoat with the fishbone pattern, grey hat and green scarf. He sets about his urgent task with the energy for which he is famous.'⁴ Mercifully, this famous energy was no longer required in the smoke-filled newsroom of *Der Angriff,* the sensation-mongering tabloid that had made his name in the early years of the Nazi 'struggle'. A sorry-looking final issue rolled off the presses in mid-February, its flimsy four pages devoid of news, analyses and readers.

When a Soviet bulletin in early February telegraphed news that Auschwitz in Upper Silesia had been captured – Allied media speculated the world would 'probably hear in a day or two whether any inmates of these camps have been liberated, or whether they have all been killed in the gas chambers and shooting yards'. As the horrors of Auschwitz were exposed, the calamitous Allied air raids increased dramatically, as did the 'achtung radio' announcements.

On 13 February, Deutschlandsender blurted out a frenzied warning of a 'bomber stream 300 miles long' striking into the German hinterland toward Dresden. That night, British and American aircraft unleashed 3,000 tons of explosives and phosphorus, killing more than 25,000 inhabitants. To make matters worse, the city's air defences had been shipped off for use in the fight against the Soviets, along with the last heavy flak battery, leaving the population with scant defence. When morning dawned, Victor Klemperer, a Jewish professor who had been keeping a record of the war, stood amid the chaos and horror: 'Building after building was a burnt-out ruin. Crowds streamed increasingly between these islands, past the corpses and smashed vehicles, up and down the Elbe, a silent agitated procession.' Along with the baroque eighteenth-century Zwinger Palace and the Semper Opera, the main RRG transmitters at the city hall – including the antenna, which stretched between city hall tower and Church of the Cross, as well as the Broadcasting House on Beuststrasse – were destroyed.

Meanwhile, as the exodus of Germans from East Prussia, and the Polish Corridor continued, the hospital ship *Wilhelm von Gustloff* keeled over during on an evacuation mission when a

Soviet torpedo struck it off the coast of Pomerania, killing 5,348 German refugees in icy waters.

Things weren't much better in Berlin, where amid the smashed walls and burning buildings, former *Chicago Tribune* reporter Donald Day was at his wit's end. Having thrown his lot in with the Nazis, his weekly talks on the RRG US Zone appeared to be going awry as he soberly blithered that homes and hotels in Berlin lacked heating and hot water, but the dominant feeling, he thought, was one of stoicism:

> Eight weeks' food coupons must last for nine weeks, and we must make-up with un-couponed vegetables. The horrors of life are enhanced by the air raids, and the need to dress in a cold room at every alert... I thought so little of Berlin had been left to bomb that these large-scale raids would cease but I was mistaken. Sleeping in a room with no windows in freezing weather is not pleasant. Life would be unendurable, but for the unostentatious heroism of everyone.[5]

As hundreds of tonnes of bombs continued to be dropped on the Reich, Hitler's forces rumbled in constant retreat, falling to pieces bit by bit. The Russians, for their part, swept over territories vital to the replenishment of the German war engine, while the Americans and British advanced to the banks of the Rhine. By 5 March, except for a small bridgehead, the entire left bank territory of the Reich was occupied by the Western Allies. Two days later, Köln fell, allowing British and American troops to cross the Rhine.

That very same week, Eugen Hadamovsky, by then an SS tank commander, was killed during a Soviet bombardment on the village of Hölkewiese in Western Pomerania. Characteristically, Deutschlandsender – the station he had spent a decade moulding – lauded his 'magnificent and invaluable' work while stating he 'died a soldier's death leading an SS company'. While Goebbels received the news with numbed indifference, he noted, 'I tell the Führer that Hadamovsky has been killed on the Eastern Front, he is deeply shocked.'

On 15 March Albert Speer told Hitler, 'German industry was bound to come to a standstill in a matter of six to eight weeks.' The prediction was more than Hitler could stand, prompting an order for the destruction of all industrial and utility facilities on Reich territory. As Speer left Hitler poring over maps, he privately vowed to destroy nothing of national value. As this was happening, the advance of the Allies continued at a frightening pace, with Koblenz conquered by a huge pocket of the US 3rd Army in mid-March, leaving the way wide open for an Allied advance into the heart of the Reich.

Fuelled by growing angst in Berlin, Erich Hetzler, the acting head of the foreign-language shortwave service, passed the order to transport studio equipment to Apen, 400 kilometres west on the Dutch border. From there, he hoped the English and Irish programmes might be able to endure a little longer. This development added to William Joyce's growing list of problems: 'Slept badly, cigarettes have given me catarrh and generally affected my health,' he confided to his diary. 'Dietz insists on our going to Apen as "anything may happen". I don't know what he expects to happen but still, I suppose he has his grounds... Margaret does not want to come, like me she values the club cellars, but they won't last long anyhow.'[6]

At the same time, the trials and tribulations of the RRG continued as another group of radio employees from the Orient and US Zones fled for Landshut, north of Munich, to continue their work from a requisitioned hotel. During the packing, frustrations flared – leading to arguments about what to take amid ever-deepening chaos. On the same day that Himmler ordered all male occupants of houses displaying white flags be shot, Joyce's diary shows he was a man thoroughly fed up with life. 'Goebbels is a genius – brilliant beyond words, but his henchmen are putrid they might be masons or in enemy pay,' he complained. 'Half of them look like yids and the other half like idiots. Maybe they are not paid enough. I don't know – anyhow they let him down to use a vulgarism.'[7]

Barry Jones, Ralph Powell and Edwin Schneider were also dispatched to Apen at the same time as Joyce, who, lubricated by the last of the wine supply, continued to complain bitterly about his predicament.[8] 'I loathe to think that these may be my last hours in Berlin, a city which I love, despite its swine and despite the heartaches it has brought me,' he lamented. 'Berlin is a composite part of my life, and I do not yield it up gladly.'[9] Several other diary entries from that week show he was almost within sight of the truth:

> I regard Apen as the last ditch. Its only merit is our tenancy of it won't last long. I find it hard to write with complete frankness, for if I did, the diary would not be very helpful if it fell into the wrong hands. But I loathe to think that these may be my last hours in Berlin.

Similar hurried departures played out across Berlin as food, medicine and fuel supplies dwindled. After an arduous journey to the wilderness of Apen, Hetzler set up studios at the drab two-storey Bremer's Hotel and hooked up to transmitters in Hamburg, Osterloog, Norden and Wilhelmshaven. Only a small antenna on the hotel roof gave a hint that something electronic was happening inside. The dining room became an office; in the lounge, tables were littered with records and scripts. In several rows of grey filing cabinets, a salvaged archive of grubby index cards recorded the names of staff, contacts and production notes, while a lone recording studio cobbled together in a first-floor suite and a live studio in the basement represented the epicentre of Hitler's foreign-language services.

Joyce's absence, due to his journey from Berlin to Apen, was duly noted by the British press: 'Haw-Haw had a bad patch one evening last week, for his *Views on the News* had to be read for him by an announcer. When he did return to the mike, a couple of nights afterwards, he seemed very subdued.'[10] The enforced migration meant from then on, daytime newscasts on shortwave were presented from Apen while evening bulletins, as well as the half-hour *Jerry Calling* programme directed at British Forces, arrived via landline from Berlin. In Joyce's corner office on the second floor, he clacked out scripts for his 22.30 transmission of *Views on the News*, while factually slipshod newscasts were read by Jones, Powell or Schneider at 17.30, 20.30 and 21.30 to a dwindling audience.

By this point, even the paper strength of the German Army had terrified General Dittmar, the familiar and resilient voice of the High Command. Although stoic in nature, he finally bowed to reality. Whist puzzling over how to end the nightmare, he asked radio listeners if there was any sense in continuing the fight, given the Rhine barrier had been overcome by the enemy:

> We cannot close our eyes to the serious threat brought about by Patton's success. Once again we are confronted with the threat of having the south of Germany severed from the north — a plan which is now being executed with the most up to date means.[11]

Dittmar's bout of clarity, or nervous hysteria, was enough to start a rumour (peddled by the Russians and foreign press) that he had committed suicide after the broadcast.

The end was closer now. On 29 March Soviet armour leapt forward crossing the former Austrian border, opening the Vienna Offensive a few days later. 'The Russians are approaching Vienna,' screamed Gauleiter Baldur von Schirach in an appeal on Reichssender Vienna. 'Everyone must now do his duty to hold Vienna – a bulwark of the south-east'.

A few days later, the same station interrupted patriotic songs to send out dramatic reports that the city was being shelled. 'Without pause, the ear-splitting gunfire goes on,' said the breathless announcer. 'Flak is flying over our heads, above St Stephens Cathedral, the Town Hall, the heavily damaged State Theatre, and the Imperial Castle of Schoenbrunn.'[12] The reports were so intense, that monitors listening in London reported hearing the battle noises, along with the rumbling of guns and the explosions of shells.

For Nazi diehards, a short-lived thrill arrived when the underground 'Werewolf movement' turned up the volume on guerrilla attacks against the Allies. Although the Nazis denied any connection with the group, the effort was coordinated and bankrolled by the SS. 'The Werewolves have emerged by themselves, and are not prepared to now bow to enemy terror,' Deutschlandsender noted.

In an effort to muscle in on the action, the ever-excitable Goebbels helped by propagandist Horst Slesina, set up 'Radio Werewolf', allegedly transmitting from 'somewhere in the enemy occupied territory', but in fact being beamed from the vast Reichspost transmitter station at Nauen in Brandenburg, west of Berlin. From the outset, the station was one of the most curious offerings ever presented to the German public; its own theme song, played at the beginning of transmissions, was equally ludicrous:

> I am so savage; I am filled with rage,
> Hoo, Hoo, Hoo,
> Lily the werewolf is my name,
> Hoo, Hoo, Hoo,
> I bite, I eat. I am not tame,
> Hoo, Hoo, Hoo,
> My werewolf teeth bite the enemy,
> And then he's done and then he's gone,
> Hoo, Hoo, Hoo.

Ostensibly, the station purported to be the standard-bearer for Werewolf activities, but in reality, it had scant contact with the organisation. Transmissions opened on 1 April with an order for Germans to stand their ground against Allied armies, 'who are preparing to enslave Germans':

> Every Bolshevik, every Englishman, every American on our soil must be a target for our movement. Any German, whatever his profession or class, who puts himself at the service of the enemy and collaborates with him, will feel the effect of our avenging hand. A single motto remains for us: 'Conquer or die'.

Allied observers easily deduced Werewolf was either a 'Himmler or Goebbels affair',[13] but initially feared it might prove a menace. To spread the message further, Deutschlandsender obligingly began quoting 'Werewolf Radio' at any given opportunity. On 1 April, it reported the group's inaugural proclamation (repeating it throughout the evening), and then on 2 April it announced the movement was 'getting more active', claiming resistance in Frankfurt began immediately after the entry of American troops. 'During that night,' the station stated, 'three high-ranking American officers were found dead in the streets of Frankfurt.'[14] The assassination of the mayor of Aachen was also attributed to the Werewolves, as were countless petty incidents, such as cutting telegraph wires and power lines. By 5 April the bubble had burst when it became clear Werewolf posed no real threat. 'Werewolf radio may make ridiculous claims to the achievements of the largely fictitious Werewolves, and a few civilians may attempt obstructionist tactics,' a leader article in the *Birmingham Mail* noted, adding, 'these are the exception rather than the rule'.[15] Early the next morning, 'Werewolf Radio' railed that resistance fighters were slowing the Allied offensive, while, at the same time, sending out increasingly fanatical messages:

We must become flame to lick and burn the enemy.
We must become dynamite to blow up the foe.
We must become poison to poison the enemies.
We must become knives to cut up the opponents.
We must continue the fight until the last enemy soldier has been driven from the Reich or the last enemy soldier has been buried in a mass grave in Germany.[16]

To ensure the nation fought to the bitter end, Werewolf used the same desperate technique to spread horrific stories of 'Bolshevik hordes' raping, pillaging and torturing captives. To complement the Werewolf rhetoric, printing presses in Berlin worked overtime printing posters urging the public to 'Stand fast. Remember Frederick the Great.' Other variations included 'German women are your loot', 'Digging will ensure victory' and 'Chatterboxes are the enemies of the brave'.

Over in Stuttgart, as unbelievable as it may seem, Charlie and His Orchestra made a heroic effort to strum propaganda jazz until 5 April, when the station was blown to smithereens by the RAF. The fate of Reichssender Stuttgart was sealed the following morning when SS troops detonated explosives at the transmitter, leaving a 5-foot-by-6-foot hole in the ground.

Six-hundred kilometres north, the tidal wave of starving and ragged refugees continued to snake into Berlin from East Prussia and the Polish Corridor seeking food and shelter, and bringing the fear of epidemics with them – pneumonia and influenza were rampant. Evacuations from the east had evolved into a chaotic flight with somewhere between 600 and 1,000 merchant vessels ferrying about 900,000 refugees and 350,000 soldiers across the

Baltic to Germany and Denmark between January and April. The once-proud radio channels at Danzig, Konigsberg and Breslau were still broadcasting on their usual wavelengths, but operations had long upped sticks to safer areas.

Against this harrowing scene, Albert Speer became the grandmaster of the macabre by assembling the Berlin Philharmonic from its nomadic existence to give one final performance. Although their instruments were in Bavaria for safe keeping, Speer found an assortment of old violins, flutes, cellos, horns and clarinets to ensure the performance could proceed. On the afternoon of 12 April, just after 17.00, the surviving ranks of the orchestra with soprano Gertrud Runge filed into the Beethoven-Saal on Köthener Strasse, opposite the ruins of the Philharmonic. Oddly, at variance with his talent, Speer found it impossible to broadcast the concert and even struggled to secure electricity to light the auditorium. With Furtwangler having fled to Switzerland, the concert was held under the baton of Robert Heger and Georg Schumann. It included the gnarly roar of Brünnhilde's last aria, the finale from Wagner's *Götterdämmerung*, and the ghostly quavers of Richard Strauss' *Death and Transfiguration*.

'It was unforgettable,' gushed Nicolaus von Below, Hitler's Adjutant. 'I sat with Speer and Admiral Doenitz and listened to Beethoven's Violin Concerto, the finale from *Gotterdammerung* and Bruckner's Romantic Symphony.' The most striking example of this desperate time came with the long-passed-on rumour that Hitler Youth members offered the audience cyanide capsules in the immediate aftermath of the performance, which, understandably, created a substantial stir.

The end was closer now. Gallows humour shone, with the 'joke du jour' being that it would soon be possible to travel by Berlin's local tram from the eastern to the western front. By mid-April virtually the whole of north-eastern Holland had been liberated, where 'Moaning Max' Blokzijl, the Dutch Nazi voice of Hilversum, was arrested on 18 April and marched into a trial for treason.[17]

The Soviets launched their final push on Berlin two days later on Hitler's 56th birthday. From this time onwards, Deutschlandsender spluttered as technicians in Königs Wusterhausen prepared for the end. Dr Richard Fischer, manager of the Berlin Electricity Company, was ordered to maintain an electric supply to Königs Wusterhausen until it was taken by the enemy. Early the next morning, feeling surplus to requirements, Hans Fritzsche dissolved the broadcasting department of the Propaganda Ministry. A few hours later in the same building, Goebbels recorded his chilling farewell speech as the sound of artillery boomed from behind the Russian lines. For those listening – and there can't have been many – he assured them that he and his staff would remain in Berlin: 'Also my wife and my children are here.' Goebbels calmly read the text, unflustered by the destruction raging outside, even when a shell blasted out the office window, as his assistant observed:

> Every one of us at least winced, the general quickly crawled under the desk, but the minister continued with his speech, undismayed as though nothing had happened. All he did was lift the page of the manuscript he was reading and shake off the powdered plaster. When we all listened to the recording, we could actually hear the explosion and the flow of Goebbels' voice, which had not changed, not even for a fraction of a second. [18]

He wrapped up by instructing Berliners to fight and make 'war without mercy ... at the walls of our city, the attack of the Mongols must and will be halted'. Unsurprisingly, Goebbels' appeal fell on deaf ears as the Russians swept into the heart of Berlin's once-bustling old town.

That same day, Albert Speer arrived at Reichssender Hamburg where technicians had set up a small recording studio in a bunker. From there, he composed a different type of speech urging an end to the destruction of infrastructure and the release of political prisoners and prisoners of war. Once mastered, the recording was passed on to Gauleiter Kaufmann with the strict instruction to broadcast it 'at the right moment', meaning preferably after the death of Hitler.

Back in the capital, Werewolf Radio was attempting to forge a population of revolutionaries:

> Together with the monuments of culture there also crumble the last obstacles separating us from the fulfilment of our

revolutionary task. Now that everything is in ruins we are forced to rebuild Europe. In the past private possessions tied us to bourgeois morality and mentality; these possessions have gone now and with them all our bourgeois restraint. Far from killing all Europeans, the bombs have only smashed the prison walls which held them captive ... In trying to destroy Europe's future; the enemy has only succeeded in smashing the past and with it, everything old and outward has gone. The crumbling of the facade of tradition has only revealed the inception of a new revolution, and all who are strong and healthy realise their task, which is that of a revolutionary.[19]

Werewolf barked that the German people would defend Berlin to the last, claiming new divisions were marching to its defence on 22 April: 'These tested units,' it boasted, 'have been ordered to intervene in the battle for Berlin and the first of them has already reached the capital periphery. There is no doubt a few days, perhaps a few hours, will decide this battle.'[20] Airtime was also devoted to the fact Hitler remained 'steadfast and resolute' in Berlin, alongside an appeal to German soldiers to follow his 'brave example':

> Hitler leads the fight from Berlin, undisturbed by the fact that the enemy already has come close to the centre of the city. You have a brave and courageous leader before you, the bravest and most courageous who ever has led German soldiers. He did not flee to south Germany, and has not left millions of Berliners in the lurch.[21]

A few hours later, the Russians overran the Nauen transmitter, pulling the plug on Radio Werewolf for good. To the north, Reichssender Hamburg picked up where Werewolf had been interrupted: 'The Führer is directing the Battle of Berlin, surrounded by military and political advisers. He himself makes the necessary decisions.' It also disclosed 'fantastic street battles' were underway on the Frankfurter Allee in north-east Berlin where Russian infantrymen advanced along rooftops and the ground. At the same time, a report claimed all railway and underground lines had been mined and could be 'blown up at a moment's notice'. A few hours later, Deutschlandsender quoted a desperate message telegraphed from Hitler to Mussolini:

> The struggle for our very existence has reached its climax. Employing vast masses of material, Bolshevism and the troops of Jewry are staking all with the object of combining their destructive forces in Germany to precipitate our Continent into chaos.[22]

The message was one of the last long-distance telegraphs to leave the bunker. Speer noted communications were 'going to pieces' as Reichspost engineers failed to patch up crumbling phone circuits, leaving Berlin virtually cut off from the world by telephone and, for the first time in the war, the Overseas News Agency fell silent, muting a vital propaganda service.

The following morning, Soviet tanks penetrated the Berlin districts of Teltow, Lichtersfelde and Mariendorf. As this was happening, British monitors listening in from afar observed 'not a sound' had been heard from Reichssender Berlin since 16.00 on the previous Sunday, which, they said, was 'conclusive proof of the chaos into which the enemy's entire broadcasting system has been thrown':

> The long list of 'dumb' stations started with the Russian offensive in January and has reached its present figure by leaps and bounds within the past week or two. It includes such names as Stuttgart, Hilversum, Leipzig, Coblenz, Breslau, and Frankfurt.[23]

The same report noted broadcast quality worsened daily and, apart from announcements, the wireless was 'probably attracting little attention from the Germans'. In the face of incredible odds, Deutschlandsender managed to put out spasmodic programmes, while 'Haw-Haw had not yet missed his nightly broadcast, although his attempts at invective become increasingly feeble'. The report also accurately stated RRG was attempting to split stations still at their disposal into three separate networks: North (which included Deutschlandsender), south-west and south-east. The plan was scuppered when Russian troops overran the transmitters at Königs Wusterhausen and Zeesen on 27 April, ending the transmissions of Deutschlandsender and many shortwave services. A Russian military communiqué relayed by Reuters confirmed the capture, meaning only the Tegel transmitter of Reichssender Berlin remained in Nazi hands in the Berlin area. 'We still had a connection from the Haus Des Rundfunks bunker,' Baier recalled. 'So, as far as things stood, we were pretty much a lone voice. But I'm not sure if people were listening.'

On 28 April, Benito Mussolini met an inglorious end when he was captured, shot and strung up by Italian partisans while trying to flee Italy. The news came as a bitter blow to Joyce, who gave an emotional broadcast:

And, for the personal point of view, if that be allowed to me, I can only say that when I joined the first Fascist movement in Britain on 6 December 1923, I saw that night in Battersea the mob violence, the Red Flags, the broken heads and the broken bodies, the typical evidence of the disruption which Communism can bring into a nation; and while I heard the dismal wail of the 'Red Flag' intoned by the men out for blood, I thought of Mussolini and of what he had been able to do for Italy. I was not pro-Italian, I was merely pro-human; there were many millions of people throughout the world at about that time who had the same thoughts; and when I look back upon these 20 years, I can only say that Mussolini has, in that period, become one of the greatest figures in history. The shades of the great Romans up to the time of Augustus, and unborn generations of Italian people, can pay homage to this great leader whose stature in time can only increase.

Meanwhile, defenders in Munich were giving no ground easily on 29 April as US troops attempted to storm through the outskirts of the city, eventually liberating Dachau concentration camp and shuttering Reichssender Munich. Over the course of the next few days, brutal street fighting near Landshut caused the Orient and US Zones to fall into disarray and their stations fade into oblivion.

While clashes still raged in the last remaining pockets of resistance outside northern ports, Reichssender Hamburg reported on 29 April the Battle of Berlin had reached its climax, while German-controlled Radio Oslo gave more detail: 'The centre of Berlin from the Zoo to the Alexanderplatz and from the Belle Alliance Platz to the Reichstag is one blazing inferno.' At the zoo, the scene was apocalyptic. Trenches had been dug across the grounds; trees were cut down to create anti-tank barriers while Russian artillery shells had killed most of the animals. The Elephant Gate became a makeshift cemetery – with a mass grave.

By now, the Russians controlled 19 city districts in Berlin, and were rolling toward Charlottenburg, where at the Haus Des Rundfunks, Werner Naumann, the state secretary at Ministry of Propaganda, descended into the bunker on Soorstrasse to press men, women and children to defend the city to their last breath. Bizarrely, as this was going on, Goebbels phoned in from Hitler's bunker at the Chancellery to order the remainder of the RRG sound archive be evacuated but was stunned to discover the Russians were just a few blocks away from the studios.

In another twist, later that day news filtered through that General Dittmar, the military commentator was, in fact, alive and very talkative in Allied captivity: 'I am absolutely convinced that Hitler's death will be followed by a total collapse of resistance within a very few days,' he told the French news service. He wasn't wrong. Albert Speer described the last days in the bunker as a bizarre mixture of hope and despair, as Hitler sat poring over maps, talking about victory and moving non-existent divisions. Late on 29 April, Soviet artillery turned its attention to the Tiergarten area near Hitler's bunker and the Propaganda Ministry. That evening, deep underground, the Führer married his long-time girlfriend Eva Braun just after midnight, before dictating his testament. Outside, withering mortar, artillery and machine-gun fire was accompanied by a street-by-street battle of terrifying small encounters.

By this point, William and Margaret Joyce, with Edwin Schneider, transferred from Apen to the Reichssender Hamburg studios, where Schneider observed Joyce at work:

Joyce used to prepare his script, sometimes assisted by Margaret. I saw him on several occasions in his office (door No. 82) typing his own script. I also saw his wife type some of it. They had two or three typewriters which had been sent from Berlin, and Joyce a small portable one of his own which he took away with him. Mr and Mrs Joyce also used one of the studios in the 'bunker' (air raid shelter) as an office and they had a typewriter there too.[24]

In Hamburg, Joyce prepared for the end. 'What a night! Drunk. Drunk. Drunk!' he recalled, before rattling off his final speech, aided by a bottle of schnapps. 'I shed tears as I left the Funkhaus. I fear I made a recording of an (indecipherable) speech. But what it was, I don't know. Well, perhaps it was best to finish thus,' Joyce told his diary. The speech – his final drunken *Germany Calling* – was devoid of energy and enthusiasm, but his acidic tongue remained in working order:

> Now, in this most serious time of our age, I beg you to realise the fight is on. You have heard something about the Battle of Berlin. You know that there a tremendous world-shattering conflict is being waged. Good. I will only say that the men who have died in the Battle of Berlin have given their lives to show that whatever else happens, Germany will live. No coercion, no oppression, no measures of tyranny that any foreign foe can introduce will shatter Germany. Germany will live because the people of Germany have in them the secret of life, endurance, and will of purpose. And therefore I ask you in these last words – you will not hear from me again for a few months.
>
> I say 'Es lebe Deutschland' Heil Hitler and farewell.[25]

After the recording, which, incidentally, was never broadcast, Joyce prepared for the last act. 'Went with a car to the hotel and brought back baggage. All was ready and the driver was waiting. ... Dietz rang up and M (Margaret) said goodbye to him. I'm sure we shall meet again soon.' Edwin Schneider had dined with the Joyces at the Vier Jahreszeiten Hotel earlier in the evening before the couple left by car for on unknown destination. 'He gave me his bank book and his passport, saying that he might be back before the end of the year.'[26] Other than the occasional group of refugees and worn-out soldiers, the streets of Hamburg were almost devoid of a human presence.

Back inside the Hamburg studios, Dr Karl Scharping from the Propaganda Ministry delivered his last broadcast with the promise that 'Germany... is a force which grows'. His message – carried by the transmitter at Wilhelmshaven – fizzled out soon after.

True to form, even with Hitler's death, the Nazis continued to betray their countrymen. Instead of disclosing the Führer's suicide with a pistol on a chaise lounge sofa – his anointed successor, Admiral Doenitz, told listeners their heroic leader had 'fallen at his post ... fighting to the last breath against Bolshevism and for Germany.[27]

> German men and women, soldiers of the German Wehrmacht —
> Our Führer, Adolf Hitler, has fallen. The German people bow
> in deepest mourning and veneration. My first task is to save the
> German people from destruction by Bolshevism. If only for this
> task the struggle will continue.

Once Doenitz had finished lying, the Hamburg transmitter celebrated the resplendence of Hitler's rule with Wagner's *Twilight of the Gods* followed by the slow movement of Bruckner's *Seventh Symphony*.

As for Goebbels, his demise did not unroll exactly as anticipated. While some followers expected he would direct a sputtering counter-revolution, he opted to end his starring role in Hitler's bunker with wife Magda and their six children. Gruesome details of their fate were later revealed by Artur Axmann, the former Nazi Youth leader, who disclosed how he sat with the Goebbels family in the bunker in the late afternoon of 30 April watching the children 'playing about merrily'. An hour later they were dead, poisoned by their mother's hand. The following day, Magda and Joseph committed suicide in the Chancellery garden, their hasty cremations turned out to be a half-baked effort given the lack of gasoline. Soviet photographs provide gruesome details showing their charred corpses, which fittingly, for someone who so thrived in the eye of the media, were later discovered by a news crew filming in the Chancellery garden.

While Hitler may have been history, Berlin city commander General Weidling gave the order to destroy the Haus Des Rundfunks – an order ignored by those inside who refused to allow meaningless destruction. At the same time, SS soldiers preparing to make a final stand at the radio studios gave up the idea before it even began.

On 2 May, Richard Baier delivered his last newscast in Berlin, and then announced the 'Greater German Broadcasting Service is closing down'.

As I remember it, Hitler's death was officially announced in the Wehrmacht report on May 3, 1945. We were the last two news anchors: Elmer Bantz and me. I closed down the Grossdeutscher Rundfunk and Bantz delivered the last Wehrmacht reports.

Then, while heading out for fresh air, he bumped into Ernst Himmler 'when he was on the narrow courtyard between the bunker and the Haus Des Rundfunks on the way to a car packed with luggage. He came up to me and wished me a good luck during this difficult situation' before disappearing into the night.

Not long after, units of the Soviet Army reached the Haus Des Rundfunks, where its few remaining defenders offered no resistance. On entering, the Russians discovered hundreds of refugees huddled in the offices, under stairwells and in the basement. 'The Russian troops paid no heed to the lives of those who fled there. What happened there can hardly be described,' Richard Baier remembered. Among them were scores of demoralised foreigners who had worked for the overseas shortwave services. Baier clearly recalls Major Popov, the Russian commander, was familiar with the building, having worked there a decade earlier:

I later learned from him that he was a German–Russian exchange employee in the Haus Des Rundfunks from 1934 to 1935, and therefore knew the place well, inside out. He spoke fluent German and had a friendly manner with all contacts with German employees. I was officially dismissed by him and my concern of being arrested as a civilian when leaving the Haus Des Rundfunks was solved when he handed me a card in the Russian language for safe passage. I also remember that Ernst Himmler died with the Volkssturm during fierce fighting in early May.

In the north, Reichssender Hamburg signed off at 13.00 on 3 May with a brief farewell: 'It is doubtful if we will come on the air again with a news bulletin. We take leave of the Hamburgers herewith.'[28]

Time magazine eloquently described Nazi propaganda as stumbling 'through its death scene to musical accompaniment' and finally dying away piecemeal. 'Berlin began broadcasting in spasms, grew fainter and fainter, fell silent. With Berlin and Bremen silent, Hamburg became the official broadcaster of the German High Command's daily communiqués.'

Germany's greatest port fell to the British 7th Armoured Division without a shot being fired. Major I. Anderson, of the 'Desert Rats', was the first officer to reach the Funkhaus on Rothenbaumchaussee, which returned to life as a station of the Allied Military Government on 5 May, with a relay of the BBC news in German. Scottish reporter Doon Campbell leafed through dozens of discarded *Views on the News* scripts that day, all signed by Joyce. 'There are up-to-date copies of every British national newspaper, and there is also a book called *Jewish Influence in British life*,' Campbell reported. A few days later, the British Forces Network occupied the famous Laeiszhalle – the concert hall that was once Hamburg's cultural centre – and before long, Arthur Askey and Vera Lynn records echoed where great composers such as Richard Strauss and Igor Stravinsky once played.

26

RECKONING

Joyce's prediction that the day of retribution would come grew closer as he scuttled for sanctuary in northern Germany, with Margaret in tow. British and Allied intelligence set the goal of finding every last radio renegade to stand trial with the effort underway before the Nazis surrendered. In mid-April, John Amery became one of the first to be collared by Italian partisans near Como and handed over to the British. The entire RRG unit had long vanished by the time US soldiers swept into Apen on 7 April. Guy Della-Cioppa from the US Psychological Warfare Division made a beeline for Bremer's Hotel:

> The studios were in a terrible condition for they had been 'vetted' by the Polish troops, who had generally smashed up everything and had thrown all documents, scripts and files into a huge mass in one big room. We noticed that certain key equipment was missing, notably the valuable magnetaphone recorders, in the end, we suspected that the Polish soldiers were not clever enough to realise the value of this equipment, and in all probability had not removed it themselves.[1]

As this was going on, the Soviet military administration ordered all transmitters and antennas in Zeesen to be dismantled and sent to Russia as reparations. When completed, the Soviets began to blow up the buildings and antenna foundations – the whole area was reduced to rubble and craters.[2]

Canadian counter-espionage men captured Eduard Dietz on 20 May. An Allied reporter noted Dietz was among several higher Nazi officials called out of the ranks to be photographed. 'A small insignificant man with glasses, he fell over himself trying to be helpful and was quite willing to answer any questions.' Luckily for Dietz, the British decided against prosecuting him as a renegade on the condition he remained in Germany.

One can only speculate if Dietz provided the Canadians with information regarding the whereabouts of Joyce, who, as it happened, was picked up by chance the following week in a wood on Danish frontier near Flensburg. His arrest was hailed as 'a sensation even in the midst of all the sensations of those wonderful days'. British Captain Alexander Adrian Lickorish described how at 19.00 on 28 May, when with another officer named Lieutenant Perry, Lickorish was gathering branches and twigs for fuel:

A little earlier we had seen an individual, a man who was also in the wood and as we were collecting logs at 7:00pm he turned towards us and waving his stick indicated some wood in a ditch. Thereafter, he remained near us and presently spoke to us in French but we ignored his remarks except to thank him in German. After a while he said in English 'Here are a few more pieces'. I immediately recognised his voice as that of a broadcaster on the German radio known as William Joyce. I desired to confirm my suspicions and had a discussion with Lieutenant Perry. We evolved a plan as a result of which when the man was placing the wood on our truck Lieutenant Perry taxed him by saying 'You wouldn't happen to be William Joyce would you?' He put his hand in his pocket and Perry shot at his hand. Joyce fell to the ground saying 'My name is Hansen'. I rushed to him and searched him with a view to disarming him. Joyce said 'I am not armed'. Looking through his pockets I found in the inner jacket pocket a Reisepasse in the name of Wilhelm Hansen and a Wehrpasse in the name of William Joyce. We treated his wound by giving first aid, later handing him over to the appropriate military authorities.

When Joyce – lying on a stretcher in his pyjamas – arrived at the British Army headquarters in northern Germany, a reception of Tommies yelled, 'Traitor, blasted traitor.' Margaret was detained a few hours later, clutching her worldly possessions – 2,000 German marks and an envelope stuffed with snapshots of Wehrmacht soldiers. After intensive interrogations, Joyce was packed off to London to stand trial for high treason and tried at the Old Bailey on three counts:

1. William Joyce, on 18 September 1939, and on other days between that day and 29 May 1945, being a person owing allegiance to our Lord the King, and while a war was being carried on by the German Realm against our King, did traitorously adhere to the King's enemies in Germany, by broadcasting propaganda.
2. William Joyce, on 26 September 1940, being a person who owed allegiance as in the other count, adhered to the King's enemies by purporting to become naturalised as a subject of Germany.
3. William Joyce, on 18 September 1939, and on other days between that day and 2 July 1940 [i.e., before Joyce's naturalisation as a German subject], being a person owing allegiance to our Lord the King, and while a war was being carried on by the German Realm against our King, did traitorously adhere to the King's enemies in Germany, by broadcasting propaganda.

During the trial, Joyce's American nationality became a key argument for the defence, but Attorney General Sir Hartley Shawcross successfully argued Joyce's possession of a British passport meant he owed allegiance to the King at the time he began working for the Germans during that fateful September of 1939. His defence unsuccessfully argued he was born in the USA and remained an American citizen and therefore could not possibly be a traitor.

As this was happening, Leo Amery had engaged some of the best psychiatrists in the land to testify his son John was insane, but to no avail. His trial on 28 November 1945 at the Old Bailey lasted just eight minutes when he pleaded guilty to eight counts on a high treason indictment that he aided the enemy. His executioner, Albert Pierrepoint, described the renegade as one of the bravest men he ever killed: '[He] walked unassisted to his fate after thanking the prison chaplain and warders for their unfailing courtesy.'

As for William Joyce, he was convicted of one count of high treason and sentenced to death; Pierrepoint was also on duty at His Majesty's Prison Wandsworth to dispatch the verdict. A notice outside the gaol stated, 'Lord Haw-Haw of the German Radio had paid the penalty of his treachery.'

Ballie-Stewart dispensed his memories in tell-all memoir, published weeks after he dropped dead in a pub.

At the Nuremberg Trials, Ribbentrop was sentenced to death and hanged, while Hans Fritzsche was charged with conspiracy to commit crimes against peace, war crimes, and crimes against humanity, but was acquitted on all counts. Former CBS reporter William Shirer was stunned that Fritzsche held such a lofty spot on the Nazi Party totem pole: 'No one in the courtroom, including Fritzsche, seemed to know why he was there – he was too small a fry – unless it were as a ghost for Goebbels.'

In contrast to Joyce, Mildred Gillars got off lightly with a prison sentence of 10 to 30 years for treason. A former US paratrooper who had been coaxed to send messages on her *Invasion Hour* testified at her trial, 'she was very cheerful, passing out cigarettes and laughing and talking'. He revealed one of two civilian men accompanying Gillars had told him the group was from the International Red Cross.

Kurt Dittmar, the 'Radio General' who gave weekly broadcasts and was then rumoured to have committed suicide, was detained and assigned as a farmhand in the Glamorganshire village of Merthyr Mawr in Wales.

For his sins, 'Lili Marlene' composer Norbert Schultze was ordered to work in the Berlin sewers for a year and banned from the German stage. British newspaper reports suggest when he attempted a comeback singing his own compositions, he was booed out and settled into obscurity.

As for the singer Lale Andersen, she later toured British music halls and performed on the BBC's *Workers' Playtime*, before representing Germany at the 1961 Eurovision Song Contest with the song 'Einmal sehen wir uns wieder'.

After the war, Richard Baier worked as a freelance journalist at RIAS, the station in the American sector of Berlin. He reported from East Berlin on the popular uprising in June 1953 but was arrested in 1955 by East German State Security for 'agitation' and sentenced to 13 years behind bars on jumped-up charges of 'espionage'. Nowadays, he lives in a retirement home on the outskirts of Berlin.

Peter Meyer, the young singer from the Rundfunkspielschar Berlin, helped defend his town when US troops approached and was wounded. 'In 1952, I emigrated to Chicago and was drafted into the US Army during the Korean conflict. Thankfully the Korean War ended soon enough so I was returned to Germany as a member of the US occupation forces.' Nowadays, he lives in quiet retirement in South America.

APPENDIX A

Original Nine Broadcasting Stations

Station Name	Location	Established	Opening
Deutsche Stunde in Bayern GmbH	Munich	18. Sep. 1922	30. Mar. 1924 (485 m, 250 W)
Funk Stunde AG	Berlin	10. Dec. 1923	29. Oct. 1923 (400 m, 250 W)
Mitteldeutsche Rundfunk AG (Mirag)	Leipzig	22. Jan. 1924	2. Mar. 1924 (452 m)
Nordische Rundfunk AG (Norag)	Hamburg	16. Jan. 1924	2. May 1924 (395 m, 700 W)
Ostmarken Rundfunk AG (Orag)	Konigsberg	2. Jan. 1924	14. June 1924 (463 m, 500 W)
Schlesische Funkstunde AG	Breslau	4. Apr. 1924	26. May 1924 (416 m)
Süddeutsche Rundfunk AG (Sürag)	Stuttgart	3. Mar. 1924	11. May 1924 (437 m, 250 W)
Südwestdeutsche Rundfunk AG (SWR/Süwrag)	Frankfurt am Main	7. Dec. 1923	1. Apr. 1924 (470 m, 1500 W)
Westdeutsche Funkstunde AG (Wefag), 1927:	Munster	15. Sep. 1924	10. Oct. 1924 (407 m, 700 W)

APPENDIX B

Deutschlandsender Schedules
(Various 1934–1939)

Monday 24 December 1934
15:00 Orchestra from Köln 16.00 Evensong from St Matthew's Church, Berlin 17:00 Merry Christmas – programme by soloists, the Fehse Quartet, the Leipzig Thomaner, the Bariuss Church School of Augsberg, the Station Chamber Choir, the German Oratorio Choir, and the Augmented Station Orchestra. Address by the station director 20:00 Munich relay 20:20 Extracts from *Hansel and Gretel* – fairy tale opera 21:15 Christmas music 23:00 Stuttgart relay.

Tuesday 29 January 1935
15:00 Hamburg relay 16:00 Baritone recital 18:20 Waltz Records 19:15 Ernst Moritz Arndt sequence (Burghardt) 20:00 *Der Schwarmer*, Political Cabaret by Orchestra and Soloist 22:00 Variety.

Saturday 22 February 1936
16:00 Variety from Köln 17:00 Folk Songs and Dances 18:00 Wind Instrument Concert 19:10 Carnival programme from Frankfurt 21:30 Bass and piano recital 22:00 The Robert Gaden Dance Band, with Songs.

Monday 11 October 1937
15:00 Popular Orchestral Music 17:00 Music for Children
(Recorded) – Soprano and Piano Recital 17.25 Records 18:15
Variety Concert from Stuttgart 19:00 Beethoven Chamber music
by a Wind Instrument Ensemble of the Berlin Philharmonic, with
Piano Soloist 20:30 The Kaufmann Band, with songs 21:30 The
Bauschke Band.

Saturday 13 August 1938
16:00 Act 1 of *The Valkyrie* – Opera (Wagner) from Munich
17:30 Piano Recital 18:00 Act II of *The Valkyrie* – Opera
(Wagner) from Munich 19:45 Piano recital 20:30 Act III of *The
Valkyrie* – Opera (Wagner) from Munich 22:30 Minuets and
Bagatelles, Op.126 (Beethoven) for Piano 23:25 Dance music
from Munich 00:00 Midnight concert by the Station Orchestras
on records from Breslau.

Saturday 29 April 1939
15:00 Records 15:30 Orchestral concert of Swedish music 18:30
Vocal and instrumental recital 19:00 Airmen's Band 20:15 Italian
National University Orchestra with violin soloist 23:00 Light
music and dance music.

Saturday 02 September 1939
14:00 Light music 15:00 Records 16:00 Vienna Station Orchestra
(recorded) 17:45–23.35 *The Mastersingers* (Wagner) from
Nuremberg.

APPENDIX C

Paul Nipkow Television Rooms in Berlin (Open Daily 20.00–22.00)

Charlottenburg
Leipziger Strasse 13
Artilleriestrasse 10
Berliner Strasse 62–64
Haus Des Rundfunks, Masurenallee

Lichtenberg
Dottistrasse 12–16

Neukolln
Richardstrasse 119–120

Pankow
Wollankstrasse 134

Reiniekendorf-West
Haus der DAF, Berliner Strasse 99–100

Schoneberg
Hauptstrasse 97–29

Steglitz
Bergstrasse 1
Geisbergstrasse 7–9

Potsdam
Am Kanal 16–18 (Postamt)

APPENDIX D

Reichssender Controllers and Studio Locations (as of 1940)

Reichssender Berlin: Berlin-Charlottenburg 9, Masurenallee, Ruf: 93 6911. Intendant: Goetz Otto Stoffregen; Sendeleiter: Heinz Kyschky.

Reichssender Böhmen: Prag 12, Foohovai 6, Ruf: 32151, 25537. Intendant: Günther Marek (kommissarisch); Sendeleiter: Sedlatschek.

Reichssender Breslau: Breslau 18, Waldenburger Str. 8, Ruf: 82391. Intendant: Hans Otto Fricke; Sendeleiter: Günther Meyer-Goldenstädt.

Reichssender Frankfurt: Frankfurt a. M., Eschersheimer Landstr. 33, Ruf: 5191 91. Intendant: Kapitän Paul Lambert Werber; Sendeleiter: Ferdinand Thürmer.

Reichssender Hamburg: Hamburg x3, Rothenbaumchaussee 132, Ruf: 55 92 51. Intendant: Gustav Grupe; Sendeleiter: Harry Moß.

Reichssender Köln: Dagobertstr.38, Ruf: 70801. Intendant: Dr. Anton Winkeinkemper; Sendeleiter: Dr. Friedrich Castelle.

Reichssender Königsberg: Adolf-Hitler-Str. 2I–25, Ruf: 242 21. Intendant: Dr. Alfred Lau.

Reichssender Leipzig: Leipzig, Markt 8, Ruf: 72921. Intendant: Carl Stueber; Sendeleiter: Wilhelm Hartseil.

Reichssender München: München, Rundfunkplatz 1, Ruf: 5209. Intendant: Dr. Hellmut Habersbrunner; Sendeleiter: Dr. Manfred v. Eyb.

Reichssender Saarbrücken: Wilhelm-Heinrich-Str. 33–35, Ruf: 293 71–75. Intendant: Dr. Gerhart von Westermann (kommissarisch); Sendeleiter: Franz Köppe.

Reichssender Stuttgart: Danziger Freiheit 17, Ruf: 235 32. Intendant: Dr. Alfred Bofinger; Sendeleiter: Walter Reuschle.

Reichssender Wien: Argentinier Str. 30a, Ruf:45550. Intendant: Karl Mages; Sendeleiter: Theodor Ehrenberg.

Landessender Danzig: Winterplatz, Ruf: 25048. Intendant: Reginald Buse.

Die Deutfehe Arbeitsfront: Zentralbüro, Propagandaamt, Abteilung Runöfunli Berlin W 50, Rankeftrasse 4 Ruf: 91 91 31 Drahtanfchrift: Daeuni; Berlin

APPENDIX E

Broadcast Frequencies
(as of 1939)

Deutschlandsender – 191 kHz (1571 metres)
Bremen II – 224 kHz (1339 metres)
Salzburg – 549 kHz (578 metres)
Nürnberg – 519 kHz (578 metres)
Innsbruck – 519 kHz (578 metres)
Stuttgart – 574 kHz (522.6 metres)
Wien – 592 kHz (506.8 metres)
Prag I – 638 kHz (470.2 metres)
Köln – 658 kHz (455.9 metres)
München – 740 kHz (405.4 metres)
Bremen I – 758 kHz (395.8 metres)
Leipzig – 785 kHz (382.2 metres)
Berlin – 841 kHz (356.7 metres)
Posen – 868 kHz (345.6 metres)
Klagenfurt – 886 kHz (338.6 metres)
Graz – 886 kHz (338.6 metres)
Hamburg – 904 kHz (331.9 metres)
Donau – 922 kHz (325.4 metres)
Breslau – 950 kHz (315.8 metres)
Danzig I – 986 kHz (304.3 metres)
Krakau – 1022 kHz (293.5 metres)
Königsberg I – 1031 kHz (291 metres)
Böhmen – 1113 kHz (269.5 metres)

Brünn – 1158 kHz (259.1 metres)
Kassel – 1195 kHz (251 metres)
Trier – 1195 kHz (251 metres)
Koblenz – 1195 kHz (251 metres)
Frankfurt – 1195 kHz (251 metres)
Kattowitz – 1204 kHz (249.2 metres)
Görlitz – 1231 kHz (243.7 metres)
Troppau – 1231 kHz (243.7 metres)
Saarbrücken – 1249 kHz (240.2 metres)
Linz – 1267 kHz (236.8 metres)
Memel – 1285 kHz (233.5 metres)
Bregenz – 1294 kHz (231.8 metres)
Freiburg i. Br. – 1294 kHz (231.8 metres)
Danzig II – 1303 kHz (230.2 metres)
Unterweser – 1330 kHz (225.6 metres)
Flensburg – 1330 kHz (225.6 metres)
Hannover – 1330 kHz (225.6 metres)
Magdeburg – 1330 kHz (225.6 metres)
Stettin – 1330 kHz (225.6 metres)
Stolp – 1330 kHz (225.6 metres)
Litzmannstadt – 1339 kHz (224 metres)
Königsberg II – 1348 kHz (222.6 metres)
Mährisch-Ostrau – 1348 kHz (222.6 metres)
Warschau – 1384 kHz (216.8 metres)
Kaiserslautern – 1429 kHz (209.9 metres)
Dresden – 1465 kHz (204.8 metres)

APPENDIX F

Shortwave Schedules
(as of 1943)

Asian Programmes

7.00 DSZ Ansage – Deutsches Volkslied – Programmvorschau
7.10 U-RPR: Frühkonzert 7.30 Nachrichten (englisch) 7.45
Musik zur Unterhaltung 8.00 Nachrichten (deutsch) 8.15
Sozialismus und Auslands-deutschtum 8.30 „Ankerspill" 30
Minuten für unsere Seeleute 9.00 Nachrichten und Zeitgeschehen
(englisch) 9.30 Symphonie Nr. 5 in B-dur von Franz Schubert
(WK 1262) 10.00 „Von Finnland bis zum Schwarzen Meer –
Gib acht, Kamerad, und höre her!" 10.30 Vom deutschen
Herzen 10.45 Vortrag (deutsch) 11.00 Deutschlandecho 11.30
Nachrichten (deutsch und englisch) 11.45 Kulturvortrag
(englisch) 12.00 Deutsches Volkskonzert 13.00 Aus der Welt
der Oper (WK 1161) 14.00 Nachrichten (englisch) 14.15 Zum
Sonntag-Abend 14.30 Für jeden etwas 15.00 Nachrichten
(deutsch) 15.15 Sozialismus und Auslands-deutschtum 15.30
Luise Walker spielt Gitarre (WK 4292195) 15.45 Vom deutschen
Herzen 16.00 Nachrichten und Zeitgeschehen (englisch)
Nachrichten (niederl.) 16.13 Grüße an niederl. Freiwillige
16.15 Polit. Wochenübersicht (niederl.) 16.30 Vortrag (deutsch)
Nachrichten (hindustani) 16.45 Kulturvortrag (englisch)
17.00 „Von Finnland bis zum Schwarzen Meer – Gib acht,
Kamerad, und höre her!" 17.15 Nachrichten (bengali) 17.30
Deutschlandecho 18.00 Absage

Programmes for Africa

17.20 DSZ Ansage – Deutsches Volkslied – Programmvorschau
17.30 Nachrichten (englisch) 17.45 Zum Sonntag-Abend 18.00
Nachrichten (afrikaans) 18.15 Deutsches Volkskonzert 19.00
Orgelkonzert (WK 1273) 19.30 Nachrichten (afrikaans) 19.45
Nachrichten (deutsch und portug.) 20.00 Vom deutschen Herzen
Nachrichten (französisch) 20.15 Nachrichten (englisch) 20.30
Es wird weiter gerommelt! 21.00 „Ankerspill" 30 Minuten für
unsere Seeleute 21.30 'Deutschlandecho 22.00 Nachrichten
(deutsch) 22.15 Sozialismus und Auslands-deutschtum 22.30
Joh. Chr. Bach; Sinfonie in B-dur (WK 1263) Nachrichten und
Kulturvortrag (englisch) 22.45 Nachrichten (portug.) Für jeden
etwas 23.00 Symphonie Nr. 5 in B-dur von Franz Schubert
(WK 1262) 23.30 Absage

North America Service

23.50 DSZ Ansage – Deutsches Volkslied – Programmvorschau
0.02 Deutschlandecho 0.30 Vom deutschen Herzen 0.45
Nachrichten (deutsch) 1.00 Deutsches Volkskonzert 2.00
Sozialismus und Auslands-deutschtum 2.15 Trough a woman's
eyes 2.30 „Ankerspill" 30 Minuten für unsere Seeleute 3.00
Nachrichten und Vortrag (englisch) 3.30 Zum Sonntag-Abend
3.45 Vortrag (englisch) 4.00 Orgelmusik 4.05 Grüße an deutsche
Internierte 4.15 Nachrichten (deutsch) 4.30 Deutschlandecho
5.00 Nachrichten (englisch) 5.15 Deutsche Jugend singt und
spielt (WK 1262) 6.00 Nachrichten und Vortrag (englisch)
6.30 Spätmusik 7.00 Nachrichten (englisch) 7.15 Nachrichten
(deutsch) 7.30 Absage

South America Service

23.50 DSZ Ansage – Deutsches Volkslied –Programmvorschau
0.02 Deutschlandecho 0.30 Vom deutschen Herzen 0.45
Nachrichten (deutsch) 1.00 Deutsches Volkskonzert 2.00
Sozialismus und Auslands-deutschtum 2.15 Luise Walker spielt
Gitarre (WK 4292195) 2.30 „Ankerspill" 30 Minuten für unsere
Seeleute 3.00 Nachrichten und Zeitfunk (spanisch) 3.30 Zum
Sonntag-Abend 3.45 Grüße an unsere Hörer 4.00 Nachrichten

(spanisch) 4.15 Nachrichten (deutsch) 4.30 Deutschlandecho 5.00
Nachrichten (spanisch) 5.15 Deutsche Jugend singt und spielt
(WK 1241) 6.00 Nachrichten (spanisch) 6.15 Absage

Programmes for Brasil

23.30 DSZ Ansage – Deutsches Volkslied –Programmvorschau
23.40 Musikalisches Zwischenspiel 23.45 Eine kleine Hausmusik
bei Tia Liloca 0.02 Deutschlandecho 0.30 Vorn deutschen Herzen
0.45 Nachrichten (deutsch) 1.00 Deutsches Volkskonzert 2.00
Nachrichten (portug.) 2.15 Luise Walker spielt Gitarre (WK
4292195) 2.30 „Ankerspill" 30 Minuten für unsere Seeleute
3.00 Nachrichten (portug.) 3.15 Notas c Pipocaṣ 3.30 Zum
Sonntag-Abend 3.45 Grüße an unsere Hörer 4.00 Sozialismus
und Auslands-deutschtum 4.15 Nachrichten (deutsch) 4.30
Deutschlandecho 5.00 Absage

15.51 Zu Bildvorspann von Dia Schallplatten
16.00 Sender-Ansage Bild des Tages – 125. Geburtstag von
Heinrich Goebel, dem Erfinder der elektr. Glühlampe (Leit. S. A.
Szymanski)
16.01 Ansage „Dame Kobold" Regie: H. Küpper (1)
17.01 Absage-Ansage „Wunder der Kugel" (Ufa) (2)
17.12 „Die Lyriaden-Sternschnuppen – Sprecher: Dr. Wegener
Zeichner: Axel Jäger Leitung: Sylvester Albert Szymanski (3)
17.26 „Die schöne Mark" (RRG) (4)
17.43–18.00 „Die Sieger von Charkow" Sprecher: Hugo Landgraf
Leitung: Sylvester Albert Szymanski (5)
18.52 Programm-Vorschau – Zu Bildvorspann von Dia
Schallplatten (6)
19.00 Ansage – „Das Übermikroskop" Sprecher: Prof. Bodo v.
Borries, Prof. Ernst Ruska, Prof. Helmut Ruska Leitung: Sylvester
Albert Szymanski (7)
19.30 „Nante" (RRG) (8)
20.08–21.26 „Zwei in einer großen Stadt" (Tobis) (9)
21.27 Programmvorschau
21.35 Senderabsage
Abendregie: Annelies Kuhnke"

ENDNOTES

1. *The Darkening*

1. There is no other recorded occasion of Hitler making such a broadcast. For instance, he never visited the state radio studios to deliver a talk; neither did he ever grant a one-on-one broadcast interview.

2. The regional broadcasting stations in the Weimar Republic were largely constructed as joint stock companies. Shares in them were held both by private shareholders with a maximum of 49 per cent of the business shares and by state trustees with 17 per cent each and a total of 51 per cent. In January 1933 the broadcasting companies were transformed into limited liability companies (GmbH). Private shareholders were forced out of the system as early as 1932.

3. *See* Appendix A.

4. *Leeds Mercury* – 23 February 1927

5. Schubotz, H., *Die Deutsche Welle GmbH.* (Jahrbuch der Deutschen Welle, 1928)

6. Large professional organisations supported the broadcasts, including as the Reich Committee for Medical Education, the Reich Association of Dentists, the Head Office of Housewives Associations and the Reich Association of Agricultural Housewives. Trade, industry, the general German civil servants' association were also involved. German foreign affairs were carried out according to proposals submitted by the German Foreign Institute in Stuttgart.

7. *Aberdeen People's Journal* – 30 December 1939

2. *Radio Revolution*

1. Hadamovsky, Eugen, *Dein Rundfunk. Das Rundfunkbuch für alle Volksgenossen.* (München 1934)
2. Deutsches Rundfunkarchiv / DRA / File: B004890967
3. Heingartner, Robert, *An American Witness in Nazi Frankfurt: The Diaries of Robert W. Heingartner* Entry: 31 January 1933 (Peter Lang, 2011)
4. Hadamovsky was appointed the director of Deutschlandsender in March, and in July of the same year, chief of broadcasting and director of the RRG.
5. The weekly organ of the *Reichsverband Deutscher Rundfunkteilnehmer.*
6. *Western Mail –* 1 March 1933
7. Hadamovsky, Eugen, *Propaganda and National Power,* ed. Christopher Sterling (ARNO Press, 1972)
8. 'Der Deutschlandsender', *Handbuch Des Deutschen Rundfunks 1938.* p.153
9. 'Volkverbundener Rundfunk'. *National-Funk,* July 1934.
10. Goebbels, Joseph *Der Rundfunk als achte Grossmach,* (NSDAP Zentralverlag, 1938)
11. Kris, Ernst and Speier, Hans *German Radio Propaganda.* (Oxford University Press, 1944)
12. Grunberger, Richard, *A social history of the Third Reich.* (Weidenfeld and Nicolson, 1971)
13. On 1 January 1938, 13.4 per cent of the population was already registered with the Radio Licensing Bureau representing over 9 million people. The listening peak was finally reached 16.2 million in 1943.
14. 'Der Volksempfänger, ein Erfolgsmodell'. *Traunsteiner Tagblatt,* 24 November 2007
15. Ettlinger, Harold, *Axis on the Air.* (The Bobbs-Merrill Company, 1943).
16. Deuel, Wallace R., *People Under Hitler.* (New York: Harcourt, Brace and Co., 1942), pp.330–331.

3. *Cleansing*

1. Bauernfeind, Wolfgang, *Tonspuren: Das Haus des Rundfunks in Berlin.* Links (Christoph Verlag, 2010) p.45
2. Bredow's sentence was reversed by a higher court in 1937. Soon afterwards, Goebbels called of the campaign against former radio officials.
3. Klepper, Jochen, *Unter dem Schatten deiner Flügel.* (Brunnen, 2002)

4. Bauernfeind, Wolfgang, *Tonspuren: Das Haus des Rundfunks in Berlin*. (Christoph Verlag, 2010) pp.44–45
5. Letter from Eugen Hadamovsky to Herbert Antoine, 31 July 1933. 'The termination announced on 11. 4. 33 and effective on 31. 12. 33, will be based on the reasons described in the letter of termination from 11.4.33, as well as §§ 2 and 4 of the 2nd Implementing Regulation of the Law on the Restoration of the Professional Civil Service. The continuing payout of the salary will take place according to the legal regulations only up to a duration of three months, therefore you are no longer entitled to additional benefits starting 1.8.1933. You have the right to object to this decision to the highest Reich authority, the Reich Ministry for Information and Propaganda, which, according to § 5 (5) of 2.270, decides only on the payouts to be made.'

4. *Drunk on Culture*

1. At the same time, Otto Stoffregen continued to serve as the controller of Deutschlandsender.
2. Reichssender Breslau was the recipient of regular reception reports from as far afield as New Zealand, Japan and Manchuria.
3. British United Press/*Daily Herald* – 3 September 1932
4. Testimony from Hans-Jürgen Meier (*1936).
5. OH/2405. Christel Hertenstein interview, 17 February, 1994. Center for Oral and Public History, California State University, Fullerton.
6. A favourite hymn featured the lyrics: 'Now let the banners flutter, towards the flaming dawn, Which either guides us to new victories or will be our funeral pyre'.
7. Cerff, Carl *Die Hitler Jugend in Rundfunk*. (Archiv Fur Funkrecht 1934/35)
8. The organisation headed by Robert Ley fell under the auspices of the Labour Front.
9. *Handbuch des Deutschen Rundfunks* (Hans Joachim Weinbrenner, 1939) pp.222–226
10. *Leeds Mercury* – 6 December 1935

5. *This Is Berlin*

1. The Reichs-Rundfunk-Gesellschaft was using the shortwave service to beam the well-known programme *The German Hour* in 1932 all over the USA (via NBC) every fortnight, where German notables spoke in English, including the Nobel Laureate Friedrich Bergius, industrialist Carl Friedrich von Siemens and Chancellor Heinrich Brüning.
2. Deutscher Weltrundfunk auf kurzenwellen, *Handbuch des Deutschen Rundfunks*. (Hans Joachim Weinbrenner, 1939) pp. 66–68

3. Weinbrenner, p.68
4. Lubbers, Schwipps *Sendungen in Afrikaans und Arabisch*. (1970) p.42
5. Potter's Corner, *Leeds Mercury* – 25 June 1935
6. Deutscher Weltrundfunk auf kurzenwellen, *Handbuch des Deutschen Rundfunks*. (Hans Joachim Weinbrenner, 1939)
7. *Coventry Evening Telegraph* – 15 December 1937
8. *Nottingham Evening Post* – 25 October 1937

6. *The Olympic Dream*

1. The games should have been held in Berlin in 1916, however, when preparations were in full swing, the First World War broke out. But in 1931 Berlin was chosen over the only other candidate Barcelona to host both the 1936 winter and summer games.
2. Hadamovsky, Eugen, *Olympia Weltsender*. (Berlin, 1937) p.17
3. Ibid, p.16
4. 37 reporters from 21 countries including France, Great Britain, Canada, USA (CBS and NBC), Argentina, Finland, Latvia, Poland, Japan, Norway and Sweden covered the event.
5. 'Olympic Games to be used for Nazi propaganda', *Yorkshire Post and Leeds Intelligencer* – 27 June 1936
6. *Nottingham Evening Post* – 24 August 1936
7. 'Der Rundfunk zu den Olympischen Spielen gerüstet', *Völkischer Beobachter* – 15 July 1936
8. RRG experimentation with outside broadcasting from vehicles had been underway for some time. One of the most daring tests was at the AVUS racetrack when a station engineer drove a car at 180 Km/h whilst a sports reporter sitting beside him delivered a running commentary. Another test was the commentary of a man rushing down the slopes of a hill on skis, whilst a third consisted of a reporter on a bob-sleigh speeding down the Olympic Games course at Garmisch.
9. 'Größte Rundfunk Übertragungsanlage Deutschland fertiggestellt. Olympia-Weltsender auf dem Reichsportfeld', *Völkischer Beobachter* – 12 July 1936
10. 42 broadcasting companies – including NBC and the BBC – were in attendance, which posted an entourage of 150 representatives.
11. TV transmissions took place from 10.00 to midday and 15.00 to 17.00, then highlights of the day aired between 20.00 and 22.00.
12. *Der Radio-Händler*, Issue 1, 1938, p.17
13. Hadamovsky, Eugen, *Olympia Weltsender* (Berlin, 1937) p.3
14. Ibid.
15. Der Deutschlandsender, *Handbuch Des Deutschen Rundfunks*. (1938), p.155

7. *The Television Miracle*

1. 'Berlin sah und hörte Nürnberg!' *Berliner Tageblatt* – 8 August 1937.
2. Else Eister, Annemarie Beck and Ursula Patzschke were favourites.
3. 'Berlin Broadcast Test' *Belfast Telegraph* – 11 April 1935
4. An example of this occurred in April 1937 when a Saturday afternoon concert starring Lena Haustein, Carla Spletter and Fritz La Fontaine – along with a children's choir: the Fritz Weber dance orchestra and the KdF musicians – were on both TV and radio between 16.00 and 18.00.
5. The programmes included 'Aktuelle Bildbericht', 'Zeitdienst' and 'Die Kriminalpolizei warnt'.
6. '300 Mann in der guten Stube', *Der Spiegel* – 7 April 2015

8. *The Road to War*

1. For many Germans, the impossible had become a reality given that after the Habsburg monarchy crumbled at the end of the Great War, Germany was forbidden from entering into a union with Austria. The ban – according to the propaganda screamed out by Goebbels – was a blatant 'breach of the people's right to self-determination'. It was only when London signalled a willingness to compromise on the issue that Hitler seized his chance. The previous month, by threatening to invade with the Wehrmacht, Hitler had forced the Austrian Chancellor, Schuschnigg, to subordinate his foreign policy to Berlin and appoint Nazi Arthur Seyss-Inquart as Austrian Interior Minister. Schuschnigg's appeal for help fell on deaf ears in London, Rome, and Paris and he resigned on 11 March. It was on that day that Hitler gave the order to move in.
2. Osterreichische Radio-Verkehrs AG, the privately owned company and the state's broadcasting monopoly.
3. Reiss, Erwin, *Wir senden Frohsinn, Fernsehen unterm Faschismus* (Elefanten-Press-Verlag, 1979)
4. Our Own Correspondent. *The Observer* – 20 March 1938
5. The station even published an 80-page book, *Verda Staeio: Esperanta Ahnanako la Chekoslovska Radio*, which contained a chapter on the Czechoslovak State and its radio service.
6. As this was happening, former Deutschlandsender official Guenther Marek was installed as commissioner for Prague Radio, which was renamed Reichssender Bohemia with a vast signal covering the Sudetengau. The station employed around 60 people at studios in the Prague suburb Karlin Karoline Valley.
7. Wenzel, Rolf, 'Der Rundfunk im Protektorat', *Handbuch Des Deutschen Rundfunks.* (1938), p.157

8. Between 1936 and 1937, the first German television tower was built on the Brocken summit but the facility was never used. Instead the Luftwaffe took over operations in 1939 for aircraft tracking.
9. *Daily Herald* – 26 April 1939
10. On 23 March 1939
11. On 22 March 1939
12. *Northants Evening Telegraph* – 21 August 1939
13. *Der Deutschen Kurzewellensender im Urteil der angelsachsischen Welt*. (RRG Berlin, 1938)
14. Ibid.
15. *Birmingham Mail* – 30 October 1939

9. Poland

1. Proclamation by Adolf Hitler to the German Army, 1 September 1939. *The Origins of the War*, (British Foreign Office, 1939)
2. Later Lieutenant General Kurt Dittmar represented the Army.
3. The first four propaganda companies were established on 16 August 1938 by order of the Army High Command. Their first assignment was in October 1938 when the Germans invaded the Sudetenland. While Goebbels had initially claimed sovereignty over state propaganda even in the event of a military conflict, the Wehrmacht considered an effective reporting impossible without incorporating correspondents into military structures. The decisive factor for this attitude was the pronounced mistrust that the military showed towards the civilian war correspondents in the First World War, who, in their eyes, had failed to report properly. After the Wehrmacht had been able to assert itself on this fundamental question, an agreement concluded in the winter of 1938/39 on the implementation of war propaganda between the High Command of the Wehrmacht (OKW) and the Ministry of Propaganda established the competencies: the propaganda companies were militarily subordinate to one Wehrmacht Propaganda Department established in the Wehrmacht High Command (OKW).
4. Goebbels, Joseph, 'PK', *Das Reich* (Nr.20,1941), pp.1–2
5. Piotrowski, Stanislaw, *Hans Frank's Diary*. (Warszawa Panstzwowe Wydawnictwo Naukowe, 1961), pp. 110–111. The meeting was held on 31 October.
6. *Dundee Courier* – 27 January 1940

10. Germany Calling

1. Delmer, Sefton, *William Joyce*. Retrieved from https://www.psywar.org/delmer/2040/1001
2. 'Fascism and Jews', *Yorkshire Post and Leeds Intelligencer* – 11 May 1934

3. Baillie-Stewart, it seems, was something of a linguistic genius and later translated the words of the popular song 'Lili Marlene' from German to English.
4. Baillie-Stewart, Norman, *Officer in the Tower*. (Leslie Frewin, 1967), pp. 148–9

11. 1940

1. Diller, Ansgar, *Rundfunkpolitik im Dritten Reich 1943* dienten allein im Heer ca. 5,000 Soldaten in den PK. (Deutscher Taschenbuch Verlag, 1980), p.339
2. Originally transmitted from 01.30 to 02.00 over Deutschlandsender and the regional transmitters at Lodz and Bremen.
3. 'Kameradschaftsdienst Dienst', *Volksfunk* – 4 February 1940. p.6
4. Letter from Wilhelm Keitel to Hans Goedecke, 29 November 1940, cited in *Wir beginnen das Wunschkonzert für die Wehrmacht.* (Neibelungen Verlag, 1940).
5. Ibid
6. Goebbels despised the political radio drama, deeming it stilted, phoney and ineffective.
7. *Gymnastik* had been a cornerstone of breakfast radio since the early 1930s. The shows were produced by Reichssender Berlin with the support of the Health Ministry.
8. *Analysis of German Propaganda, January 1–15 1940*. National Archives, CAB 68/4/37
9. Wolf, Josef, *Presse und Funk im Dritten Reich. Eine Dokumentation.* (Gütersloh, 1964)
10. 22 January 1940 – Reichssender Hamburg
11. *Daily Herald* – 24 May 1940
12. Hall, J. W., *Trial of William Joyce.* (William Hodge, 1946), p.110
13. Joyce, William, *Twilight Over England.* (Internationaler Verlag, Berlin, 1940), p.12.
14. The Irish shortwave service of the RRG.
15. Francis Stuart Interview, RTE Radio, Dublin – 29 January 1976
16. 'Some More Tricks of the Trade', *The Scotsman* – 17 April 1940. p.7
17. 'As Goebbels Sees Us', *Thanet Advertiser* – 13 August 1940
18. 'Deutschlands Soltz, Englands Sorge', *Die Surag*, Sudwestdeutscher Radio Zeitung – 25 February 1940. In the September issue, aerial photography of the British capital burning sat under the headline 'Harte Schlage auf London'.

12. *Grumbles*

1. 6 April 1940 – Deutschlandsender, monitored by the Press Association

2. The issue topped the agenda at the Reich Propaganda Directorate conference in Berlin in April 1940.
3. 'Warum Eigentlich Fremdsprachige Nachrichten', *Volksfunk* – 14 April 1940
4. Deutschlandsender – 17 March 1940. 22.30
5. Sennerteg, Niclas, *Tyskland talar: Hitlers svenska radiostation.* (Lund, 2006), pp. 60–61

13. Hitler's Winning Streak

1. Despite a gallant stand, the Dutch Army surrendered two days after the Germans occupied Hilversum.
2. *Voices in the Darkness: The Story of the European Radio War.* (Secker and Warburg; second edition, 1943)
3. *Civil Affairs Handbook: Germany*, Volume 12. United States. Army Service Forces
4. Fraenkel, Heinrich and Manvell, Roger, *Doctor Goebbels: His Life and Death.* (Frontline Books, 2010), p.196.
5. *Reichsrundfunk Journal* – 22 June 1941
6. *Voices in the Darkness: The Story of the European Radio War.* (Secker and Warburg; second edition, 1943)
7. Ibid
8. Radio-Humanité and La Voix de la Paix ceased operations in late June.
9. *Voices in the Darkness: The Story of the European Radio War.* (Secker and Warburg; second edition, 1943)
10. Dorothea Günther (1914–2010): Der Krieg 1939/40 – Lemo/ Lebendiges Museum

14. Britain

1. 'Propaganda Tricks'. *The North China Herald and Supreme Court & Consular Gazette* – 25 December 1940. p.483
2. KV 2/2861
3. IBid
4. 'Propaganda Tricks'. *The North China Herald and Supreme Court & Consular Gazette* – 25 December 1940. p.483.
5. 'Hail Caledonia, says Nazi Radio', *Aberdeen Evening Express* – 17 September 1940. p.5.
6. Bremen (home programme), 23 September 1940.
7. 'More Turbulent talk from Berlin', *Daily Gazette for Middlesbrough* – 26 January 1940. p.1.
8. The idea was based on a successful radio hook-up which took place between army garrisons on 28 March 1939. Units in Tilsit, Mülheim an der Ruhr, Oldenburg, Mährisch-Schönberg, Flensburg and Graz

took part. *Der Deutsche Rundfunk* – 26 March 1939. A similar effort connected troops from the North Cape to the Bay of Biscay on 1 September 1940.

9. Richard Baier interview with Nathan Morley, 2019

15. *Farewell America*

1. Smith, Howard K., *Last Train from Berlin*. (Cresset Press, 1942)
2. BBC – 16 September 1940. 17.00
3. Eventually, the Ministry of Propaganda and the intelligence services became involved when the service was incorporated into Interradio AG, an entity subordinate to both the Foreign Ministry and the ProMi but even then, the competencies of each master remained obscured.
4. Unsurprisingly, during 1941, the Vatican Radio was very briefly forced to broadcast some programmes in slow dictation after being jammed by Germany. Another notable Vatican programme was the regular visits to camps for prisoners of war and internees in Italy; some of the internees talked over the Vatican Radio and sent messages home. Among the news broadcasts other programming, of course, included Mass celebrated by the Pope at St Peter's, along with the Christmas Eve message to the world.
5. Having stated his views, Goebbels enlisted intelligence chief Admiral Wilhelm Canaris to investigate the Seehaus on suspicion of defeatism, urging him to restrict the dissemination of reports to senior figures. It later emerged that Goebbels had been right on the button, when scores of Seehaus monitors were unmasked as members of the 'sabotage club' resistance movement.
6. *Angriff Auf Kreta* transmitted on all German stations on 25 May 1941. Transcript from the *Reichsrundfunk Journal* 20 July 1941.

16. *A Single Voice*

1. Along with the longwave transmitters in Friesland and Vistula
2. 'Aus Der Arbeit der Deutschen Europasender', *Deutschesrundfunks Journal*, 22 June 1941
3. Rundfunk Archive, March 1942
4. *Hartlepool Northern Daily Mail* – 27 May 1941
5. 24 June 1942. 22.00
6. *Netherlands News Digest* – March 1942
7. When Goebbels appointed Toni Winkelnkemper as the foreign director of the RRG, the former head of the department, Horst

Cleinow, became the deputy director of the shortwave station, whilst the former head of the wireless service, Walter Wilhelm Dittmar, became intendant of the European service, and former head of department Walter Kamm took charge of the 'Office for International Broadcasting'.

8. Clienow, Horst, 'Deutschland's Stimme in die Welt', *Reichsrundfunk Journal* – 22 June 1941

9. BBC Monitoring – 12 July 1941

10. Edwards, John Carver, *Berlin Calling: American Broadcasters in Service to the Third Reich.* (Praeger, 1991), p.12.

11. On the upper floors of the Adlon Hotel, translator Dorothea Günther was busy in the English section of the Foreign Ministry Linguistic Service, making sure the world, via all the RRG foreign-language radio services, was being clued in to what was happening. She recalled the translations that morning were examined word for word: 'The decision on the most appropriate formulation sometimes had to be made by Dr Paul Schmidt, the chief interpreter. Hitler once said with pathos: "This bloody war ..." innocently, the English translated it as: "This bloody war ..." which sounded more like "this shit war".' Incidentally, just a few rooms away in the same hotel, the English novelist PG Wodehouse – the creator of Jeeves and Bertie Wooster – was presumably deep in slumber after being freed from a civilian internment camp and moved to Berlin. He had opted for a more comfortable life by agreeing to broadcast on RRG's American shortwave service, although the Nazis insisted 'he was under no compulsion regarding his broadcast talks'. Wodehouse, who was then 60, had been in German hands since the collapse of France, and was compared to William Joyce when his broadcasts were finally transmitted.

12. Berlin, KWS in German received in the USA, 23 June 23, 1941 United States Foreign Broadcast Information Service (Transcript). File: RG262

13. Karl Holtzhamer's PK report from 23 June 1941. Transcript of broadcast on Deutschlandsender as published in *Reichsrundfunk*

14. KWS shortwave to America, 29 June 1941, 21.00 UTC. 'Jane Anderson and Musical Programme'. United States Foreign Broadcasting Information Service

15. Belgrade Radio broadcast from 19 February 1942, as cited by *Edinburgh Evening News* on 28 February 1942

16. Rundfunk Archive, April 1942

17. Ibid.

18. *Daily Herald* – 25 May 1942

19. *Belfast News-Letter* – 15 August 1944

17. *Calling Africa and the Middle East*
1. KV 2/2085 P117a
2. MD, RG262. KWS to the USA, 11 October 1941. United States Foreign Broadcast Information Service archives
3. *Western Morning News* – 15 October 1941
4. Speech from 9 December 1941 presumably transmitted on Deutschlandsender. Cited in *German Radio Propaganda; Report on Home Broadcasts during the War*. (Oxford University Press, 1944) p.338

18. *The Turning Tide*
1. 'The Invisible Men', *Liverpool Echo*, 3 January 1942
2. At the outbreak of war, the actor Jack Trevor was engaged in making a film on a German boat on the Baltic Sea. After being arrested and interned, he was taken to Berlin where the Propaganda Ministry coaxed him to work on the English-language broadcasts.
3. *Daily Herald* – 15 October 1941
4. Chandra Bose in June 1943 (WO 208/3812)
5. KV2 / 3902 Arathil Chandeth Narayanan Nambiar file
6. KV2 / 3902
7. The report *Arbeits und Finanzplan für die deutsche Auslands-Rundfunk-Gesellschaft Interradio* focuses on the operation and finance plan for the foreign broadcasting company 'Interradio AG' as cited in *Missbrauchte Mikrophone. Deutsche Rundfunkpropaganda im Zweiten Weltkrieg*. (Wien, 1967), p.150.
8. Ettlinger, Harold, *Axis on the Air*. (The Bobbs-Merrill Company, 1943)
9. Peter Meyer interview with Nathan Morley, 2020
10. Ibid.
11. Ibid.
12. Fredborg, Arvid, *Behind the Steel Wall* (Harrap, 1944).
13. Rundfunk Archive, May 1942.

19. *New Ideas*
1. *Dundee Evening Telegraph* – 5 January 1942
2. Befehl 2688/42
3. Swift, John, *Adventure in Vision, the First 25 Years of Television*. (1950, Lehmann)
4. Goebbels, Joseph, *The Goebbels Diaries, 1942–1943*. Entry from 11 February 1942. (Praeger, 1970)
5. KV2-250 Edwin Schneider statement at Radio Hamburg.
6. Ettlinger, Harold, *Axis on the Air*. (The Bobbs-Merrill Company, 1943)
7. Ibid.

20. *1943*

1. *The secret conferences of Dr Goebbels, October 1939–March 1943* Entry from 4 January 1943. (Weidenfeld & Nicolson, 1970), p.313.
2. KV 2/2861
3. West End actor Henry Mollison was captured while returning to Britain from a business tour, he remained in a POW camp for the duration of the war. On returning to England, he featured in the classic films *Whisky Galore!* and *The Man in the White Suit*, alongside Alec Guinness.
4. *Nottingham Evening Post* – 6 December 1943
5. *Derby Daily Telegraph* – 29 September 1943
6. *Evening Despatch* – 3 June 1943
7. The upshot of these speeches saw Ley find his name splashed across a 'mood report', compiled by the security services, which noted he was audibly 'drunk or tipsy' during a broadcast, while a member of the public confessed: 'I am often overcome by quiet fear of how matters are to go on if such people continue to remain in leading positions.'
8. BBC – 9 February 1943
9. *The Secret Conferences of Dr Goebbels, October 1939–March 1943*. (Weidenfeld & Nicolson, 1970), pp.315–316
10. A news script from December 1943 preserved in the Foreign Office archives shows that in one bulletin alone, every item concerned the war: There were details of Rommel visiting defence facilities, the opaque situation in the Mediterranean, General Smuts' views about the long way to the end of the war, the fate of Finland and the Arabs as natural allies of Germany.
11. At the same time, the Luftwaffe attempted to requisition all shortwave transmitters used on the USA services for military purposes, and issued a directive forcing Reichssender and Deutschlandsender to switch off their transmitters every time enemy planes approached.

21. *Stalingrad*

1. 'Francis Stuart – The Truth', *Sunday Independent* (Dublin) – 14 December 1997
2. Speech on Deutschlandsender – 6 February 1943
3. Warrant Officer Hughes broadcast propaganda talks in Welsh for the Welsh troops in Italy on Radio Metropol between 10 April and 8 August 1944.
4. Ettlinger, Harold, *Axis on the Air*. (The Bobbs-Merrill Company, 1943)
5. Alfred Müller, *Stiftung Deutsches Historisches Museum*

6. The following people were on the editorial staff of Radio Moscow or made contributions: Anton Ackermann, Martha Arendsee, Rudolf Appelt, Johannes R. Becher, Lilly Becher, Becker Lene Berg, Bertold Brecht, Willi Bredel, Ernst Busch, Heinrich Evers, Martha Esche, Ernst Fabri, Ernst Fischer, Magda Fischer, Philippine Fischer and Walter Fischer.
7. BBC – 16 March 1943
8. D02 98/501 / LeMO

22. *The Show Goes On*

1. The campaign had claimed the lives of 40,000 men since November 1942 and was considered a second Stalingrad, which paved the way for the invasion of Sicily.
2. BBC – 19 September 1943
3. BBC – 26 November 1943
4. US Department of Justice, file 146-7-51-1708
5. Station operation report. October 1943. FO 898/51
6. *Goebbels Diaries* 1943, p.384
7. *Nottingham Evening Post* – 18 May 1943
8. Reuters report, citing German Radio – 16 June 1943
9. *Daily Record* – 12 September 1942
10. Interview with Nathan Morley, 2019
11. Rundfunk Archive, May 1942
12. 'Goebbels's Dishwater Broadcasts', *Aberdeen Evening Express* – 20 August 1943. p.8. The newscast was transmitted on Friday 20 August
13. *Hartlepool Northern Daily Mail* – 12 October 1943
14. *Nottingham Evening Post* – 28 December 1943
15. Dagmar, Brita, and the other Swedish radio propagandists received 30,000 letters in which Swedish listeners, among other things, called for more Jew-baiting – 'it would be good if you could put more anti-Semitic propaganda in the broadcasts'. 'Kafferep för Hitler', *Aftonbladet* – 24 September 2005
16. *The Times*, Shreveport, Louisiana – 5 December 1943
17. Sennerteg, Niclas, *Tyskland talar: Hitlers svenska radiostation.* (Lund, 2006). pp.167–171

23. *1944*

1. Sebastian, Mihail, *Journal 1935–1944: The Fascist Years.* (Ivan R. Dee, 2000)
2. *Shields Daily News* – 25 January 1944
3. *Aberdeen Press and Journal* – 15 February 1944
4. *Shields Daily News* – 8 February 1944

24. D-Day

1. Europasender – 7 June 1944, 23.00
2. Reichssender Hamburg – 22 June 1944
3. Off-air recording, 12 September 1944, 21.15 EST
4. Europasender – 21 June 1944, 22.30
5. Until early October 1943, the total losses of PK propaganda troops stood at 546 killed or missing in action, 480 wounded and 32 taken as POW.
6. Von Oven, Wilfred, *Mit Goebbels bis zum Ende*. (Grabert, 1974)
7. Longmate, Norman, *The Home Front*. (Chatto and Windus, 1981)
8. 'Radio: Operation Annie', *Time Magazine* – 25 February 1946

25. Shouting into the Abyss

1. *Liverpool Evening Express* – 15 March 1945
2. *Western Daily Press* – 31 January 1945
3. *Hull Daily Mail* – 31 January 1945
4. *Hartlepool Northern Daily Mail* – 7 February 1945
5. BBC Monitoring – 24 February 1945
6. A reference to the wine cellar at the Press Club on Leipziger Strasse, a favourite haunt of the Joyce's.
7. Joyce, William, *Diary* – 14 March 1945. (National Archives)
8. Powell and Jones were translators, and occasional announcers at the Haus Des Rundfunks.
9. Joyce, William, *Diary* – 14 March 1945. (National Archives)
10. *Nottingham Evening Post* – 19 March 1945
11. *Daily Record* – 30 March 1945
12. *Daily Herald* – 7 April 1945
13. *Aberdeen Evening Express* – 6 April 1945
14. *Daily Record* – 3 April 1945
15. *Birmingham Mail* – 5 April 1945
16. *Daily Herald* – 7 April 1945
17. Blokzijl was executed by firing squad on Saturday 16 March 1946.
18. *Völkischer Beobachter* – 23 April 1945
19. Perry Biddiscombe, Alexander, *Werwolf!: The History of the National Socialist Guerrilla Movement, 1944–1946*. (University of Toronto Press, 1998)
20. *Boston Globe* – 24 April 1945
21. *New York Herald Tribune* – 24 April 1945
22. Ibid
23. *Aberdeen Press and Journal* – 24 April 1945
24. KV2-250. Statement of Edwin Schneider at Radio Hamburg, 21 May 1945.
25. KV3-250

26. Ibid.
27. On 30 April, the Fuhrer appointed Grand Admiral Doenitz as his successor.
28. *Hull Daily Mail* – 3 May 1945

26. Reckoning

1. KV2-250. Guy Della-Cioppa statement, recorded on 23 May 1945.
2. A document in the Zeesen community archives notes that the rubble was used in road construction in the district.

BIBLIOGRAPHY

Baird, Jay W, *The Mythical World of Nazi Propaganda: 1939–1945*. (University of Minnesota Press, 1974)

Balfour, Michael, *Propaganda in War 1939–1945: Organisations, Policies and Publics in Britain and Germany*. (Routledge & Kegan Paul, 1979)

Bartov, Omer, *Hitler's Army: Soldiers, Nazis, and War in the Third Reich*. (New York: Oxford University Press, 1992)

Bauernfeind, Wolfgang, *Tonspuren: Das Haus des Rundfunks in Berlin*. (Christoph Verlag, 2010)

Bell, P. M. H., 'Censorship, Propaganda, and Public Opinion: The Case of the Katyn Graves', *Transactions of the Royal Historical Society*, Fifth Series, Vol. 39 (1989)

Berkhoff, Karel, *Harvest Of Despair: Life and Death in Ukraine Under Nazi Rule*. (London and Cambridge: The Belknap Press of Harvard University Press, 2004)

Bidlack, Richard, 'The Political Mood in Leningrad during the First Year of the Soviet–German War'. (*Russian Review* Vol. 59, 2000)

Braithwaite, Rodric, *Moscow 1941: A City and its People*. (Vintage: New York, 2006)

Burds, Jeffery, 'German Fifth Column in Chechnya, 1942–1944'. *Journal of Contemporary History*, Vol. 42. 5 (April, 2007)

Clark, Alan, *Barbarossa: The Russian–German Conflict, 1941–1945*. (New York: Harper Collins, 1985)

Edwards, John Carver, *Berlin Calling: American Broadcasters in Service to the Third Reich*. (Praeger, 1991)

Farndale, Nigel *Haw-Haw: The Tragedy of William and Margaret Joyce*. (Macmillan, 2005)

Forster, Jurgen, 'Barbarossa Revisited: Strategy and Ideology in the East,' *Jewish Social Studies*, Vol. 50 (Winter, 1988–Spring, 1992)

Fox, John P., 'Der Fall Katyn und die Propaganda des NS-Regime,' *Viertaljahfshefte fur Zeitgeschiste*, Vol. 30 (1982)

Fraenkel, Heinrich and Manvell, Roger, *Doctor Goebbels: His Life and Death*. (Frontline Books, 2010)

Glantz, David M., *Zhuvok's Greatest Defeat: The Red Army's Epic Disaster in Operation Mars, 1942*. (University Press of Kansas, 1999)

Grabowski, Jan, 'German Anti-Jewish Propaganda in the Generalgouvernement, 1939–1945: Inciting Hate through Posters, Films, and Exhibitions,' *Holocaust and Genocide Studies*, Vol. 23. 3 (Winter, 2009)

Gombrich, Ernst H., *Mythos und Wirklichkeit in den deutschen Rundfunksendungen der Kriegszeit*. (Stuttgart, 1983)

Grunberger, Richard, *A Social History of the Third Reich*. (Weidenfeld & Nicolson, 2013)

Herf, Jeffrey, *Nazi Propaganda for the Arab World*. (Yale University Press, 2009)

Herzstein, Robert E., Anti-Jewish Propaganda in the Orel Region of Great Russia, 1942–1943: The German Army and Its Russian Collaborators', *Simon Wiesenthal Center Annual* Vol. 6 (1989)

Joyce, William *Twilight Over England*. (Internationaler Verlag, Berlin, 1940)

Kaufmann, Johannes, *Rundfunkkrieg: Deutsche Und Britische Radiopropaganda Im Zweiten Weltkrieg*. (Diplomica Verlag GmbH, 2013)

Lomagin, Nikita, *Soldiers at War: German Propaganda and Soviet Army Morale During the Battle of Leningrad, 1941–44*. (University of Pittsburgh Press, 1998)

Longerich, Peter, 'Joseph Goebbels und der Totale Krieg. Eine unbekannte Denkschrift des Propagandaministers vom 18. Juli 1944,' *Vierteljarhshefte fur Zeitgeschichte*. (Volume 25, 1987)

Longerich, Peter, *Propagandisten im Krieg: Die Presseabteilung des Auswirtigen Amtes unter Ribbentrop*. (Studien zur Zeitgeschicte, 1987)

Lower, Wendy, *Nazi Empire Building and the Holocaust in the Ukraine*. (Chapel Hill: University of North Carolina Press, 2005)

Lubrich, Oliver, *Travels in the Reich 1933–1945: Foreign Authors Report from the Reich*. (Chicago: University of Chicago Press, 2010)

Martin, Terry, *The Affirmative Action Empire: Nations and Nationalism in the Soviet Union, 1923–1939*. (Cornell University Press, 2001)

Merridale, Catherine, *Ivan's War: Life and Death in the Red Army 1939–1945*. (Metropolitan, 2006)

Messerschmidt, Manfred, *Die Wehrmacht im NS-Staat. Zeit der Indoktrination.* (Schenk, 1969)

Michlic, Joanna, 'The Soviet Occupation of Poland, 1939–1941 and the Stereotype of the Anti-Polish and Pro-Soviet Jew,' *Jewish Social Studies,* Vol. 13. 3 (2007)

Morley, Nathan, *Hitler's Home Front: Life in Nazi Germany during the Second World War.* (Independent, 2019)

Pleshakov, Constantine, *Stalin's Folly: The Tragic First Ten Days of World War II on the Eastern Front.* (First Mariner Books, 2005)

Quinkert, Babette, *Propaganda und Terror in Weißrußland 1941–1944: Die deutsche 'geistige' Kriegsführung gegen Zivilbevölkerung und Partisanen. Krieg in der Geschichte.* (Schöningh Paderborn, 2008)

Sennerteg, Niclas, *Tyskland talar: Hitlers svenska radiostation.* (Lund, 2006)

Schubotz, H., *Die Deutsche Welle GmbH.* (Jahrbuch der Deutschen Welle, 1928)

Smith, Howard K., *Last Train from Berlin.* (Cresset Press, 1942)

Shirer, William L., *The Rise and Fall of the Third Reich.* (Rosetta Books, 2011)

Snyder, Timothy, *Reconstruction of Nations: Poland, Ukraine, Lithuania, Belarus, 1569–1999.* (Yale: Yale University Press, 2003)

Steinberg, Jonathan, 'The Third Reich Reflected: German Civil Administration in the Occupied Soviet Union, 1941–4.' *Holocaust and Genocide Studies* 110 (1995)

Stites, Richard, *Russian Popular Culture: Entertainment and Society since 1900.* (Cambridge: Cambridge University Press, 1992)

Taylor, Fred, *The Goebbels Diaries 1939–1941.* (G. P. Putnam's Sons, 1983)

Trevor-Roper, Hugh, *Final Entries 1945: The Diaries of Joseph Goebbels.* (G. P. Putnam's Sons, 1978)

Tyaglyy, Mikhail, 'The Role of Antisemitic Doctrine in German Propaganda in the Crimea, 1941–1944.' *Holocaust and Genocide Studies* 18.3 (2004)

Uziel, Daniel, *The Propaganda Warriors: The Wehrmacht and the Consolidation of the German Home Front.* (Bern: Peter Lang, 2008)

Welch, David, *The Third Reich: Politics and Propaganda.* (Routledge: New York, 1993)

Werth, Alexander, *Russia At War.* (E. P. Dutton and Company, 1964)

Zeman, Z. A., *Nazi Propaganda.* (Oxford University Press, 1973)

INDEX

Also available from Amberley Publishing